A Practical Heathen's Guide to

ASATRU

About the Author

Patricia is a Troth-certified Godwoman. She has been a heathen for approximately seventeen years and a pagan for twenty-four. She is a proud member of both The Troth and Two Ravens Kindred, and a founding member of Bjornsal, a seidh group which ran from 2001 through 2008. She has served The Troth since 2002 as a Steward, High Steward, Godwoman, Rede member, and former Steerswoman. She is also the founder of The Troth's Lore Program and served as its Provost. Patricia is currently a Dean in the Lore Program and an active Freyjasgythja.

To Write to the Author

If you wish to contact the author or would like more information about this book, please write to the author in care of Llewellyn Worldwide, and we will forward your request. Both the author and publisher appreciate hearing from you and learning of your enjoyment of this book and how it has helped you. Llewellyn Worldwide cannot guarantee that every letter written to the author can be answered, but all will be forwarded. Please write to:

Patricia M. Lafayllve
℅ Llewellyn Worldwide
2143 Wooddale Drive
Woodbury, MN 55125-2989

Please enclose a self-addressed stamped envelope for reply,
or $1.00 to cover costs. If outside the USA, enclose
an international postal reply coupon.

Many of Llewellyn's authors have websites with additional information and resources. For more information, please visit our website at http://www.llewellyn.com.

A Practical Heathen's Guide to

ASATRU

PATRICIA M. LAFAYLLVE

Llewellyn Publications
Woodbury, Minnesota

FIRST EDITION
Seventh Printing, 2019

Book design by Bob Gaul
Cover art: Background © iStockphoto.com/12530110/loops7
Cover design by Kevin R. Brown
Editing by Ed Day

Llewellyn is a registered trademark of Llewellyn Worldwide Ltd.

Library of Congress Cataloging-in-Publication Data
Lafayllve, Patricia M.
    A practical heathen's guide to Asatru / Patricia M. Lafayllve. --
FIRST EDITION.
        pages cm
    Includes bibliographical references and index.
    ISBN 978-0-7387-3387-6
        1. Neopaganism. I. Title.
BP605.N46L34 2013
299'.94--dc23
                                                                    2013025848

Llewellyn Publications
A Division of Llewellyn Worldwide Ltd.
2143 Wooddale Drive
Woodbury, MN 55125-2989
www.llewellyn.com

Printed in the United States of America

To my grandfather, Leon Louis Lafaille.
A better man I could not know.

Acknowledgments

No work exists in a vacuum. Scholarship must be cited. Permissions must be granted. What we seldom notice are the small comments, the one-liners, the inspirations around a campfire, or the running conversations on an e-mail list. A community is built on these small things, on mutual acceptance, humor, and an ability to quietly get along, even when the person next to you might be at her most vexing. I want to acknowledge you, my community here in the Northeast region of the United States, and also you whose communities have made me welcome across America. Our religion is nothing without solid, committed, upstanding, and often hilarious people standing together in it. Hail the community.

Contents

PART TWO

Pronunciation Guide

The author has decided to use the commonly accepted Anglicized terms throughout the majority of this work. This is done in an attempt to decrease inconsistency and increase understanding of the concepts under discussion. However, quotes will appear as the quoted author intended. Thus, it seems prudent to offer a basic pronunciation guide in order to assist people new to the language. This should not be seen as complete nor definitive—merely helpful. The words given as examples following pronunciations are words commonly found in Old Norse passages quoted in the text.

Vowels:

- á: "ow" as in "house" (Ásatrú)

- a: "ah" as in "Father" (Vanir)

- e: "eh" as in "enter" (Brisingamen)

- í: "eh" as in "men" (Íslendingur)

- i: "i" as in "pin" (Egil) or "ee" as in "fleece" (Vanir)

- ó: "oh" as in "boat" (Blót)

- ö: similar to the "u" in "slur" (Örlög)

- o: "o" as in "pot" (Od)

- ú: "oo" as in "moon" (Ásatrú)

- u: "u" as in "turn" (Hyndluljod)

Diphthongs and consonants:

- ei (also ey, eng, enk): "a" as in "came" (Heimdall)

- æ (also ae): "i" as in "eye" (Æsir)

- ð: hard "th" as in "the" (Oðinn)

- þ: soft "th" sound as in "think" (Þorr)

- j: the j is nearly always pronounced as a "y" sound, as in "youth" (Njord). It is also sometimes substituted with the letter i (Niord).

- v: as it sounds in standard English (Van, Vanir)

- w: in Old Norse remains as a w sound (wan). However, in Old English or continental Germanic languages the w replaces the v sound. Therefore in Old Norse, a word such as Van in Old English or Germanic sources becomes Wan. This can cause some confusion when translating texts. Wherever possible, the author has chosen to stay with the Old Norse words, as they are arguably more commonplace in their anglicized forms.

- y: the y is typically pronounced with a "y" sound (Freyja). However, when it is used to replace an i, the sound is pronounced as "i" as in "pin" (Ydalir).

Generally speaking, in Old Norse the accent is on the first syllable of any word. Accented vowels indicate an accented syllable where the letter is placed, thus Ásatrú is OW-sah-troo (the second accented vowel also gets emphasis, but not as strongly as the first). Two-syllable words generally have the accent placed on the first syllable as well; hence, Vanir is VAH-neer rather than vah-NEER.

Introduction

Some call it Ásatrú. Some call it Theodism. It is known by a host of other bynames, including Odinism, Forn Sed, and tribalism. In fact, many of these labels are not merely names, but strong variations based around a few central tenets. This is why many of us refer to our religion and culture as Heathenry or Heathenism, and call ourselves Heathen. Sometimes we get specific and refer to what we do as "Pan-Germanic" or "Northern European Heathenry." Whatever we choose to call it, what we do can be summed up thusly: we are members of a primarily reconstructionist, polytheistic, animistic faith that reflects the cultural and religious paradigms of our pre-Christian, post-Proto-Indo-European ancestors.

We will discuss all of these terms in detail. Let me start here with "reconstruction." Reconstruction is a method by which we interpret our primary source materials, secondary scholarship, historical documents, and the archeological record in order to piece together details about what ancestral heathens did, how they did it, and why they did it. Then we bring those practices and beliefs, as we understand them, forward to the modern era and apply them to our lives. If you've ever been in a room of scholars debating any given topic, you'll understand just how complex this process is and how much ire it can induce in people using the same translations to produce entirely different findings.

Welcome to Ásatrú.

Ben Waggoner coined what are often called the two tenets of heathenry. The first is "You are not the boss of me." The second is "You are doing it all wrong." These are meant to be humorous, and they get big laughs. At the same time, heathens are, by and large, a strong-minded, opinionated group of people who, from the outside, can look like they are saying precisely those two things over and over again. That is not typically the case. Actively engaging in the reconstructive method can cause a lot of heated debate. You will find that sometimes the hardest, loudest debaters are actually the very best of friends.

Let me say from the outset that this book contains my interpretations, my reconstructions, and my experiences as someone who has been heathen for nearly two decades. I began looking into paganism generally at age eighteen and became heathen roughly in 1994. I am a longtime member of The Troth, a heathen organization, and have served in many of its offices, including Steerswoman. I also teach and give lectures throughout the United States and have been doing so for over a decade. In other words, I have been exploring heathenry from the inside as well as practicing the religion and living with a heathen worldview as best I can for quite some time. However, there are a great many heathens who have been doing this longer than I have, and a great many that are relatively new. We all have our opinions. At some point, some heathen reading this book will roll his or her eyes and sigh, thinking "she's doing it all wrong." That's okay, because that heathen is not the boss of me.

In many ways, heathens owe the biggest debt to the Germanic Iron Age and early medieval people of Iceland. They took the time to write things down to preserve their cultures and folkloric identity. Modern Icelanders led the way here in the modern world, gaining recognition for Ásatrú in the 1970s. Many Icelanders look askance at Americans and our attempts to develop heathenry—sometimes with good reason. After all, we are not, by and large, Icelandic. Most of our families came from

Northern Europe generally, from Scandinavia to Denmark, England, Germany, France, and Ireland. But not all of us can trace our ancestry—and not all of us should. America, like any other culture, puts its own unique stamp on everything it touches. So are we heathen? Can we be heathen? What is "being heathen" all about?

This book explores these questions. It has been divided into two parts. In the first, I explore what is known about heathenry through the surviving mythology, folklore, and sagas. In this section I compare what we know about pre-Christian heathenry to our modern practices. Part Two deals with specific rituals for holidays, life-status changes, and ways to create rituals on your own. Remember, my own opinions and worldview are, essentially, American, and more specifically Northeastern American. Heathenry in all its glorious varieties is found across the world. I am fortunate enough to know people outside of America, and when I can, I've consulted them and asked their opinions, and will do my best to point out where the varieties of culture affect our faith. But I can't get too far out of my own head, despite my best efforts, so to the reader I say: "Understand my bias is unintentional, and I avoid it wherever I can."

What I can do is boil down some of our complexities and try to point out some of our constants. I can use words old and words new, words from other philosophies, and words from our own source materials in order to express the ideas we're just now beginning to explore as a faith. I can offer a point of view that is, in its essence, a synthesis of all these things, coupled with my own continuing research, scholarship, and the practices I have observed and participated in. This book is an effort to explore all of these things in ways that are relevant and practical for newcomers to heathenry and also offers thoughts for heathens to mull over.

Imagine if you will a large campfire. Many people are sitting around it, and horns of mead are being passed around. Everyone is talking. Come. Have a seat here at the fire. Read on with me, and let's see what we can find.

PART ONE

I am heathen because I am.

One

An Introduction to Heathenry

Let's start with a simple question. Why be heathen? The easiest answer might run along the lines of "why not be heathen?" There's more to it than that. Heathenry is a faith of many variations. Heathenry requires a certain level of personal commitment to one's community, however small it may be. Heathenry is often called "the religion with homework" because heathens tend to read and interpret materials on their own. Heathenry is not a mystery religion where secrets and practices are revealed as one advances. The information is all there for us to engage in, and reconstruct, as best we can.

Ásatrú (also Asatru, the spelling I will use for the remainder of this book) is usually broken down into two words: "asa," or "As," referring to the gods and goddesses, and "tru," meaning true or loyal. Asatru, then, is for the most part defined as "true or loyal to the gods and goddesses." Typically people will add "of Northern Europe" to specify exactly which pantheon is being referred to. A specific, richly detailed cultural worldview can be found among heathens, who generally live by a family-focused, community-based ethos and share actual or chosen kinship ties.

Heathens share a deep and abiding connection to the gods and goddesses of Northern Europe—Odin, Frigga, Thor, Frey, Freyja, and all the others. Heathens are also committed to their ancestors, and ancestor worship is a continuing thread through the heathen community at large.

There are two main heathen rituals—blót (also blot) and sumble. *Blót*, a word which relates to "blood," typically involves an offering or sacrifice of some sort. This can be as simple as pouring out a drink or as extensive as forging a sword, then bending it in half and throwing it into a bog, pond, or other body of water. Many of the rituals found in this book are blóts in one form or another.

Sumble, on the other hand, is about forging the bonds of community. It is a ritualized drinking occasion. The horn is either passed by a cup-bearer or from hand to hand, and there are typically three rounds. The first is a round of welcome for the gods and goddesses. The second is a round to the ancestors or, in some cases, personal heroes. The final round is referred to as an "open" round during which stories, songs, toasts, and even bragging occur. Bragging about one's actions is acceptable among heathens, as long as the facts are true. If someone is bragging about themselves and they happen to be exaggerating or lying, you can almost always bet that someone in the room knows better, and will speak up about it.

In terms of reconstruction, the era from which we get most of our information spans time between the late Bronze Age, through the Migration and Viking Ages, and into early Medieval European sources. We will cover history in more detail later, but it is important to remember that heathens tend to be skeptical about source materials. Unlike other faiths, there is no one true book containing the words of the gods themselves, although the *Poetic Edda*'s "Hávamál" (also called "The Sayings of Hár," after one of Odin's bynames), a few other poems, and parts of the sagas may come close. Still, Asatru is not a revealed religion with secrets being passed to those who have worked through various levels. That said, another reason for skepticism is that very few of our remaining sources are from the period itself, and fewer still are from internal sources. The Roman Tacitus, for example, a historian, wrote a book about the Germanic peoples in 98

CE. However, as a Roman, his view was, ultimately, from the outside looking in.

Another important source is Snorri Sturluson. The Icelandic historian lived from roughly 1179–1241 and was thoroughly Christian. Snorri's goal was to preserve what he could of the pre-Christian myths, stories, and various poetic meters used in traditional Icelandic poetry. We know that Sturluson was the author of the *Prose Edda*, a series of stories, myths, and all the traditional Icelandic poetic meters, and the *Heimskringla*, the sagas of the Norwegian kings. However, he also altered some myths based on the classical education he had, and so Snorri Sturluson must, like most of the surviving material, be viewed with respect, but also with some skepticism.

The span of time is not the only issue heathens need to confront— heathens collect information from various geographical sources as well. Northern Europeans explored and settled area from the Arctic down through Norway, Sweden, Iceland, continental Germany, into Great Britain, back up and over to Greenland, and onto the North American continent. Early heathens got around—and left archeological records, writings, grave goods, and graffiti where they went. History and the saga records are studied as well, to form a fuller picture of what the pre-Christian worldviews of varying tribes looked like.

Some heathens focus their reconstruction primarily on one group of tribes or geographical era—the Anglo-Saxons, for instance—while others do their best to look for the similarities among the varying sources to form a "Pan-Germanic" heathenry. This is an important point. For the most part, there was no "one heathen religion" in the Pre-Christian era. There were a great many interpretations and practices. While there was an emphasis of a kind when it came to public offerings made at gatherings like the Althing, in each household the "rules" or "traditions" were those of that household. Groups would form shared beliefs and practices as well, but geographically—even locally—heathen practices varied a great deal. This is true in the modern era as well. *Siðu* is an Old Norse word very roughly relating to "tradition," and every heathen group has its own *siðu*. Regions have a kind of group *siðu*, but there is no one central "Asatru religion."

By and large, heathens are polytheists. They believe that the gods and goddesses are individual and distinct. Each deity has his or her own triumphs and foibles, and they are complex entities in their own right. Most heathens do not believe in one great god or goddess; there is no synthesis between, say, Frigga and Freyja. They share commonalities, but are by no means one and the same. Archetypes are also not found in the majority of heathen belief—there is little to no evidence of a maiden/mother/crone tripartite goddess in Northern Europe.

Animism is a popular belief among heathens. In many ways, this is a natural outgrowth of the heathen worldview. They believe in multiple, individual gods and goddesses in the presence of their ancestors and heroes and that there are many types of wights, so why not believe that everything has some sort of "soul" or "energy" that makes up that particular item? *Wight*, by the way, is a word used to refer to any being at all. Humans are wights. The spirits of the land are wights. There are apartment wights, and house wights. Animals are also wights. Our ancestors, and even our gods and goddesses, are called wights. Remember that animism does not equate to all wights being able to communicate in human fashion. It simply means that there is a spiritual component to every animate—and inanimate—thing in the universe.

The use of the word "wight" underscores one difficulty in reconstructionism. If, as we've seen, the word can be used to refer to any living thing, then how to we distinguish which is which? The answer can be very confusing. Words are often substituted for other words in our source materials. This is especially true in poetry, where the number of syllables or accents had to be adhered to. A woman, for instance, is a wight. In poetry or the saga record, she might be referred to as a woman, a lady, a mother, a sister, or a daughter. These are fairly straightforward terms that we use today. However, a poet might call a woman a *dis*—a word referring to a female ancestral spirit—or a Valkyrie, one of Odin's servants in Valhalla. This does not mean the woman is a dis or Valkyrie, but simply that the poet has chosen to use that term to refer to her. Sometimes the best answer is to look at the surrounding content. If a man is standing in his lord's hall and declaring his love for Thora, and calls her "that Freyja of the long, golden hair," we can know this is referring to Thora, and not the goddess Freyja. On the other hand, sometimes context is not enough, and heathens reconstruct as best they can.

I can tell you that heathens often have no hard answers for some of the questions asked. Nor should heathens, really—most world religions spend their first thirty to fifty years figuring out just what they are, and how they work. Heathen reconstruction is only now entering its fifth decade, and modern heathenry is right where it should be. It's young in terms of history and entering those awkward teen years when we see a lot of rebellion, constructive criticism, schism, sects forming, and acne. Still, heathens need to strive—to seek out terms they can agree on, practices they can point to, cultural ethics that will inspire modern heathens and their progeny. Because that's what it is all about, you know. Progeny. If there are no second- or third-generation heathens, if heathenism stays where it is now, our religion will die with us. And no one wants that.

History is what we make of it.

Two

A Brief History

What does history have to do with anything? Well, as you will find, heathens live by looking to the past. History provides the context by which heathens can understand where they came from, and how they came to be there. Before delving into the mythology, we need to understand just which people were creating the myths. Additionally, a brief history will help us center ourselves on what is, and what is not, relevant to heathen reconstruction.

This is where Proto-Indo-European (PIE) studies come into play. We do not know a lot about the Proto-Indo-Europeans, except as speakers of a family of reconstructed languages. Philologists have traced languages back from the modern era toward the past, to see where languages converge with one another. Proto-Indo-European is a theoretical language and culture existing in Europe prior to all other cultures and language groups.[1] Pronunciation is hard to determine. Since these words are reconstructed, an asterisk is used before the word to denote its status. As an example, *per*, meaning "forward" or "chief," is the root form of the word that later became Freyja. It is possible to link the meaning of *per* with Freyja's status as one of the chief goddesses in the Norse pantheon. We can trace Proto-Indo-European back to approximately 4000–1800 BCE. From the words that they used, we know they were a cattle-focused cultural group and that their cultural structure may have been organized into households or people related by ancestry much as their descendants, the Viking-era peoples, were. We also see a focus on ancestor worship and a concept of the holy which included "feeding the dead" in their tombs. There are also deities such as the *Dyeus pater*, an ancient father-god who evolves through the centuries to become the Greek Zeus, the Roman Jupiter, and the Germanic Tyr.[2] Thus we can see that the origins of our gods trace quite a long way back into human history.

Following Proto-Indo-European, the next major language family we are most interested in is called "Germanic." Broadly speaking, many of the Northern European languages trace back to what is called the "Germanic" language family, which developed from Proto-Indo-European. A great many languages evolved out of the Germanic language group, including Old Norse, Old Icelandic, and Anglo-Saxon, which became Norwegian, Icelandic, and English, respectively.

In terms of history, archeological evidence indicates the slow advancement of the Bronze Age throughout the world. The Nordic, or Northern, Bronze Age occurred roughly between 1700 and 500 BCE. Most of the information we have regarding this particular era comes from rock carvings found in Scandinavia. There is not much evidence of religion, per se, although there are rock carvings of a man holding a spear, which could be Odin or Tyr, and a male figure holding an axe, which might, or might not, be a representation of Thor.

One interesting artifact is the Trundholm Sun Chariot. Found in a bog near Sjælland in 1902, this artifact has come under fascinating archeological scrutiny. It seems that this is one of the earliest horses represented in Europe and dates to the late Bronze Age. The image is striking—for one thing, spoked wheels were not generally considered Bronze Age technology. For our purposes, however, it indicates something far more relevant. In Norse mythology, the goddess Sunna drives across the sky in a chariot.

In that chariot is a "spark from Muspellheim," or a fiery rock, that the gods placed in the sky and called the sun. In the *Poetic Edda*'s "Lay of Vafthrúthnir," the horse is listed as a male. In fact, we have a name for Sunna's horse: he is called "Skínfaxi," and his mane is gold.[3]

Could the Trundholm Sun Chariot be an early depiction of Sunna and her horse? That is a matter of speculation and cannot be confirmed. What can definitely be said is that, in the Bronze Age, solar worship featured prominently enough that art images like this were made, and then offered as sacrifices. This speaks strongly toward the development of sun worship in the Viking Age.

The next area of history, in terms of heathen reconstruction, comes with the advancement of Rome into Europe. Julius Caesar crossed the Rhine River and entered what was known then as "Germania" in roughly 55 BCE. He wrote about his experiences, and while his writings are mostly of his military successes, he does mention many of the "Germanic" tribes by name. Later, in 98 CE, the Roman Tacitus wrote the *Germania*, a book describing what he knew and had experienced regarding the Germanic tribal peoples. This book is considered very important to the heathen reconstruction because it contains, among other things, the first mention of the goddess Nerthus and the rituals surrounding her worship. Nerthus is often considered an earth-goddess who brings peace and prosperity wherever she goes. According to Tacitus, her priests would bring an idol of her, carefully covered so that no one might look upon it, off of her island. The idol was carried in a wagon drawn by cows throughout the region. When Nerthus arrived, weapons would be put down and rejoicing would begin. When her travels were complete, Nerthus would be returned to her island and ritually cleansed. The slaves that tended to the idol would then be sacrificed.

From Tacitus's account, we skip forward in time again. Over time, the Nordic Bronze Age faded with the adoption of iron and iron-working tools and weapons. Some of the various "Ages" we are discussing overlapped one another. The Germanic Iron Age, for example, ran from approximately 600 BCE to 800 CE. These dates occur amidst the Conversion Period in Europe, which expanded from roughly 300–1000 CE.

As can be seen, several important historical events were happening at roughly the same time period—the Germanic Iron Age, the rise of Christianity, and the migration of many Germanic-language family tribes down from the north and spreading throughout Europe. The Age of Migration occurred from approximately 300–600 CE. The migrations, which coincided with the arrival of the Huns and fall of Roman territories in Europe, are accepted to end approximately in conjunction with the crowning of the Frankish King Clovis and subsequent Frankish conquest over much of continental Europe.[4] Migrating tribes included the Goths, Vandals, Frisians, Suebi, and others first mentioned by Julius Caesar and later by Tacitus, many of which shared cultural and mythological characteristics found throughout the Germanic language family.

We know that *Beowulf*'s origins are in the eighth century, closely following the Migration Age. *Beowulf* seems to coincide with the recorded evidence of King Hygelac's attack on Frankish-controlled Frisia, a country once found along the modern-day coastal regions of the Netherlands, into Germany, and northward approximately to the Denmark border. *Beowulf* is an epic poem and a work of fiction, but it does contain remnants of history and some descriptions of Migration Age culture which have proven accurate. As an example, during the sumble that King Hrothgar holds in honor of Beowulf, Unferth performs a flyting. He uses the fact that Beowulf once failed a contest he boasted he would win in order to question Beowulf's current boast to slay Grendel.[5] *Flyting* refers to a process whereby a person could challenge another in a kind of reciprocal insulting. It was used as a means of maintaining or lessening one's status in the community, and also as a way to ease tensions before blood feud occurred—an ancestral "blowing off steam" of sorts. A similar thing occurs in the *Poetic Edda*'s "Lokasenna,"[6] a poem telling a story where the gods and goddesses gather in the giant, Aegir's, hall. We also see records of flytings in the saga record. Therefore, while heathens know that *Beowulf* is fictional, they can look to it for some supporting evidence of earlier practices that continued into the Viking Age and have become accepted modern practices.

The so-called Conversion Period, the time in which polytheism was replaced by Christianity, was a gradual process. In order to give perspective to this process, the Conversion Period begins at around 300 CE and ends roughly in 1000 CE—directly mirroring the Germanic Iron Age and the early part of the Viking Age. Iceland was the last country to convert; according to *Njal's Saga* and according to the historical record, this occurred in 1000 CE.[7] This, in part, explains why so much of our remaining material comes from Iceland—when Snorri Sturluson wrote his *Edda*, also called the *Prose Edda*, he was writing a mere 200 or so years post-Conversion. Many of the sources he used are now missing to us. This is why, although he was a Christian and a classically educated man, Snorri Sturluson is invaluable to us for simply writing down myths and poetic meters before they were lost to history.

Our final historical time period, as you might expect, is the Viking Age. Many scholars place the beginning of the Viking Age at the raid of Lindisfarne Abbey—June 8, 793 CE. Seldom are the openings or closings of eras so specific, but this is the single earliest record of a raid and, as Lindisfarne was an important center for learning, the record starts here. After this, the Northmen raided coastlines, up rivers, and wherever the pickings were good through the eleventh century CE. (*Vike* is a term for what they did, which was later, and somewhat falsely, applied to the Northern European peoples.)

Most modern heathens use source material rising from the Iron Age generally, and the Viking Age specifically. It is vital to remember, however, that no part of history exists in a vacuum. The beginning of an era marks the end of the era prior to it, and as we have seen, evidence such as the Trundholm Sun Chariot show that solar worship in the Bronze Age may very well have influenced solar worship in the Viking Age. Modern heathenry places a great deal of importance on the past, as we shall see in later chapters. However, it is vital to remember that the past, in itself, also has a past. While focusing on a particular set of circumstances for the purposes of reconstruction is necessary and expected, the wise heathen remembers to put the past in its proper context.

Connecting to the Sun—Meditation on Sunna

As we have seen, solar worship is a vital part of early religious practice. In Germanic tradition, the sun is driven across the sky by Sunna. This meditation is designed to help the newcomer to connect with the sun and Sunna herself.

Find a quiet, sunny place where you can be safe. Be sure to wear your sunscreen! Sit or stand comfortably. Inhale for four beats, pause for two beats, and exhale for four beats. Repeat this rhythm, gradually relaxing your muscles from the toes to the top of your head. As you relax, feel the sun's warmth on your skin, your face, your head. Allow the sun's warmth to help you relax as you continue to breathe deeply in and then out again.

Visualize the sun's warmth as sunlight itself. As you breathe, imagine that the sun's light is permeating your muscles and helping them relax. Then, visualize Sunna. She is driving her cart across the sky. It is hard to see her past the sun's blaze in her chariot, but she is there, and as you watch you can see her using the reins to guide her horse into the now-familiar path across the skies. They move at a full gallop, although from this distance it may seem like they are not moving at all, much as the sun appears motionless as the earth rotates on its axis. You may call out her name, either out loud or as part of your visualization. "Hail Sunna!" you cry as she passes. She turns her face to you and raises one hand in greeting.

You slowly become aware of your own body. The sun's light fades, and the sun's warmth is now outside of you. Inside you are aware of yourself, relaxed, and somewhat energized from the sun's light. When you open your eyes you are standing or sitting in the same place you started. Thank Sunna for her time, and head inside. If you are able, offer something up to Sunna in thanks—this can be as simple as a favorite pebble, or a splash of beer, mead, or apple cider offered to her by being spilled onto the ground. The idea is to form a reciprocal relationship with Sunna—by thanking her and giving her something, you acknowledge the gift she has given to you.

Other Practices

1. In order to connect yourself with the sun's rhythm, track sunrise and sunset in your area. This is easily done by searching the Internet. Try your best to be awake at sunrise, and hail Sunna as she rises in the skies. Thank Sunna at sunset, as she fades into the west. This can be done even in bad weather, where the sun is not evident—Sunna is there, above the clouds.

2. A simple prayer to the sun can be made out of the Valkyrie Sigdriffa's words to the hero Sigurd in the Saga of the Volsungs: "Hail Day, and Hail the Sons of Day" begins the prayer; you can add "Hail Sunna on her travels" as well, making the prayer:

    Hail Day! Hail the Sons of Day! Hail to Sunna on her travels!

    You can recite this at any time you see the sun, from the moment you wake up until sundown.

3. Simple votive offerings are signs of the relationship you are developing with the sun and the natural order of daylight and darkness. Offerings of grains, liquids, or portions of your meals are always appropriate. Place the items out in the sunlight—in a sunny window, perhaps, or outside in the sun—and hail Sunna, thanking her for her presence in our lives. The "typical" time to leave these out is twenty-four hours, or one full solar cycle; after that time they may be discarded.

Notes on Chapter Two

1. John Algeo and Thomas Pyles, *The Origins and Development of the English Language*, Fifth ed. (Boston: Thompson Wadsworth, 2005). For an excellent overview of English and its origins, I recommend reading this college-level textbook. While it is focused on English as a language, its first few chapters delve directly into this topic. It is a readable text, and the chart tracing Proto-Indo-European to modern languages is invaluable.

2. Gundarsson, et al, *Our Troth Volume One: History and Lore* (North Charleston, SC: BookSurge, 2006), 22–43. The book does a good job outlining this period in history from a heathen point of view.

3. Lee M. Hollander, trans., *Poetic Edda*, Second Ed. (Austin: University of Texas Press, 2004), 44.

4. Edward James, *The Franks* (Oxford: Basil Blackwell, 1998). Mr. James's research is extensive and related directly to this period of history, from the Frankish point of view.

5. Seamus Heaney, trans., *Beowulf*, Bilingual edition (New York: W. W. Norton, 2007), 33–41.

6. Carolyne Larrington, trans., The *Poetic Edda* (Oxford: Oxford University Press, 1996), 84–96.

7. Robert Cook, trans., *Njal's Saga*, (London: Penguin Books, 2001). *Njal's Saga* describes this in detail; the lawspeaker went "under his cloak" to consider the matter, and asked not to be disturbed until he emerged. His decision was that, while Iceland would formally convert to Christianity, each

household was legally allowed to maintain whatever forms of personal worship they practiced. It was a rather clever compromise, all things considered.

*A complex cosmology needs
equally complex deities.*

Three

Gods and Goddesses

Before we go too much farther, it is time to discuss how heathens view their gods and goddesses. One thing our modern world tends to do is attempt to categorize everything into a neat series of boxes. Though efficient, this way of thinking is at odds with the mythic world, where the lines continually blur. Instead, try thinking of the gods and goddesses in more humanistic terms—just as you and I, as individuals, are more than the sum of our parts, so are the Norse deities. It is unfair to refer to Odin, for instance, as "the" god of war, or even as "a" god of war. In the first case, he is by far not the only god or goddess associated with warfare. In the second, he is so much more than that—his purview encompasses wisdom, knowledge, memory, magic, war, poetry...you see the point. The gods and goddesses are multifaceted.

There are two groups, or tribes, of deities: the Aesir and the Vanir. Both words are plural—the singular forms are As and Van, respectively. Some scholars theorize that the tribes are distinct and that one existed before the other "took over." Others feel that the Aesir and Vanir are more akin to "classes" of deities that developed simultaneously. The Aesir, for the most part, live in Asgard while the Vanir live in Vanaheim. In the myths, there was once a war between the two groups. This war continued until both sides realized they shared a common enemy—the chaotic and destructive fire and ice giants, or *thursar* (singular *thurs*). The Aesir and the Vanir ended the war by exchanging hostages and were allies from that point forward. This hostage exchange explains why the Vanir Njord, Frey, and Freyja have halls in Asgard now, as well—they were a part of the hostage exchange that ended the Aesir-Vanir war.

Many of the deities are related, or married, to one another. Among the Vanir, we see that Njord is the father of Frey and Freyja. We do not know who Frey and Freyja's mother was. Some speculate that she may be Nerthus, but there is no evidence to support this. We do know that Njord later marries the giant Skadhi, although they end up divorced. Frey marries the etin-bride (*etin* is a word for "giant") Gerdh, and they have no children. Freyja marries Ód, who later leaves her. They have a daughter together, named Hnoss. As we can see, it is fairly easy to lose track of just who is related to whom, and how. Additionally, not all of the gods and goddesses are faithful to one another. On the Aesir side, Odin, for instance, is married to Frigga. Their son is Baldur. Odin has more than one son—he fathered Thor, Vali, and Vidar from three different mothers.

Heathens, as ancestor worshippers, place a great deal of importance on family and the ancestral line. A brief look at any Icelandic saga will reveal that characters are most often introduced by reciting the names of their ancestors. While quite confusing, especially at first, it is important to know which As (the singular form of Aesir) or Van (plural Vanir) belongs to which lineage. We do not know many of the Vanir, as seen above, so it is slightly easier to keep track of them—Njord, Frey, and Freyja are the three key Vanir members (Nerthus is also often included); the "in-laws" Gerdh, Skadhi, and Ód, and the child Hnoss.

Things get increasingly complicated with the Aesir, as we can see with Odin. It may be helpful to remember that we know who our own families are. We know our grandparents, parents, aunts, uncles, brothers, sisters, and cousins. We can list each of them, who their parents are, and how they relate to us personally. In large families, the lists of relatives can sprawl across time, generations, and geographical locations, but ask any member of that family who he is related to, and he can tell you without hesitating. It is precisely the same thing when it comes to the Aesir and Vanir. Kinship is important, and while it can be difficult for an outsider to track, each knows who the other is related to.

Snorri Sturluson, in his *Prose Edda,* relates that there are twelve gods and twelve goddesses. That number is actually more fluid, depending on which deities are counted. (The criteria used to determine deity status can vary among heathens). For the most part, the gods and goddesses are the denizens of Asgard. Some, like Skadhi, live in their own lands, and others are controversial, to say the least. This chapter covers the major deities and a few of the minor ones, detailing their familial relationships along with mythic information about them to help you get a feel for each one. Remember, in some cases we know only the name and perhaps one line of mythic text about the deity. Vali and Vidar, for instance, are Odin's sons by Rind and Grid, respectively. We do not know if these sons married or fathered offspring. Rather than speculate in the descriptions of the Aesir and Vanir that follow, I have attempted to simplify and clarify the relationships among the gods and goddesses.

The deities are distinct entities. The heathen belief system is polytheistic—they believe that each god and goddess is his or her own individual deity. There is no evidence for an archetypal symbol set—maiden, mother, crone is the most obvious example, as is hunter, father, sage—in the Norse mythic system. When heathens speak of the gods, they speak of them as just that—deities who may be their original mythic ancestors and are worth respect and worship. Some heathens believe the deities contact us directly through visions, dreams, or seidh (a trance-based magical practice), and some believe that the gods are too remote and cannot be directly contacted. Some believe that the gods intervene directly in our lives; others believe the gods are far too busy for that kind of minutia. What most agree on is that the gods are real.

The Norse gods are neither infinite, nor immortal. Idunna, one of the Aesir goddesses, is known as the keeper of golden apples. The gods and goddesses eat these apples in order to stay young—and without the apples they would wither and die. Most of the gods do perish in Ragnarok. As seen in both the *Prose* and *Poetic Eddas,* Ragnarok, often referred to as the "twilight of the gods," deals with a final battle during which many of the deities are slain, and the world is set afire. Odin is consumed by the Fenris wolf. Tyr is slain by the hound, Garm, who guards Helheim, the land of the dead. Frey is killed by Surt, a giant who is bent on destruction. Surt later sets fire to all of the worlds, and everything is burned except for a few gods and goddesses and two humans who take refuge inside the World Tree, Yggdrasil.

Ragnarok is interesting in terms of time simply because we do not really know when it happens, or if it has even happened yet. Some theorize that Ragnarok occurred with the final adoption of Christianity, indicating that the old gods were dead, or at the least no longer worshiped. Others believe that the final battle has not yet occurred but will occur at some point in the distant future. There are also heathens who believe that, since time is cyclical in nature, there may have been more than one Ragnarok, and that another may be approaching. Ultimately, there is no specific answer to the question of Ragnarok except to say that it does occur, and the gods die.

Similarly, Norse gods and goddesses are not all-knowing, or omniscient. The myths prove that they make mistakes just as we do. Odin may know more than anyone else, but even he is not infallible—his wife Frigga tricks him on more than one occasion. Heathen gods, as you have seen and will continue to see, are also not all-good, or omnibenevolent. They express wrath, use trickery and deceit to get their ways, and have their own agendas. This is not to say that the gods are tough, rude, and inaccessible—that is hardly the case. Frigga, in particular, seems to be a very compassionate figure, as is Thor's wife, Sif. In one myth, Odin asks Loki to steal Freyja's necklace, Brisingamen. When she asks for it back, Odin says he will return it to her—if she starts an eternal war between two tribes of humans. She complies. While she is, in essence, being coerced into this action, the point is that no omnibenevolent goddess would not stoop to such tactics.

Finally, the gods are not omnipresent. Sometimes they are in one place or sometimes another, but they are almost never in more than one place at one time. These concepts are all important to the heathen religious worldview—our gods are not immortal, not all-knowing, not all-good, and, frankly, not always there. In short, the gods are realistic examples that heathens can turn to in order to improve their own lives. All humans make mistakes along the way, but no wight, human or otherwise, is perfect, not even a goddess. Heathens can learn how to handle their successes and mistakes because the gods are more realistic examples to follow than any single omniscient, omnibenevolent, omnipresent deity. This is, in itself, a comforting thought, and one that allows heathens to show compassion to themselves and to others.

History and archeology show us that no one god held sway over every part of the Norse world. Odin, Thor, and Frey idols are often set up in sacred *hofs*—a word referring to a hall, or other sacred building—together, but the order seems to shift geographically. Frey is the central god at Uppsala, Sweden, for instance, while Thor is the central god elsewhere in Europe. While Odin is specifically called the "father" and the "king" of the gods, it is important to remember that local practice varied and that he was not always the central god worshipped. A tribe might dedicate itself to a deity like Forseti, and hold him as their central figure instead of Odin, while another might hold its allegiance with Frigga. In modern practice, this holds true among groups as well as individual people deciding who they are, or are not, closest to. A *fulltrui* relationship is one in which a person swears to be closest friends or allies to a god or goddess. This is not the same as being dedicated to one deity to the exclusion of all others. Rather, it is more like "first among many." Taking an oath to a deity begins that fulltrui relationship, and it is more common to hear "I am sworn to Freyja" than it is to hear "Freyja is my patroness." Not all heathens take this relationship on; many do not hold themselves closer to any one deity or the other, but respect them all equally. The choice is up to the individual, and heathens tend to be very independent people. In any case, people can develop their own relations with the gods.

The list that follows covers what is best known about each deity. Keep in mind that not all deities were worshipped in all places. I have included some alternate spellings and names, as appropriate. These myths come from the *Prose Edda*, written by Snorri Sturluson, and the *Poetic* or *Elder Edda*, a collection of poems, songs, and heroic lays with no one author prominent, nor even known. Remember, Asatru is not a revealed religion. Heathens use the same materials to reconstruct heathenry. Therefore, I recommend that the reader spend time with both *Eddas*. The Anthony Faulkes translation of the *Prose Edda* is the most complete; it contains the *Hattatal* section, which is meant for traditional Icelandic poets in order to retain the Icelandic poetic forms. Many translations omit it as irrelevant, but it is worth reading through because the *kennings*—poetic devices used to refer to various things—can reveal more about how the gods and goddesses were seen by the pre-Christian heathens. The *Poetic Edda* is compiled from various manuscripts; of the translations I find that Carolyne Larrington's is the most accessible to new readers, although Ursula Dronke's translations are more directly from Old Norse to English. Several, although not all, available translations are listed in this book's bibliography.

The Gods and Goddesses

Odin

Odin is far and above the most active player in the source material, and is called Sky-Father and All-father as well as Valfather, or "father of the slain." He was broadly worshipped in pre-Christian times and is among the most commonly worshipped gods in the modern era as well. He is a complex figure, and a great deal can be said of him.

Odin is one of the three creator gods who order the universe, set the worlds in place, put the sun and moon in their positions, and ultimately create humankind. He and his brothers slay Ymir, the founder of a race of giants, and use his body to create Midgard, an act of transformative magic that clues us in to the power of this god. Odin transforms himself into a snake to sneak in and steal the mead of inspiration from Gunnlod, showing that he is also a shapeshifter. He also has truck with the dead—*Voluspa* translates roughly to "the Prophecy of the Volva." A Volva is a kind of witch or seeress, and "Voluspa*"* begins when the deceased Volva, buried in her grave-mound, is summoned by Odin, who says he knows the runes needed to bind the dead to his will. He is a god of the crossroads, a god of death, magic, shamanic practices, language, poetry, wisdom, battle, war, and kingship, and despite his prominence as a leader among the Aesir and Vanir, he dies at Ragnarok.

Odin is married to Frigga, although he is certainly not monogamous; his lovers include Gunnlod, Jord (Iord), Rind, Grid, and Freyja. He laments about women and their deceitful natures to Loddfafnir in "Hávamál," one of the poems found in the *Poetic Edda*. While this certainly does not mean women are inherently deceitful, it does mean that Odin has had enough bad experiences to urge caution. He fathers Thor with Jord (the earth goddess), and Baldur with Frigga. Rind gives him Vali, who avenges Baldur's death. Vidar, who comes from Grid, is destined to avenge his father when Odin is slain by the wolf, Fenrir. Victorian sources used to favor calling all the gods Odin's sons, due to his appellation All-father, but this is not the case, as can be seen in the source materials left to us.

It is Odin who rules over Valhalla ("slain-hall," just as Val-father means "father of the slain"). This is where the chosen battle-slain, warriors handpicked by Odin's Valkyries, come to live their afterlives. They feast and celebrate all night, then battle with one another endlessly during the day. This is done to prepare the war-band—called the Einherjar—for Ragnarok, the end-game battle on the Vigrid Plain when the giants come to destroy the nine worlds. This connection to the dead, and his leadership over them, reinforces Odin's ability to command the dead in general. He hangs himself from a tree for nine days and nights, wounded by Gungnir, his spear. Some scholars view this as a mythic example of shamanic initiatory experience. The myth has many points, but ultimately means he has died, sacrificed to himself, and come back to life again. In this case, he comes back with the runes—after hanging over a pool and seeing them, he finally reaches to grasp them and falls back screaming. This could be a sign of pain or a sign of shamanic ecstasy—it is certainly a sign of the runes' power and magic. Odin then tells us that he knows bind-runes for a number of workings, which also cements his role as a magic-god. This is not Odin's only shamanic-style role—he also plucks out one of his own eyes and tosses it into Mimir's Well. Having that eye in the bottom of the well gives him all of Mimir's wisdom. Mimir is known in the *Eddas* as a giant in charge of his Well, although *Heimskringla* notes that he is one of the two hostages the Aesir sent to the Vanir as surety against further bloodshed.

As a battle-god, Odin is the keeper of Valhalla, the hall of the slain, which is where warriors who prove themselves in battle go. The Valkyries are said to swoop down over battles and choose the most heroic warriors, who are then killed in battle and taken up to Valhalla. The Valkyries are under Odin's purview and are known to serve the Einherjar warriors meat and mead in the hall. In Valhalla, Odin is said to drink only wine, which was a luxury in Northern Europe, and it could be that this description of him has as much to do with his wealth and status as it does separate him from his Einherjar. Odin is also known for starting battles, and a spear was often thrown over the ranks of the enemy to dedicate the battle and the enemy souls to Odin. His purpose here is clear—it is Odin who is preparing the dead for the final battle at Ragnarok, where he will die, swallowed by the wolf, Fenris (also Fenrir).

Hugin (thought) and Munin (memory) are Odin's ravens. He sits upon his high seat, Hlidskjalf, and watches over all the worlds. Hugin and Munin are his eyes-on-the-ground; they fly everywhere, and report what they learn back to Odin. He has said that the two are vital, but that he would miss Munin more. This speaks directly to the importance of memory not just as a brain function that helps us shape ourselves, but also to the presence of Wyrd and his ability to know it. Wyrd is discussed in detail later in this book, but for now it can be seen generally as the pattern of every individual's life. He also has two wolves, Geri and Freki. Both of their names mean "ravenous," and it seems that they are present to underscore Odin's connection with battle. Wolves and ravens were commonly seen at battle sites, scavenging bodies not yet burned or buried. He is also the rider of Sleipnir, the eight-legged horse spawned by Loki. Sleipnir is the only horse who can ride not only through all the living worlds but into the underworld. Some modern heathens suggest that Sleipnir is a coffin, with its legs representing the legs of four coffin-bearers. There is no evidence for this, but it is a notion that implies Odin's ability to ride into and out of the lands of the dead.

Odin leads the Wild Hunt, and rides Sleipnir at the head of the pack. According to folklore, the Wild Hunt occurred in winter, while storms and winds rushed over the heads of the people. Members of the Wild Hunt, who may have been lost or unnamed souls as well as deities, hunted across the skies, flying just over human heads or along the ground. Seeing the Wild Hunt was thought of as a dire omen—it often preceded major catastrophes or, at least, the death of the person who saw it riding by. During Autumn festivals, traditional folklore says that the last sheaf of grain harvested should be left in the field, to "feed Sleipnir." The continental Germanic goddess Holda, discussed in more detail below, is also a member of the Wild Hunt. This may provide a tenuous connection between the god and goddess.

Odin is known by many names. In the Old Norse he is Óðinn. His Anglo-Saxon name is Wode. In Old High German he is known as Wodan, which gave us the Modern German Wotan. This is not all, however; in the *Grimnismal,* or *The Lay of Grimnir,* he lists all of the following as his names: Grím (hood/cowl), Grímnir (hooded one, in disguise), Gangleri (Mask or Way-weary), Herjan (which may mean War-god, Warrior, or Wanderer), Hjálmbreri (Helm-wearer or -bearer), Thekk (the Welcome One), Thrithi (Third, which connects him to the High, Most-High and Third of the *Prose Edda*), Thuth (or Thund), Uth (or Ud), Helblindi and Hár (One-Eyed: The *Poetic Edda's* Hávamál translates as the "Sayings of Hár"), Sath (Truthful or Sad), Svipdal (Changeable), Sanngetal (Truth-finder), Herteit (Glad in Battle, War-Merry), Hnikar (Thruster—especially of spears), Bileyg (One-Eyed), Báleyg (Firey-Eyed), Bolverk (Bale—or Evil-Worker), Fjolnir (Concealer), Glapsvith (practiced seducer), Fjolsvith (wisest of the gods), Síthhott (Long-Hood), Síthskegg (Long-Beard), Sigfather (victory-father), Hnikuth (Spear-Thruster), Alfather (Father of All), Valfather (Father of the chosen slain), Atríth (possibly Attacker by Horse), Farmartyr (Lord of the Boatloads—Odin is known as a cargo-god), Jálk (gelding), Kjalar (possibly "the god who gives carrion-eaters something to eat," referring to himself as a war-god), Thrór (Strife-Stirrer), Vifthur (weather-god), Óski (wish-fulfiller), Ómi (the "noisy" or "superior" one), Jafnhár (Just-as-High), Biflindi (potentially "the one with the painted shield"), Gondlir (Bearer of the Wand—potentially a magic wand), Hárbath (Harbard, Grey-Beard), Svithur (spear-god), and Svithrir (Wise).

Frigga

Frigga, also Frig, is the wife of Odin and the mother of Baldur. She is a prominent goddess and, as Odin's wife, is the first in rank. Her name derives from the Proto-Indo-European *pri, meaning "to love." The word frith, a kind of inviolable peace, share this root word. It is here that we see one reason why she is called "Beloved of Odin." As a well-known goddess throughout continental Germanic sources, it is most likely that Friday was named for her, just as Wednesday was for Odin (Woden). Some scholars believe she and Freyja are one and the same, but it seems unlikely given the differences in the Proto-Indo-European root words of their names.

There are not many myths where she is an active player, but she is always listed among the gods and goddeses, wherever they are gathered. Her hall is Fensalir, which means "fen (or bog) hall." When Baldur was born, Frigga got all the beings of all the worlds to swear never to harm Baldur. She forgot only one—the mistletoe, which seemed harmless enough. An old woman called on Frigga, who then told her the story. This was Loki in disguise, and he hastened off to make a mistletoe dart. He convinced Hod to fire the arrow, helping him with aiming, and struck down Baldur. Loki, then, is most responsible for Baldur's death—a fact he brags about to Frigga in the "Lokasenna." This is called Frigga's "first grief."

Frigga's second grief comes when Odin falls at Ragnarok. Like all of the goddesses, we have no evidence for what happens to her at the end of days. She is best known as a mother and a wife. That said, in *Heim-skringla* she helps the Langobards win a battle by tricking her husband into favoring them and is said to be their patroness. She is also known for marrying Odin's two brothers after Odin's disappearance, which has led to charges of adultery against her. Some scholars suggest that this story may be a remnant of something older, perhaps a story about sovereignty. She sits at Odin's High Seat, Hlidskjalf, and she is known to prophesy but never speak what she knows. She urges Loki to discretion in "Lokasenna"; he does not comply.

What we know of Frigga's attributes comes from her handmaidens. As Frigga's servants, they cover a range of domestic affairs. This is what has led to the modern interpretation of Frigga as a goddess of the hearth, home, and social order. She is also a spinner and weaver of cloth. Examining what the handmaidens do can reveal Frigga's character as well as the roles of ranking women in Norse society. They are listed below. Remember that the handmaidens are less well known, and often only a single line remains for us to understand them by.

Frigga's Handmaidens:
Eir

She is known as a healer. That said, Eir's name translates roughly to the word "mercy," and in addition to being one of Frigga's handmaidens, she is listed among Odin's Valkyries. This has led some modern heathens to speculate that, in addition to her healing skills, she was the source of "mercy on the battlefield," which, depending on the circumstances, could mean a clean death for those already dying from their wounds.

Fulla

Not much is known about Fulla. She is called a virgin and goes about with her hair unbound and flowing. She wears a gold band around her head. She carries Frigga's casket, a small chest, and also cares for Frigga's shoes. She is considered someone with whom Frigga shares her secrets. Fulla may be the Volla listed in the Second Meresburg Charm, Frigga's sister, or, potentially, Frigga herself.

Gefjon

Gefjon has four sons, whom she changed into oxen in order to carve land for herself out of Denmark; folklore has it that Zealand is Gefjon's property. Her name means "giver," and this has caused her to be confused with Freyja, whose byname, Gefn, means the same thing. However, as Frigga's handmaiden, she protects maidens and unmarried women. This, taken along with the myth about Zealand, is enough evidence to suggest that she is a goddess in her own right.

Lofn

Lofn is the handmaiden who clears the way for permission to be granted for marriages, particularly those marriages which would otherwise be seen as forbidden.

Sága

Sága is an interesting character. Her hall, Sökkvabekk, refers to sunken benches, the implication being a bog or fen. Frigga's hall is Fensalir, which also involves a fen. Frigga is married to Odin; Sága is known to sit with Odin in her hall and drink mead with him. In fact, there are so many similarities between Sága and Frigga that many scholars contend that they are one and the same, and that Sága is one of Frigga's bynames. The *Prose Edda* mentions her as one of Frigga's handmaidens.

Sjofn

Sjofn helps turn the minds of men and women to love.

Snotra

Snotra is known to be wise and courteous.

Syn

Syn is known as the handmaiden who bars the doors to the hall and guards against those who are forbidden to enter. It is also said that she can stand in assembly as a party for the defense, in cases that involve her.

Var

Var is most concerned with hearing the oaths people make, particularly the marriage oath.

Vor

Vor is also known to be wise, but she asks questions, and nothing can be concealed from her. Vor is the last of Frigga's handmaidens that we have record of, so here we will return to the other Norse gods and goddesses.

Thor

Thor is described as having a red beard. Thor is the son of Odin and Jord (Iord), who is the embodiment of Earth, the planet beneath our feet. He is the slayer of giants and the friend of man who stands ready to defend Midgard with his hammer, Mjolnir. He is married to the goddess Sif and has two sons, Modi and Magni. The rainbow bridge links Asgard to Midgard, and is protected by Heimdal. Thor is said to be so powerful that he cannot stride on the rainbow bridge, or he would break it. When Thor travels to meet with the other gods, he has to walk, fording rivers as he goes. He drives a cart with two goats in the traces.

Most of the myths involving Thor revolve around his ability to kill jotnar (a name for giants). He travels to Jotunheim, land of the giants, often with Loki in tow. On one occasion, Thor first visited a peasant's house. He slaughtered the goats, Teeth-Gnasher and Teeth-Gritter, who drive his cart, and bade everyone to eat the meat, on one condition: that the bones be left alone and not cracked open for the marrow. The morning came and Thor held his hammer over the bones and called his goats back to life. One had a lame leg, so he knew someone had broken a bone. Ultimately the repayment of this damage led to Thor having two human bond-servants, Thialfi and Roskva. In this same myth, Thor and Loki meet the giant Utgardh-Loki, who challenges them to a contest; he uses trickery and sets them against the embodiments of fire, thought, the ocean, the Midgard serpent named Jormungandr, and old age. Of these challenges, Thor tried to drain a full horn and could not, although he did lower the ocean's level—Snorri tells us this is why there are tides. The Midgard serpent is Thor's mortal enemy. Later, at Ragnarok, the two fight one another. Tor kills Jormungandr, then takes several steps back and dies himself. Thor very nearly brings the Midgard serpent up out of his place circling Yggdrasil, an act of strength that shocks everyone present. Thor wrestles with a nurse called Elli; she is actually the embodiment of old age. Utgardh-Loki is impressed that Thor did as well as he did, nearly breaking the Midgard serpent's back and almost defeating old age. This story shows us the prowess of Thor as much as it does the realities of life: the sea will have tides, and old age comes to us all, no matter how we wrestle with it.

Mjolnir has significance as a cultural item to this day; Scandinavians wear it, regardless of their specific religion, to show their pride in their countries. Heathens wear the hammer as a symbol of Thor and of heathen religion. In addition to Mjolnir's ability to raise goats from the dead—which hints at Thor's connection to life itself—it is used to bless fields before planting and to bless funeral pyres. The hammer is also placed in a bride's lap to ensure her ability to produce children. These practices, folkloric in origin, also reveal various aspects of Thor as a god who is connected to fertility.

Thor is outwitted by Harbard, a ferryman on the other side of a river Thor wishes to cross. They throw boasts and insults across the river at one another until Harbard gets the best of Thor. Many scholars point to this poem as an example that Thor is slow-witted or simply more brawn than brain. The truth is that Harbard is Odin in disguise, and there is no being in the world wiser than Odin. Saying that Thor is no match for Odin in a contest of wits does not insult Thor's intelligence in the least. He himself outwits Alvis, or "All-Wise," the dwarf Thor questions until the sun rises.

Sif

Sif is married to Thor, and is the mother of Ullr. Her long, golden hair is her main feature. Loki, in an act of mischief, cut all of it off. Thor threatened Loki, and so Loki persuaded two dwarves, brothers named Brokk and Eitri Ivaldi, to forge Sif new hair out of pure gold. At the same time,

Loki wagered his head that the dwarves could not create anything finer. Ultimately, the dwarves created the magic ring Draupnir; Frey's boat, Skidbladnir, and his boar, Gullinbursti; Odin's spear, Gungnir; and Thor's hammer, Mjolnir. Loki attempted to sabotage the forging in the shape of a biting fly, to no avail. Everyone present agreed that the dwarves had outdone themselves, and Loki had lost. As the cost of losing the wager, Loki was to lose his head. When Loki pointed out that he had given his head to the wager but not his neck, Brokk tied Loki's lips shut instead.

Sif's hair is made of that spun gold, and it grows the same way as regular hair. The *Prose Edda* refers to her as a seeress, and her name appears whenever the ranks of the gods and goddesses are present, but not much else is known. Some modern heathens associate Sif with the fertility of the fields, both for her relationship to Thor and her hair's similarity to wheat.

Frey

"Frey" is a word, and a title, meaning "Lord." We do know that Frey's name was Ing, or Ingvi/Yngvi, and the *Heimskringla* tells us he was the first king of Norway and the founder of the Ynglings, the ruling family of Norway. He held the primary position in the temple at Uppsala, and the early kings of Norway certainly saw him as a god of kingship. Frey is the son of Njord and the brother of Freyja, and is also the lord of Ljosalfheim, the land given to him by his father as a "tooth-gift" upon cutting his first tooth.

He owned a magical boar named Gullinbursti (literally, "gold bristle"), whose bristles were said to shine so brightly that he could be seen in the dark, and a magical ship named Skidbladnir. Frey is associated with wealth and plenty. It is said that when he was king over Norway, frith—a kind of inviolable peace—reigned, and the time was very prosperous for everyone. When he died, his council did not let the people know; instead they set Frey up in a burial mound, and left a "window" where scot, or taxes, could be paid to him. As such, he is associated with wealth of all kinds, and also with peace. When he saw Gerdh, the etin—a kind of giant—who would become his wife, he was so overcome by love and lust that he willingly gave up his sword and his warhorse to his servant, Skirnir, who then wooed Gerdh on

Frey's behalf. This is still another association with Frey and the maintaining of frith. However, it is vital to know that he fought Surt—a destructive giant, also called a thurs—at Ragnarok, battling him with an antler in place of his sword. Most statue depictions of him show Frey with an enlarged phallus, indicating his connection with fertility.

Frey seems to be more in line with the fertility and prosperity of the earth and all growing things than he is with childbirth, per se, although with his connection to fertility he very well could have something to do with the actual begetting of a child. Gold is associated with all three of the Vanir, and he is definitely a god who holds sway over riches and money, but he is also about bountiful harvests at the end of every season. Frey is one of the best-known gods, with names in Old Norse, Anglo-Saxon, and Old High German, indicating he was known throughout most of Northern Europe. He is referred to in many ways, including blot-goda, or ritual/sacrifice god, shining, weaponless, harvest god, chieftain, the people's ruler, mighty, providing, and beautiful in appearance. He is also called "Beli's Bane," after his battle with the giant Beli, and Beli's subsequent death at Frey's hands.

Freyja

Freyja (also Freya) is on par with Odin in terms of her complexity. Her name is actually a title, "Lady." We do not have record of any other name for Freyja. The word stems from the Proto-Indo-European root *per*, which meant "first," "forward," or "chief."[1] She is married to the shadowy figure, Ód, who traveled frequently and one day did not return. Freyja wept for her missing husband, and it is said that she wandered the worlds looking for him. They had a daughter, Hnoss, whose name means "treasure." In *Heimskringla*, Sturluson mentions a second daughter, Gersemmi (which also means treasure), but she is only mentioned one time, whereas Hnoss is mentioned more often, and never with a sister. Freyja has two cats pulling her cart. The cats do not have names.

Freyja is one of the Vanir who come to Asgard at the close of the Aesir/Vanir war. Some speculate that she is also Gullveig, "gold-greedy," who appears in Asgard and is later burned by the Aesir. Gullveig survives the burning not once but three times, each time stepping from the fire whole. If Gullveig and Freyja are one and the same, then we can see the burning as a potential representative of a shamanic initiatory experience as well as Freyja being a strife-stirrer, or someone who starts wars. Freyja does start battles in her role as a battle-goddess. She also performs (and is the goddess most connected to) seidh, a trance practice discussed later in this book. These arguments may connect Freyja with Gullveig, although there is no direct evidence connecting the two. On the other hand, the Heid mentioned in "Voluspa" is clearly Freyja—Heid tells Odin she has given him the gift of seidh, which we know is Freyja's purview. This also connects Freyja to witchcraft and magic as well as seidh. Seidh, also spelled seidhr, could be used to prophesy, heal, protect, or even unbind fetters, but it is also used to bind the fetters of the enemy, loosen their bowels, and send them nightmares. It should be said that "witchcraft" is often in the eye of the beholder. A seidhworker protecting her village by sending curses to its foes is both a *seidhkona*—literally, a seidh-woman—and a witch, depending on which village you are in at the time.

Freyja owns the necklace Brisingamen. It was forged by the four Brising brothers, dwarves, and their price for the necklace was that Freyja had to sleep with each one of them, in turn. She did just this, and the necklace was hers. In at least one story, Loki steals Brisingamen, and Freyja must go to Odin to get it returned. Odin says that he will, if she starts an eternal war between two tribes. She does this, which enhances her role as a battle-goddess. She receives the Einherjar—the chosen dead warriors—into her hall, Sessrumnir, and it is said that she gets half and the other half go to Odin. We have no record of what the warriors in Freyja's hall do. She also has charge of Folkvang, which can be seen as a plain for the people or as a battle-plain. Freyja herself never enters battle nor does she fight directly.

Freyja was prayed to in matters of love, and was seen as a goddess whose domain included sexuality. Loki charges her with promiscuity and incest during the "Lokasenna," but Njord, her father, stands to defender her and says, roughly, that it is no big deal if a woman has many lovers. Like all the goddesses, we do not know what happens to Freyja during and after Ragnarok. That said, she has strong associations with the dead, and we know that both the chosen slain warriors and women could go to her hall after death. In *Egil's Saga*, Egil's daughter, sharing her father's decision to starve himself to death out of grief, says that she will neither eat nor drink until she dines with Freyja.

Freyja has many bynames, including Syr (sow), Gefn (giver), Horn (flax), Thrund (throng), and Mardoll (sea-bright). She was not known in continental German sources, but is one of the most prominent goddesses throughout Scandinavia. The modern German *Frau* comes directly from the word Freyja.

Tyr

Tyr is the one-handed sky-god of the Norse mythic system. When the gods decided to bind the wolf, Fenris, to stop him from wreaking havoc throughout the worlds, it was Tyr who put his arm in the wolf's jaws. The rope the dwarves made to bind Fenris was suspiciously thin in appearance, and Fenris agreed to have it put on him only if someone would put his hand in Fenris's jaws. Tyr was the only one who agreed. When Fenris could not break free of his bonds, he bit Tyr's sword-hand off. In folklore, the wrist is called the "wolf-joint" because of this.

Some scholars maintain that Tyr was an elder sky-god, or father of the gods, until Odin came along and forced him out of his position. However, as Georges Dumezil points out, many Indo-European systems have two gods in the rulership position—one who is more concerned with magic and sorcery and the other who is more concerned with social justice.[2] This fits more appropriately into Germanic myths in general and the Norse myths in particular.

Underscoring this concept, Tyr is a warrior-god and is also known as the god of the Thing, an assembly where judgments would be heard. Things occurred in Iceland through the Conversion Period and beyond, and Thingvellir is an archeological site which can be visited today. Tyr therefore holds sway over judgments and legal matters of all kinds. However, he is also known as a god whose justice is fickle; this can seem insulting to Tyr unless one considers how legal matters were handled among the Germanic peoples. Often, two warring clans would challenge each other at the Thing, and wind up with a peace agreement involving some form of exchange. Unless the exchange of goods happened at the Thing, there was no real way to enforce it, nor was there any way to prevent the feud from breaking out again.

At Ragnarok, Tyr will fight Garm, the hound who guards the gates of Helheim. He will fall to Garm, as well, ranking him among the gods destroyed on the Vigrid Plain. Until then, Tyr is known to travel with Thor, dispense justice, and be a leader amongst the gods and goddesses of Asgard.

Holda

Holda, also Holde, Holle, and Dame Holda, is best known among continental Germanic source materials. She governs the act of spinning, keeps order in the hall, and rides in the Wild Hunt with Odin. She has a great deal of similarity to Frigga, which has made some scholars think the two are one and the same. This seems unlikely, given that Holda has such a prominent place in modern German folklore.

Snow is referred to as Holda shaking out her feather bed. When plague hit a village, if some died and others lived, then Holda had visited the village with her rake. If, however, everyone died, then it was said that Holda had visited with her broom. This associates her with the dead, albeit in an oblique way. She is known to keep the souls of children and, in the Christian Period, the unbaptised souls of babies as well. This in turn associates Holda with children and the caring of children's souls after death.

Njord

Njord is a Van, the singular form of Vanir, one of the two classes of gods and goddesses, and the father of Freyja and Frey. We do know some things about him, although he does not take an active role in many of the myths. His hall, Noatun, is a boatyard. He is also a god of prosperity, particularly from the shoreline—imagine longboats coming in from the sea or the fjords, laden with cargo and wealth. He is also said to have some control over the seas, the motion of winds, and fire; he was prayed to for success-ful sea ventures, from raiding to fishing.

He and Frey were the hostages exchanged to the Aesir in order to se-cure the Vanir-Aesir peace treaty. Indo-European cultures generally con-tain a twin pair; many consider the twins to be Frey and Freyja. However, there is no mention in the lore of their being twins, and the exchange was for Njord and Frey. If there is a twin pair in Norse cosmology, it is more likely to be the father-son pair of Njord and Frey.[3]

When Skadhi came to Asgard she demanded weregild, the price due to a family when a murder occurred. Thiazi, Skadhi's father, had been killed by the Aesir and Vanir, and so weregild was certainly due. Skadhi demanded two things as payment for the death of her father. First, the gods had to make her laugh, a difficult trick because she was in mouning. Second, Skadhi demanded that one of the gods marry her. Her condition here was that she have her choice of husband. The gods agreed, but with a catch: she could only look at their bare feet. Looking down, she saw a beautiful, fair, pale pair of feet and, assuming they belonged to Baldur, chose them. The feet belonged, of course, to Njord. They married. Skadhi could not tolerate the sounds of the gulls and the crashing waves at the shoreline, so they moved to her hall, Thrymheim, deep in the mountains. After a time, Njord realized he could not take the silence of the mountains, and they realized they could not remain together. They divorced over these irreconcilable differences.

Njord, too, was at Aegir's hall during the Lokasenna. Aegir is a giant whose purview is the sea, and who acts as an ally of the gods. The Aesir and Vanir are gathered for a sumble at Aegir's hall. When Loki accuses Freyja of sleeping with all of the gods, including her own brother, Njord comes to his daughter's defense. He says that there is no big deal, really, if a woman wants to have many lovers. This means two things. One, because a father defended his daughter's honor, she is most likely as promiscuous as Loki suggests, but since he does not care, then some kind of female promiscuity must have been acceptable in Norse society. Second, because Njord makes no protest at all over the accusation of incest Loki makes, he must be aware of, and have no qualms with, his children having sex together. This is born out in the *Heimskringla*, where Snorri Sturluson says that incest was common among the Vanir, as were brother-sister marriages. This is one of the distinctions between the Aesir and Vanir, and it may be assumed that, whoever Frey and Freyja's mother was, she may have been Njord's sister.

The word Njord is the masculine form of the female Nerthus. We do have specific mention of Nerthus as an early continental goddess—she was worshipped by the Suebi, according to Tacitus—and there is some scholarly speculation that the two may once have been one and the same deity. Others point to this fact and suggest that Nerthus may well have been Njord's sister and the mother of Frey and Freyja. It must be said that this is speculation—no evidence of this exists in the source materials.

Nerthus

Nerthus is not mentioned in the *Prose Edda* nor the *Poetic Edda*, but rather by the Roman Tacitus, in his work discussing the Germanic tribes. Tacitus states that the Suebi honored her, and that, in springtime, the priests of Nerthus would sense her presence and bring her forth in a cart drawn by cows, covered so that her image could not be seen. Her cart then traveled across the land, stopping at every village, and all weapons would be laid down in peace while she was there. When she returned to her island, her thralls—slaves—would uncover her, clean her, and settle her back into her shrine. After that, they were ritually drowned, connecting Nerthus to human sacrifice.

Tacitus wrote the *Germania* in approximately 98 CE, making Nerthus one of the older deities we know about. Her name is the feminine—and original—form of Njord, which makes some scholars think Njord evolved over time from the worship of Nerthus, or that the two are one and the same. Some modern heathens speculate that, since we know Njord married his sister and that Nerthus is the feminine form of his name, Nerthus must be a Van and the mother of Frey and Freyja. It must be said that there is no evidence for this.

Heimdall/Heimdal

Heimdal guards Asgard. His senses are so acute that he can hear the grass and a sheep's wool growing. Heimdal does not need to sleep. It is said that, when the thursar—the destructive giants—mount their final attack against the Aesir, he will lift his great horn, Gjallarhorn, also called the "horn of great resounding," and blow a blast to signal they are coming and Ragnarok is beginning. The exact style of the horn is unknown, although some depictions of Bronze Age rituals did feature lur horns. Some modern heathens think of it as a large horn, perhaps from an aurochs, or a long-horned cow.

We know that Heimdal has nine mothers—who are called the nine waves and said to be the daughters of Aegir—and that he has a hall of his own, named Himinbjorg, which roughly translates to "heaven-mountain," perhaps indicating his place at the gates of Asgard. His horse is named Gulltoppr, or "gold-mane."

Interestingly, Heimdal is referred to as "muddy-backed," *aurgo baki*. In the "Voluspa," verse 27, the mud from the Well of Wyrd, which the Norns feed to Yggdrasil, is referred to as *aurgom forsi*. While Loki intends to insult Heimdal by referring to him in this manner, the similarity between the two words is not accidental. This has led some modern heathens to consider Heimdal as standing with his back to Yggdrasil, near the Well at the base of the tree, guarding not only Asgard but all the worlds. He is counted among the Aesir, but some speculate that, since he has the mud of Yggdrasil and Wyrd on him, he may be a being more akin to the Norns themselves, and part of the larger cosmology than might otherwise be known.

Heimdal is also the main character of the *Rigsthula*; the prologue tells us that Heimdal came to Midgard in the guise of Rig, which means King. He visited three couples, lay with each of them, and thus fathered the enslaved thralls, the freemen, and the ruling class. This was important in Old Norse society because a more rigid social structure existed, but it still has relevance today. While Odin, Vili, and Ve created humans, Rig, by acting as he did, created human society. In fact, the couple called Great-Grandfather and Great-Grandmother welcomed Heimdal to their rough hut, after which Great-Grandmother gave birth to Thrall. Grandmother and Grandfather bore and raised Karl. Mother and Father gave birth to Jarl, raised as a warrior-ruler. What we see here is that the ancestors were also involved in crafting society from the start—why else use such specific familial names? We can say that our ancestors bore us, but we can also say that Heimdal fathered us.

Lastly, in the poem *Husdrapa*, it is said that Loki steals Freyja's necklace, Brisingamen. Heimdal chases after him and the two do battle out in the open water, transformed into seals. Heimdal defeated Loki and returned Freyja's necklace to her. Thus, we can see that Heimdal and Freyja may be allies, as Aesir and Vanir are, but that Loki is no friend to Heimdal. This is born out in the Ragnarok cycle, when Heimdal and Loki battle one another yet again.

Baldur/Baldr

Baldur is the son of Frigga and Odin, and therefore is a ranking god by birth. In the myths, Frigga asks every living thing to swear an oath never to harm him. Frigga forgets to ask the mistletoe for its promise, thinking it a harmless plant. The gods have great fun throwing various things at Baldur, since they will not harm him. When an old woman—Loki in disguise—comes to Frigga and asks about Baldur's invincibility, Frigga tells her about the oaths she receives and mentions that she missed the mistletoe. Loki goes off and makes a dart, or arrow, out of the plant. He then uses the blind god Hod to fire a dart of mistletoe at Baldur, promptly killing him. Baldur is known to reside in Hel's hall in high honor, and will return after Ragnarok to rule the new gods.

Saxo Grammaticus, who wrote *History of the Danes*, tells a different tale. He asserts that Baldur and another warrior, Hod, got into a duel to see who would win Nanna, who the Icelandic sources say is Baldur's wife. In Saxo's version, Baldur dies of his wounds and Nanna goes to his opponent instead.

Hel

Hel is the daughter of Loki and the giantess Angrboda. She is described as being half white and half black, which some speculate might mean the pale flesh of death and the rotting flesh that comes after. Some consider her half living and half dead while others point to the way the blood pools in a body after the person has died, and liken Hel's coloring to corpses. It is Hel whom Odin sent to Helheim to take leadership over the dead.

She receives Baldur and Nanna into her halls when Baldur dies, and is, presumably, a good hostess to them. When she is asked to release Baldur, she says that she will, but only if every being weeps and mourns for him. One troll—many claim this is Loki in disguise—refuses to weep, and thus Baldur remains dead in her halls. She is not mentioned in many myths, but is known to lead the dead and side with the thursar at Ragnarok, against the gods.

Forseti

When Forseti landed on an island in Frisia, he struck his axe into a stone and a spring gushed forth. He is the son of Baldur and Nanna and is considered a settler of lawsuits and other legal entanglements. He is the patron god of the Frisians and is said to have given them their laws. Historically, it is said that silence was enforced while people were gathered by his sacred spring and when drinking from it. It is also said that, as a result of Forseti's action, the beasts on the island he landed on could not be harmed.

Idunna

Idunna is the keeper of the golden apples. These keep the gods young and strong; without them, the gods would age and wither. Loki insulted a giant named Thiazi (also Thiassi, Skadhi's father) and swore to get Idunna and her apples out of Asgard in order to free himself from Thiazi's vengeance. When the gods found out, they were furious, and also began to age. Loki was then charged to bring her back again, and he did so in the shape of a bird, with Idunna transformed into a nut and held in his claws. Thiazi gave chase in the form of an eagle, and was burned to death by the gods as he flew over Asgard's gates.

Bragi

We do not know much about Bragi. He is the husband of Idunna and is associated with bards, scops (actually pronounced "shope," the equivalent to a skald, or wandering performer and poet), poetry, and storytelling in general. Loki insults him by calling him a "benchwarmer" during Lokasenna, clearly referring to him as a coward. On the other hand, being a "benchwarmer" could be a reference to the place of honor that skalds held when called into the longhall to perform. While Odin obtains the mead of poetry, some heathens suggest Bragi might be the keeper of it. There is no source in the lore for this, but it makes sense given his connection to the art of recitation. Scant evidence may suggest that there was a historical figure named Bragi who lived during the Viking Age and may have been a prominent skald, but this may in itself be a legend.

Aegir

Aegir is a giant, or etin, but one who is allied with the Aesir and Vanir. His hall lies under the sea, and he is considered by many to be an embodiment of the deeper waters, those beyond the shoreline. He hosts the gods in his hall on more than one occasion. The most famous occurs as part of the Lokasenna, or "Flyting of Loki," during which time Loki commits murder and ultimately shatters his relationship with the gods. We know from that poem that Aegir is also called Gymir. Aegir is known as a brewer, and his skills are often invoked by heathen brewers and mead makers. He is married to the giantess Ran, who keeps the souls of drowned sailors in her hall. Aegir's hall is described as glittering and gold.

Ran

Ran is married to Aegir. She is a giant, and holds sway over the deep seas. When people drown at sea, she gathers them in her net and brings them to her golden hall. They must pay her in gold, but then she keeps them with her.

Skadhi

Skadhi, also Skadi, is the daughter of the giant Thiazi. She left her home, Thrymheim, and sought weregild—a kind of payment for his murder—from the gods in Asgard. Her demands were that she be made to laugh and to be given a husband. Odin placed Thiazi's eyes in the sky as stars as a way to honor Skadhi's father. Loki tied his balls to a goat and pranced around until she laughed. Skadhi was allowed to choose her husband, but the gods pulled a sheet across them, so that the only things visible were their feet. She picked the most beautiful pair of feet, thinking they must be Baldur's—instead they were Njord's. The two eventually divorced after realizing neither could live in the other's hall.

Some sources say she married Odin after her divorce from Njord, and even bore him a son. The records are sketchy in this regard, and we do not have much detail to confirm or deny this myth. We do know that Skadhi had her own cult. Place-names in particular reveal that she was known, and likely worshipped, in eastern Sweden. This bears out her assertion that only bad advice would be given to Loki in her sanctuaries and plains. She is the first to tell Loki he is about to be bound by the gods, and she is the one who places the venomous snake over Loki's face.

She is called the Ondur-Dis, or snowshoe-goddess, which may indicate a connection between her and the winter months. This is the only connection she has to winter, and some modern heathens do not associate her with winter due to scant evidence. She is certainly known as a hunter, just as her father, Thiazi was.

Loki

Loki is a complicated figure, and modern heathens are divided as to their opinions of this god. This section will cover some of the myths known about Loki; the appendix "The Problem of Loki" goes into further examination of why many modern heathens do not worship Loki.

Loki is an etin, and Odin's sworn blood-brother. He is the father of Sleipnir, Odin's eight-legged horse, whom he bore while in the guise of a mare. Loki is also the father of the monsters Fenrir (Fenris); the Midgard

Serpent, Jormungandr; and the half-living, half-dead Hel, guardian of the underworld. We know that Loki is able to shape-shift, as well—he borrows Freyja's falcon cloak to find the location of Thor's hammer, becomes a bird to seek out Idunna when she is kidnapped by a giant, and, as stated, he becomes a mare in order to prevent another giant from completing the wall surrounding Asgard in the time period allowed by the gods. He travels with Thor from time to time, often getting Thor into trouble or stealing his hammer, Mjolnir, as he does Freyja's necklace, Brisingamen. When Skadhi comes to Asgard, demanding weregild for the death of her father, Thiazi, among her demands she says someone must make her laugh. Loki accomplishes this by tying his balls to a goat and following it around until she starts laughing.

Loki breaks frith with the gods as part of Lokasenna, when he murders a servant and then verbally attempts to cut everyone present at that sumble down to size. In one myth, he flees Thor and shifts into various shapes, among them a salmon. He is caught by a net of his own design. In another version, he is manhandled into submission. The Aesir and Vanir bind him to a rock in an underground cave using his own son's intestines. Skadhi, in an act of revenge against Loki, hangs a serpent over his face, where its venom will drip down onto him and cause him eternal agony. Loki's wife, Sigyn, holds a bowl over his face to catch the venom; her act keeps the agony from him until she needs to go empty the bowl. Folklore suggests this as the reason for earthquakes—Loki's physical response to his agony moves the world.

At the end of days, Loki breaks free of his bonds. He leads the giants in the final battle of Ragnarok, an enemy of the Aesir and Vanir.

Sigyn

We know that Sigyn is Loki's wife and the mother of Narfi and Nari. She holds a bowl over the bound Loki's face, catching the venom dripping from the snake fixed in place over him. There are some who speculate that this act may relate Sigyn to compassion.

Mani

In Germanic language and culture, the moon is masculine while the sun is feminine. Heathenry is not the only culture that believes this; many Proto-Indo-European-derived cultures believe the same. This can be difficult for those who are used to seeing the moon as a woman, or a reflection of Artemis, while her brother, Apollo, is the sun. It can be helpful to remember the phrase "Man in the Moon." The man in the moon, according to Norse mythology, is Mani.

We know that Mani is the brother of Sunna and that they both were given their positions during the creation of the world by Odin, Vili, and Ve. They are the children of Mundilfæri, and his arrogance at their beauty is what caused the gods to put them in the skies. Mani drives a wagon across the night sky; in it he carries a chunk of rock from Muspelheim that is the moon itself. His horse is called Hrimfaxi (which means rime—or ice-mane) and he is eternally chased by a troll transformed into a wolf. When Ragnarok begins, the wolf will catch up to, and devour, the moon.

The moon's impact on the tides cannot be questioned. There is no specific mention of this in the myths, but it must have been obvious to the ancestors that the tides rose and fell with the lunar phases just as they do today. This has led some heathens to speculate that Mani has an impact over the tides along the shorelines, as well. The *Prose Edda* also states that two children, Bil and Hiuki, travel with Mani, carrying a tub on a cross-pole. It is possible that this is an old story that may have its roots in the Jack and Jill nursery rhyme.

Sunna

Sunna also drives a cart across the sky, and her horses are named Árvakr (early-awake) and Alsvith (all-swift). The sun itself is a spark from Muspelheim which Odin, Vili, and Ve set into place, but Sunna is seen by most modern heathens as the personification of the sun. This makes sense in a worldview that holds the sun as feminine. She is chased across the sky by a troll transformed into the shape of a wolf. The Fimbulvintr—three years of winter—which presages Ragnarok, will occur when the wolf inevitably catches the sun and devours her.

Sun worship was prominent in the Bronze Age, as can be seen in the Trundholm Sun Chariot and in the prevalence of the sunwheel, either even-armed or as a swastika. The sunwheel is found across ancient and modern cultures all over the world. That said, it is vital to remember that the Nazi party co-opted and corrupted this ancient symbol of the sun; many modern heathens will not wear or associate with the swastika due to its ill fame. Instead they prefer the sunwheel shown as an even-armed cross inside a circle. As we discussed in chapter 1, the worship of the sun predates the Viking Age. It certainly existed during it as well, as seen in the Sunna myths.

Ostara

Ostara is another goddess with just one mention. It is said that she comes from the east, and Ostara does mean "east." In Anglo-Saxon, her name is Eostre, a word that has been carried down as the modern English "Easter." This may be an indicator that her worship was not fully stamped out during the Conversion Period. Since this is the only mention of her, we have to speculate what her worship may have looked like. The rabbit and eggs, if traceable to Ostara, indicate fertility, and the timing of her worship connects her with the spring.

Hod/Hodr

There are two versions of the Baldur myth. In the first, and the one most commonly believed by modern heathens, Hod is Baldur's brother. He is blind and is deceived by Loki into shooting a mistletoe dart at Baldur, thus committing fratricide. Hod is, himself, then slain by Vali in an act of vengeance. In his book *History of the Danes*, Saxo Grammaticus, relates Hod as a strong warrior and says that he duels Baldur over Nanna, winning her and slaying Baldur. The outcome of both myths is the same—Baldur dies, slain by Hod. This sets up the myth spoken of Baldur, that he will return after Ragnarok to rule the new gods.

Hoenir

We know almost nothing about Hoenir. He is one of Odin's brothers, and, as part of the Odin-Lodur-Hoenir trio, created mankind from driftwood; this gives him some creator god aspects. It is important to note that there are two separate records of the three original creator gods. The second trio is Odin-Vili-Ve. We do not know why there are two different versions of the same myth. This may be due to differing geographical beliefs or may simply mean that these were both written down and preserved in different texts. Hoenir is one of the hostages sent from the Aesir to the Vanir as part of their peace treaty. Hoenir is also known to be slow of speech. After Ragnarok, he returns to Asgard to take up the role of *godhi* (roughly meaning priest) for the new gods. This not only suggests that he lives through the destruction, but also leads to an interesting little speculation about Vanaheim's survival rate as well. It seems logical that an As surviving Ragnarok must have had a place to do just that, and at the time he is living in Vanaheim.

Lodur

We know next to nothing about Lodur as well. He is the third of the creator gods Odin, Hoenir, and Lodur. This also makes him one of Odin's brothers.

Ve

The word *ve* refers to a sacred structure where heathens practiced their religion and means "holiness" or "the sacred." The god Ve, then, had a great deal to do with holy or sacred things. Precisely what, we do not know, because other than his mention as one of the three creator gods, Odin, Vili, and Ve, we know nothing about him from the source materials. It is commonly accepted that Ve is the one who gave lá, or "comely hue." This will be discussed further in chapter 6, which deals with creation and cosmology.

Vili

Vili is one of Odin's two brothers, and is involved with the creation of humans. His name means "will," and he is the god who gave us the gift of Óð, called "spirit" or "inspiration."

Jord

Identified as one of Odin's lovers and the mother of Thor, Jord represents the personified Earth, the planet we stand on. She is not to be confused with Midgard, also the place we stand on. It is better to think of her as an embodiment and personification of Earth-the-planet, while Midgard is the name of a location.

Ull

Ull, or Ullr, is known as a god of both the bow and the snowshoe, indicating his connection to hunting and the winter months. His mother is Sif. His name means "glory," and he is also a god called upon prior to holmgang, or dueling. We know that his hall is named Ydalir, or "Yew-Dales"—since many bows were made of yew wood, this may also indicate his connection to hunting.

Interestingly, archeological digs happening near paces named for Ullr have unearthed rings, mostly arm-rings. The arm-ring of a chieftain was used to swear oaths on, so there may be a tenuous connection between Ullr and the swearing of oaths, as well.

Vali

Vali seems to have one purpose—slaying Hod and avenging Baldur's death. He is the son of Odin and Rind, and is called a "good shot," implying his ability as an archer. Snorri Sturluson says that Vali survives Ragnarok, and will dwell with Vidar in Idavoll.

Vidar

Vidar is the son of Odin and the etin Grid. Often referred to as the "silent god," Vidar is most clearly associated with avenging his father's death. He rips Fenris's jaws apart and kills the wolf. Folklore suggests that remnants of shoe leather were offered to Vidar to make his shoe thicker, and thus better able to step on the wolf's lower jaw.

Connecting to the Gods

Modern heathens practice blót (it rhymes with "boat" and is also spelled blot) as their primary ritual. I deal with the details of blót and blót structure later in this book, but it is important to note here because connecting with the gods and goddesses comes primarily through blót. I have written two examples. God and goddess names can be changed in order to connect with any specific deity.

Sample Blót One—Freyja

Items Needed:

Liquid offering (mead is best, although cider
    is a good nonalcoholic substitute)

Drinking horn or cup

Offering bowl

This blót is ideal for solitary practitioners or heathens who feel the need to do this on their own. It is deliberately short, sweet, and to the point.

Set up your horn and bowl, along with any other ritual items/altar set-ups you feel are needed, indoors or outdoors. Take a few calming breaths and focus on Freyja—on her bright Brisingamen, her cats, and the Lady herself. When you are focused on Freyja, begin your blót.

Pour the liquid offering into the cup/horn you are using. Hold it up and make the sign of the hammer over the top.

SAY: "Mighty Mjolnir, Hammer of Thor, bless this (drink)."

Then toast to Freyja three times. Each time, raise the horn and speak out loud, as if speaking directly to Freyja. After each toast, take a small sip yourself, and then pour a bit from the horn into the offering bowl—that is the goddess's portion.

SAY: "Freyja, Vanadis, Lady, I raise this horn to you in thanks for your many gifts. Hail Freyja."

SAY: "Lady of love and laughter, I raise this horn in your honor. Hail Freyja."

SAY: Njord's daughter, Frey's sister, boar-rider, I lift this horn to you with respect and gratitude in my heart. Hail Freyja.

Notice the repetition of the sentence "Hail Freyja." Heathens do this every time they lift a horn to someone, and it basically is a formal ending to the toast. As a less formal toast, you can also just say "Hail Freyja."

When you have done your three toasts, stop and listen quietly to the world around you. This may be very inspirational, or very simple, depending on your personality. At the end of your private thoughts, lift the horn again.

SAY: Freyja, I offer this mead to you. Hail Freyja.

Pour the liquid into the offering bowl. Take the bowl outside, or walk to a tree, and libate the offering. Pour the offering out of the bowl.

SAY: From the gods to the earth to us, from us to the earth to the gods. A gift for a gift. (This closing was originally written by Lewis Stead).[4]

This ends your simple, solitary blót to the goddess.

Sample Blót Two–Frey

This one is more ritually expressive and can be done with any number of people. If you have more than twenty people, you probably will want to do only one round to Frey instead of three—it is just as acceptable and won't take as long to complete.

Items Needed:

Altar/table

Altar cloth

Hammer (think of a hand-held sledgehammer,
    small enough to comfortably lift)

Offering liquid (again, mead or cider are best)

Horn or other drinking vessel

Offering bowl

Any icons you may have of Frey (for the altar)

Set up your altar. It is typical in heathen practice to place the altar in the north, and to face north, but this is not required. As a matter of fact, we know that Frey comes from the east when he travels, so putting the altar in the east would work just as well in this case. If you want to, you can have all the people present put something on the altar to be blessed by Frey.

Create sacred space by using the so-called "Hammer Rite," discussed in more detail later in the book. For now, know that it is a way of "clearing house," so that the land or area becomes sacred. Begin by facing north with the hammer in your hand. Lift the hammer up.

SAY: Hammer of Thor, hallow and hold this holy stead.

Then face south and repeat. Remember that north and south are the primary directions that heathens pay attention to.

Bless the mead/cider by pouring it into the horn, then lift the horn upward. Make the sign of the hammer over it, and either say the words from the Freyja blót, or as an alternative you can use any one or this whole series of kennings:

SAY: Bountiful boon of bees, blessed brew of Aegir, blood of Kvasir, carry our words into the Well of Wyrd.

At this point, you can invoke Frey by speaking about him or by calling his names/kennings out and asking him to be present. Words like these are appropriate:

SAY: Ingvi, Frey, god of the world, we ask that you come to us that we may thank you for your many gifts. Hail Frey.

SAY: We know Frey as the lord of the Alfar, as the king of men, and as the brother of Freyja. He is a god of wealth and fertility, a god of the bountiful harvest, and the husband of Gerdh. We ask Frey to join us for this rite as we honor him with our words. Hail Frey.

Pass the horn. You can do this in one of two ways—pass it from person to person, or choose one person to be the "Valkyrie" and bring the horn to everyone individually. Either way, let everyone speak a toast to Frey and take a sip from the horn. In a large group it is hard to pour out a sip for Frey every time a toast is finished, although some heathens will spill a bit out onto the ground, as the god's portion. Remember this can be one round or three, depending on the size of the crowd.

When everyone has had their turn toasting Frey, thank him for his gifts and pour the liquid from the horn to the bowl.

SAY: Frey, we offer this blessed mead to you as a gift.

Take the offering bowl to a tree and libate, pouring the mead onto a tree's roots.

SAY: From the gods to the earth to us, from us to the earth to the gods. A gift for a gift.

These words stem from the Ravenbok *written by Lewis Stead, and they are used by many heathens, particularly in the northeast region of the United States, as a way to end the ritual.*

Notes on Chapter Three

1. Patricia Lafayllve, *Freyja, Lady, Vanadis: An Introduction to the Goddess*, (Denver: Outskirts Press, 2006). For more details on this, as well as a thorough examination of Freyja, please see my book on the subject.

2. Georges Dumezil, *Gods of the Ancient Northmen*, (Berkeley: University of California Press, 1973), 26–48. Dumezil argues that Indo-European societies originally

had a tripartite religious system based upon the functions of particular gods. The first function is rulership, the second warriors, and the third based on the masses of society. This would, for instance, place Odin as first-function, Thor as second-function, and Frey as third-function gods. He specifically compares Odin and Tyr in chapter 2, titled "Magic, War, and Justice: Odin and Tyr," and argues that both fit the first function simultaneously, Odin as the magician/priest and Tyr as the god of war/law.

3. Georges Dumezil, *Gods of the Ancient Northmen*, (Berkeley: University of California Press, 1973), 66-79. Georges Dumezil was a philologist involved in the exploration into the Proto-Indo-European languages. While doing so he noticed a great many mythic parallels across various Indo-European-derived cultures. One involved a twin pair, both of whom tended to be what he called "third function" or fertility deities of some kind. There is no evidence in our lore for a twin pair, per se—there is no evidence that Frey and Freyja were twins, only siblings. However, some heathens argue that, since Njord and Frey were the hostages to the Aesir, perhaps these two derived from an earlier twin pair.

4. Lewis Stead, *Ravenbok* (http://www.ravenkindred.com/ Ravenbok.html, accessed December 14, 2011). This is an online source for information on Asatru and samples of then-Raven Kindred's blót structure.

We stand on the shoulders
of those who came before us.

four

Ancestor Worship in Heathenry

Evidence for ancestor veneration exists in nearly every culture in the world. Stone Age sites, particularly burial mounds, show evidence of food and drink left as offerings for the ancestral dead, which speaks to the longevity of ancestral cult practices.[1] Northern European tribal peoples were no exception, and a great deal of saga evidence and place names remain to reveal ancestral worship and the offering of sacrifices to ancestors, particularly the disir, during events such as Disablót and Mothers' Night.[2]

The singular word *dis* can refer to an ancestress known to guard the family line. It can also mean "woman," which is how it is frequently used. There are also times when goddesses are referred to as *disir* (the plural form of dis). Therefore, we have to use some scrutiny to determine which are the ancestral disir and which are not. Hilda Roderick Ellis Davidson agrees, discussing the term disir and adding that it "seems to include the female guardian spirits attached to certain individuals or families."[3] Du-Bois says something similar and suggests that the disir may "derive ultimately from ancestor worship."[4]

We know that the disir can appear in dreams. The Medieval Icelandic manuscript *Flateyjarbók* discusses a Winter Night's feast, where Thorhallr felt that someone would die that night and warned everyone present not to go outside. Thithdrandi answered a knock on the door anyway, and there saw nine women in white and nine in black. The women in black attacked him, and the next day he was dead at dawn. Thorhallr interpreted this as meaning that the old, heathen disir attacking were from the "old custom" and the nine in white were disir who wanted to help him, but were not able to do so.[5] We also have a tale from *Gisli's Saga* which happened in similar fashion, one *draumkona* (dream-woman) offering him advice and the other threatening him.[6] By and large, however, the disir were and still are seen as helping spirits.

The disir seem to travel directly with their descendants, offering help, volunteering advice, and generally maintaining the family's *hamingja*. Hamingja refers to a kind of ancestral or "folk soul" that flows from generation to generation, every member of a family contributing to it with their actions in life. There seems to be some evidence indicating a belief in multiple soul parts—meaning that a person's spirit is not simply one soul but a combination of many.[7] A good amount of heathens feel that the hamingja is one of the many parts to the heathen soul. Linking the disir to it, therefore, may mean that the disir are connected to the individual's soul itself. One might consider the disir as similar to a line of grandmothers stretching back to the beginning, offering both warm chocolate-chip cookies and stern corrections for bad behavior.

The male ancestral dead are harder to pinpoint. Unlike the disir, they have no specific name and seem to reside in their burial mounds or graves rather than traveling descendant to descendant. We know that the burial mounds in Uppsala, Sweden, were both large and small, and that "the outstanding ones were the graves of kings who reigned long before the Viking Age."[8] DuBois suggests that the dead "were venerated at sacred sites, often burial grounds or shines near the home."[9] This may indicate that ancestor worship was part of the sacred nature of Uppsala and other places, and may predate the Stone Age. In the modern era, most heathens call on both the disir and the alfar as ancestors, implying that the male ancestral dead are among the alfs, or elves.

There is some evidence for this point of view. Ellis Davidson tells us that "worship of the ancestors can probably not be clearly separated from that of the land-spirits."[10] We know that some notable men, after their deaths, might "become known as alfs."[11] This includes kings like Óláfr of Norway, who came to be known as *Geirstaðaálfir*, or the elf from Geirstaðr.[12] Gabriel Turville-Petre points to the same evidence and suggests that the alfar may be the "manly" counterpart to the disir.[13] Ann Groa Sheffield agrees, adding that "the practice of ship burial unites the idea and its journey into mystery with the practice of mound-burial and the veneration of buried ancestors who continue to interact with the living."[14] *Our Troth, Volume One: History and Lore* suggests that these male ancestors are considered "dark alfs" or "mound elves" and separates them from the svartalfar spoken of in detail in the next chapter.[15]

Herein lies the problem. We have different kinds of alfar (alfs). There are ljosalfar and svartalfar—light elves and dark elves—and these beings are in no way connected to the ancestral dead. There are different kinds of alfs, and it appears that the male ancestral dead may be only one kind of alf among many. We will discuss the various alfar in the coming chapter, but it must be said that there are those who call the male ancestral dead "alfar," and those who do not, because the alfar as a whole are not "only" the ancestral ones. What modern heathens tend to say is that the alfar—the male ancestors—are more connected with the land they are buried on, especially if it is the family land. There is some evidence to back this belief up as well, given that we know offerings were left at burial mounds, also called howes, at Yule and other holy times. Blood or milk seemed to be offered in times of famine as well.[16] In her book, *The Road to Hel*, Hilda Ellis Davidson speaks at length about small, hollow depressions found in stones near grave mounds. Sometimes called "elf-cups," these may have been places where the food and drink offerings were made.[17]

What does all this mean? Ultimately, it means heathenry is focused on many things, but one of its stronger focuses is ancestor worship.

Heathens take pride in the accomplishments of their ancestors. Heathens will emulate their ancestors and ask them for advice, make offerings to them, and keep heirlooms around the house. It goes deeper than that, though. The Hávamál says:

76. Deyr fé
    deyja frændr
    deyr sjálf it sama
    en orðstírr
    deyr aldregi
    hveim er sér góðan getr

76. Cattle die
    and kindred die.
    You will die, as well.
    but the reputation
    of the one who earns good renown
    never dies. (author trans.)

Clearly, this stanza is talking about two things. One is reputation—a person's reputation is what will remain long after he or she has died. The second is, by inference, immortality; if one's reputation never dies, then that person is remembered, and if their reputation is a good one, then they shall live on after death. Stanza 77 follows this up:

77. Deyr fé
    deyja frændr
    deyr sjálfr it sama
    ek veit einn
    at aldri deyr
    dómr um dauðan hvern.

77. Cattle die
    and kinsmen die.
    You will die, as well.

I know one thing
that never dies
the judgment (destiny) of those now dead. (author trans.)

Here we see that the dead have their own destinies, as well. One presumes that a good reputation will lead to a good destiny—being remembered is, after all, the one certain way to gain immortality that we heathens have. At the same time, should a person's reputation be negative, that will mean his or her destiny can be quite different. If we put the two stanzas together, what we have is a message about immortality, and perhaps the afterlife, being directly attached to a good reputation. In other words, when heathens speak the names of their ancestors, tell their stories, make offerings to them or toast them in sumble, what heathens are really doing is keeping them alive and making them immortal. An ancestor forgotten is an ancestor dead forever. It is important to remember, here, that not knowing the name of an ancestor is not the same as forgetting altogether—many heathens will toast to their family ancestors by surname when full names are not known. Deliberate forgetting means not toasting the ancestor in question, not making offerings, and never talking about that person. This can be a key point for abuse survivors—even though ancestor worship is important, not all ancestors need be honored in these ways. In some cases, perhaps the best thing that can be done is to deliberately forget to include them.

Many heathens practice genealogy, the study of one's "family tree" or direct line of ancestors. Some can trace their lines back to a god, like Odin or Frey. Linking genealogies to gods was common throughout the Medieval Period and was seen as a way for ruling families to maintain their credibility. Others can trace their ancestry back to such figures as Olaf the Fart or Harald Bluetooth. In any case, listening to these heathens recite the names of their ancestors during blót or sumble can be a powerful and moving experience. On the other hand, some heathens only know their family names back one or two generations. This is fine—not all can trace their lines—and the common practice is to list all the family names known, regardless. It can be equally moving to listen to the family names being recited.

Ancestor Offerings

When it comes to offering gifts to the ancestors, the typical approach is to offer food and drink to them. This has led to many modern heathens doing their best to offer to ancestors the foods and drinks they loved best in life. Heathens may know some of this directly, since they knew the family member while he was alive, or they may remember her favorite recipe and prepare that.

Some heathens have adapted a practice from another tradition. At festivals, blóts, or remembrance nights—such as an ancestor's birthday—an extra plate is put on the table, with a chair left empty as the place setting. This is known as the "ancestor plate" and the ancestor is served alongside the gathered people. Often the ancestors are given the first serving of every item in the meal, even dessert, and a glass of whatever is being served is given to them as well. The gathered assembly—or the solo person, in private practice—toasts the ancestor(s) being remembered and fed, and then sups with the ancestors present.

After the meal is complete, the food and drink are offered out to the ancestors. This can be as simple as leaving the plate out on the counter for an hour or two before clearing it away, or even leaving it out in the backyard or on an outdoor altar space overnight. Some heathens use their best china, silver, and crystal for the ancestor plate, so it is important to place such things where they are unlikely to be broken. I know my grandmother loved her china and might be upset if a plate got cracked!

A smaller version of this is to offer a shot glass or other small item's worth of food and drink to the ancestors, leaving it on the ancestor altar in your home. Always remember to thank your ancestors for their many gifts.

Connecting with the Ancestors

The simplest, and in some ways best, way to connect with our ancestors is by telling their stories. Speak their names in the ancestor round of a sumble, and tell the gathered people about them. Heathens believe that immortality comes mainly from being well-remembered, so in order to provide that for your ancestors, speak about them.

Another simple way of connecting with your ancestors is by keeping their mementos about the house. If your grandmother collected teacups, then keep one of hers in your house. Use it on special occasions when you are ritually connecting with her, specifically. You can design an ancestor altar out of old photographs, small mementos, or other things that remind you of your ancestors. Leave food and drink offerings on that altar from time to time to deepen that connection you feel with your own family line.

Remember that you might not know the names of many of your ancestors. That is very common in today's American societies, although in Iceland people can, and do, recite their lineage back to the original settlers of that country. In the cases where you do not know their names, use the surnames if you can—for instance, my direct ancestors come from the Lafailles and the Lowerys, so I can say "Hail the Lowerys and the Lafailles" with impunity. You can also choose to say a simple "Hail the ancestors" if that is more comfortable for you. One thing to keep in mind: as I said above, heathens venerate their ancestors to keep them alive after they've passed to the ancestral halls. The opposite is also allowable—the deliberate forgetting of an ancestor.

Sample Ancestor Blót

Items Needed:

Table

Altar cloth

Drinking horn or other vessel

Offering bowl

Small mementos, photographs, or
other images of your ancestors
A sprig off a live evergreen tree

Before the day of the blót, ask anyone attending to bring small items that remind them of their ancestors. Let them know that they will be used on the altar, but are not sacrificial offerings of any kind. Leave the table covered with the altar cloth with only the horn and bowl on it—it should start unadorned. As you gather for the ritual, ask everyone to place the items they brought to represent their ancestors on the altar. This will visually and metaphorically represent a kind of "coming together" of the various families present.

You can choose to hallow the space and make it sacred either with the hammer rite or by saying words such as these:

SAY: Here we stand in sacred Midgard, here in this place we are safe, and here our ancestors are with us. Ancestors, please guard and keep this stead while we perform our blót.

Invoke the gods and goddesses with words like these:

SAY: Aesir. Vanir. All the shining gods of Asgard, our eldest ancestors, we ask that you come here, now, to stand with us as we honor our family lines. Hail the gods.

Invoke the land-spirits (landvaettir, see chapter 5) *with words like these:*

SAY: Wights of land and wights of sky. All you who are seen and unseen, present as we stand in sacred Midgard, we ask that you share your space with us as we honor the ancestors. Hail the land-spirits.

Invoke the ancestors with words like these:

SAY: Ancient ones. Those whose bones are our bones, and whose blood sings in our veins, we welcome you. We remember you this day as on all days. We ask that you be with us, and share your wisdom and love as we gather here to honor you. Hail the Ancestors.

Bless the mead or other liquid by lifting the horn up and making the sign of the hammer over it. You can also ask Aegir to bless the brew.

Pass the horn for one round. As it comes to each person, they have the opportunity to talk about their ancestors and why they remember them. If this is a small group, consider three rounds—one round is mainly crafted to give everyone the time to speak without lengthening the ritual too much.

When the horn has been passed and everyone has said their words over it, thank the ancestors for all their many gifts, and pour the mead out into the offering bowl. Dip the evergreen sprig into the liquid and move through the gathered company, sprinkling each person with the liquid.

SAY: May the blessings of the ancestors shine on you.

When this is finished, take the offering bowl out to a nearby tree and pour it out onto the roots, saying nothing. Thank everyone for participating.

Sample Ancestor Meditation

Items Needed:

An altar dedicated to the ancestors

A drinking horn

Liquid offering (mead is the preferred liquid,
　　　but cider can also be used, or apple juice,
　　　which represent the juice from Idunna's apples)

Offering bowl

This can be performed alone or with a larger group. This is not a blót, per se, but contains the rough shape of one. The point of the meditation is to deepen one's connection to the ancestors. Othila (also Othala), the rune chanted, refers to the ancestral home lands. Many heathens also use it as representative of the ancestors.

Bless the space by using a hammer rite, a simple blessing of the land, or words like the ones below. Hight means "named." This invocation calls on the Norse creation myth to secure the space and make it holy:

SAY: Before there was time, before the beginning of things, there were but two lands. In the north lay one land, Niflheim hight, a land of cold and frozen things, of glaciers and ice, blizzards and snows. In it lay Hverglemir, the well from which all icy waters flowed.

In the south lay the other land, Muspelheim hight, a land of fires, desert heat, and hot winds. Magma flowed from it.

Between the two yawned the roaring gap. As the icy waters met the molten magma in Ginnungagap, a rime formed. Above all of this stretched the mighty ash, Yggdrasil hight, its branches stretching through all the heavens and its roots stretching down below all other worlds. Here, in Ginnungagap, Midgard was formed. Here we stand at the base of the great tree. Here we stand in sacred Midgard.

Invoke the gods, goddesses, and the landvaettir with words like these:

SAY: Shining ones of Asgard and Vanaheim. Mighty ones. Aesir and Vanir. Gods and goddesses. Be with us as we honor the ancestors, and share your wisdom with us. Hail the Aesir. Hail the Vanir. Hail the gods and goddesses.

SAY: Vaettir of this place. You who go seen and unseen. You who walk, or crawl, or swim, or fly, come to us. We ask that you share this place with us while we honor the ancestors. Hail the landvaettir.

Lift the horn and fill it with liquid. Bless the horn and the offering within it, using words like these:

SAY: Blessed boon of bees, bountiful brew of Aegir, blood of Kvasir, bear our words into the Well of Wyrd.

Take a small sip of the mead, then pour a bit into the offering bowl as the gods' and wights' portion.

SAY: At this time, in this place, we honor the ancestors by chanting.

When chanting the rune, use one entire breath per invocation. The rune should sound long and drawn out. While chanting, focus your mind and heart on your ancestors.

CHANT: Othila, Othila, Othila.

SAY: Ancient ones, hallowed ones, those who travel in our souls and along our journeys. Disir, we call on you to attend us now. Share your love, your protection, and your wisdom as we wend our ways through the world. Hail the disir.

Take a small sip, then pour out some mead as the disir's portion.

CHANT: Othila, Othila, Othila.

SAY: Ancient ones, hallowed ones, those who lay steady in their mounds. Alfar, we call on you to attend us now. Share your strength, your protection, and your wisdom as we wend our ways through the world. Hail the alfar.

Take a small sip of mead, then pour out some of the mead as the alfar's portion.

CHANT: Othila, Othila, Othila.

SAY: Ancient ones. Hallowed ones. Ancestors whose bones are our bones, and whose blood sings in our veins. Disir, alfar, shining ones. We ask that you share your wisdom with us now. We listen in silence to your words.

Spend a long moment in silence. Listen to your heart, to the emotions that stir you, to the wind as it blows or the whispers touching your ears. Hear the words of the ancestors in silence. If this is a solitary ritual, move on when you feel you have heard or felt what you needed to. If this is a multiperson ritual, sit or stand in silence even after you are done. Try to get a "feel" for the silence—when people start shifting or fidgeting a little bit, you'll know they've received their messages, too.

CHANT: Othila, Othila, Othila.

SAY: Ancient ones, ancestors, we feel your song in our hearts. We thank you for the wisdom you have shared with us this day.

Take a sip of mead, then pour some out as the ancestors' portion. Be generous.

SAY: Landvaettir, we thank you for your presence here as we honored our ancestors. Hail the landvaettir.

Take a sip of mead, then pour some out as the landvaettir's portion.

SAY: Shining gods, our ancient ancestors, we thank you for your presence here today. Hail the gods and goddesses.

Take a sip of mead, then pour out some as the gods' portion. Then hold the horn high for a moment, toasting the entities present. Pour the remaining mead into the bowl. In silence, take the bowl outside to a tree, rock, or other land feature. Libate the mead.

SAY: This rite is ended. Hail the ancestors.

Notes on Chapter Four

1. Gundarsson, et al, *Our Troth, Volume One: History and Lore* (North Charleston: Booksurge, 2006), 456.

2. John Lindow, *Norse Mythology: A Guide to the Gods, Heroes, Rituals, and Beliefs* (Oxford: Oxford University Press, 2001), 97. He explains that little is known about ancestor worship and what it might have looked like, then sets out the very evidence used to prove ancestor veneration did exist.

3. H. R. Ellis Davidson, *Myths and Symbols of Pagan Europe* (Syracuse, NY: Syracuse University Press, 1988), 106. This book compares various pre-Christian cultures, mainly the Celtic and the Norse, and looks for connections between them.

4. Thomas DuBois, *Nordic Religions in the Viking Age* (Philadelphia: University of Philadelphia Press, 1999) 51.

5. Gundarsson, et al, *Our Troth Volume One: History and Lore* (North Charleston, SC: Booksurge, 2006), 442. Chapter 22 deals exclusively with the disir and Valkyries, while chapter 23 deals with landvaettir and discusses the male ancestors and mound-folk.

6. Gundarsson, et al, *Our Troth Volume One: History and Lore* (North Charleston, SC: Booksurge, 2006), 443.

7. Winifred Hodge Rose, "Heathen Full-Souls: The Big Picture." *Idunna* issues 67–69, 2006. This three-part article covers not only multiple-souls theory but goes on to identify the various soul parts and their purposes.

8. H. R. Ellis Davidson, *Myths and Symbols of Pagan Europe* (Syracuse, NY: Syracuse University Press, 1988), 127.

9. Thomas DuBois, *Nordic Religions in the Viking Age* (Philadelphia: University of Philadelphia Press, 1999), 75.

10. H. R. Ellis Davidson, *Myths and Symbols of Pagan Europe* (Syracuse: Syracuse University Press, 1988), 121–122.

11. Gundarsson, et al, *Our Troth Volume One: History and Lore* (North Charleston: Booksurge, 2006), 456.

12. Gundarsson, et al, *Our Troth Volume One: History and Lore* (North Charleston: Booksurge, 2006), 455.

13. Gundarsson, et al, *Our Troth Volume One: History and Lore* (North Charleston: Booksurge, 2006), 456. *Our Troth* discusses Turville-Petre's views on the subject of alfar as male ancestors.

14. Ann Groa Sheffield, *Frey: God of the World* (LuLu.com, 2007), 17.

15. Gundarsson, et al, *Our Troth Volume One: History and Lore* (North Charleston: Booksurge, 2006), 452.

16. Gundarsson, et al, *Our Troth Volume One: History and Lore* (North Charleston: Booksurge, 2006), 456.

17. H. R. Ellis Davidson, *The Road to Hel* (New York: Greenwood Publishing Group, 1968), 155–156. *The Road to Hel* discusses the afterlife as seen in the history and source material, and includes a section on the mound-elves or male ancestors.

We live alongside the spirits of the land.

five

The Landvaettir and Other Wights

The landvaettir are all around us. They are the spirits of the land, rocks, trees, bodies of water, and so on. There are even house-spirits, apartment-spirits, a sauna-spirit, and a great many others. The word most commonly used for these types of spirits is "vaett" (vaettir is the plural), and so you will hear things like husvaettir (literally "house-wights") and, most especially, landvaettir ("land-spirits"). It is important to remember that a term like landvaettir refers to a number of classes of "spirits"—a cat has a spirit, and can rank among the landvaettir, but so do the alfar (singular alf). As we have seen, the word "wight" is used throughout the source material to refer to any kind of being. Wight is the word used to classify us, and not used as a color. As with the ancestors, a great deal of overlap exists among the land-wights. We have already discussed the link between the male ancestral dead and the alfar—mound-alfar may be the male dead resting in their mounds, or classified as land-wights, alfar more generally, or even the more fearful barrow-wights.

The word "alf" looks a great deal like the word "elf," and the meanings of the two words have some similarities. Given the overlap in classifying land-wights generally and the alfar specifically, we can ask ourselves if the alfar are similar to the elves and faeries spoken of in other cultural folklore. The answer is both yes and no. We do know that the word "álfkarl" (male elf) was taken into the Irish as "alcaille," meaning "ghost of the dead."[1] This may connect them with the Sidhe, who are also known as mound-dwellers.[2] It should be noted that in many cultures a mound or burial mound was considered an entry point to the Otherworld generally. While there may be a connection between the Sidhe with the ancestral dead (their home is in the mound), it is also important to remember that the mound may "only" be an entrance into the Otherworld. We also know from Anglo-Saxon folklore that alfar were known to sing and to dance, especially in an elf-ring,[3] and were able to mate with humankind. This, too, is consistent with the myths of other cultures regarding the elves.

On the other hand, similarities do not necessarily mean connections. Our ancestors, specifically the male alfar in their mounds, are not the same class of beings as the Sidhe. They behave differently according to both the saga records and folklore. Irish myth and Germanic myth developed at the same time, but in separate directions. It seems logical, therefore, to think of the Irish and German wights as fundamentally distinct from one another. As polytheists, and as animists, heathens tend to believe that each wight, alf or otherwise, is its own individual with its own quirks, behaviors, and expectations.

There are many surviving folkloric references when it comes to dealing with the alfar. Some are rules of polite behavior, and others are warnings against dealing with them at all. KveldulfR Gundarsson deals with these in detail in his book, *Elves, Wights, and Trolls*, but a few can be listed here[4]:

1. If an alf presents you with a present or token, politely
   accept it. Folklore references speak of an alf giving
   a midwife or other helper a pile of what looks to be
   worthless—often dead leaves or trash—that the midwife

discards. Later, she learned the pile of trash had been transformed into gold.

2. The alfar know when you have lied to them, or about them. Never do this.

3. Ask for permission before you set fires, move rocks, or take plants from various locations, or you risk offending them. It is common in modern Iceland to move highway projects around mounds and stones where the land-spirits are thought to live.

Naturally, there are warnings against dealing with the elves or alfar as well:

1. Dealing with the elves can cause madness, sorrow, or a wandering of the mind.[5]

2. Elves use elf-shot, or alf-shot—tiny arrows, often invisible, that cause sickness, localized swelling, sharp unexplained pain, and other diseases, even death.[6]

Many Anglo-Saxon and other folklore texts refer to alf-shot, troll-shot, and otherworldly damaging darts in terms of protecting or healing a person from them. As an example, the *Galdrabók*, a Medieval Icelandic book on magic, lists this charm:

31. Against Toll [sic]-Shot
If something comes flying toward you, read this verse as a rule: "Bumen sittimus calectimus me tasus eli siebahot elem ve a onaj."[7]

It is unclear what the phrase is specifically referring to, but it may refer to a mode of card-counting in order to win at a game of cards. Gambling was important to Icelandic peoples, and may have a connection to a personal store of luck. The charm may be meant to confuse the alf firing the shot, or as a distraction; it may connect to the luck of the alf shooting the dart. It is hard to say with certainty, but the charm as it was used survives.

The book *Scandinavian Folk Belief and Legend* has a great number of events referring to alfs or dealing with alfs. Story 47.1 deals with *tusse*, another word for alf-kind, helping with a harvest. A couple living on Austaana were having trouble getting help to bring their harvest in. It was simply too much work for only two people to accomplish. The couple brewed and baked, presuming that with food and drink available, their neighbors might help out after all. That night, however, voices were heard saying:

"Everybody can mow,
but nobody can tie the cross.
We tie it straight,
and soon we can quit."[8]

In the morning, the field had been harvested, presumably by the tusse. The method of tying they used was not the common cross-tie, but a straight tie that no one had seen before.

As another example, story 47.11 contains a more intimate, one-on-one neighborly tale. A farmer walking in his fields comes across a mound. On it is a little man filling his pipe. When the alf asks, the farmer gives him fire to light the pipe. In exchange, the farmer is allowed to fill his pipe with tobacco from the little man's pouch.[9] Legends like these reinforce an idea of the elves as good neighbors who are willing to help and to share with humankind. In a sense, they are a part of the local community and should be respected as such.

In addition to the landvaettir, house-wights (husvaettir) do exist and are recorded in folklore. There are different names for these spirits, depending on the region where humans live. The *tussen* (singular *tusse*) are from Norway and can be both house-spirits and mound-dwellers, as seen in the above story. In Denmark they are called the *nissen* (singular *nisse*); in Germany they are *kobolds*. The house-spirits are called *tomten* (singular *tomte*) in Sweden, and *brownies* in England.[10] Finally, we know from the *Poetic Edda* that Alfheim, the land of the alfar, is given to Frey as a tooth-gift.[11] We can surmise, then, that Frey is the Lord of the Alfar and has governance over them. As a god of the mound, too, Frey has a further connection with the alfar and, we can extrapolate, a connection with the male ancestral dead as well.

After the light-elves, or alfar, we have the dark-elves (svartalfar), or dwarves. The dwarves are created from the maggots emerging from Ymir's body after he is slain by Odin, Vili, and Ve. They are often described as having dark faces—this may be a reference to the color black (svart) or may have to do with the fact that the dwarves are the masters of smithcraft, and spend so much time at their forges that soot from the fires has darkened their skin. One dwarf, Dáinn, whose name translates as "the dead one," is called the leader of the alfar; this might connect him more closely to the mound-alfar than other dwarves. The "Voluspa" mentions many of the dwarves by name. Here are just a few:

Wind-elf, Thrain, Durin, Bombur, Nori, Mead-wolf, Alvis, Fili, Kili, Foundling and Nali, Loamfield, Oakenshield, Greyhair, Mound-river, Skirvir, Skafid, Fialar, Frosty, Betrayer, and Finn.[12]

As we can see, many of the dwarf-names were taken and used by J. R. R. Tolkien in his *Lord of the Rings* books. This is no surprise given Tolkien's specialty in Anglo-Saxon and Norse myths. In any event, we do have references of svartalfar being consulted, creating magic items, and exacting payment, as seen in some of chapter 3's mythology concerning the gods and their interactions with svartalfar. The only solid references we have to the appearance of the svartalfar are above—they are dark-skinned in some way and are called dwarves. Interestingly, given these descriptions, there is nothing in the lore to suggest that the dwarves are particularly short. It may make sense for them to be so, given that they tend to live underground and practice smithcraft, but there's nothing say-ing all dwarves are low in stature, nor in importance.

For example, four dwarves share the task of the holding the vault of the sky—Ymir's skull—overhead. Their names are Austri (East), Vestri (West), Sudri (South), and Nordri (North). These directions are important from a navigational standpoint, and it must be said that the Northern peoples were among the best sailors of their times. However, there does not seem to be any sort of mystic or magical connection with the directions. They are dwarves, we know that, and they hold up the sky. That is a truly important job for them to have, and many modern heathens believe that leaving them alone to do that job is best.

While not necessarily warlike, the dwarves can be violent. At least one dwarf, Alvis (all-wise), turns into a rock when the sun strikes him at daybreak. They can be forced to work via threats or after a bargain is struck with them. In order to gain the necklace Brisingamen, for instance, Freyja agrees to sleep with the four Brising brothers, each in turn. Loki wagers his head with the dwarf Brokk that he cannot forge gifts better than those the sons of Ivaldi created (Sif's hair, the ship Skidbladnir, and Odin's spear, Gungnir). Despite Loki's interference, Eitri forges the golden-bristled boar Gullinbursti, the gold ring, Draupnir, and Thor's hammer, Mjolnir. The gods agreed Mjolnir was the best of all six gifts. Loki runs away, but is captured, and then agrees to hold up his end of the bet. However, he stipulated that his neck was not part of the bargain. Unable to behead Loki, Brokk settled for sewing his lips shut.[13] What we can see from the story above is that the dwarves create the greatest gifts for the gods, and exact their payment.

Our final classification of wights is the etin. Etins, also called *Jotnar* (singular Jotun), resemble the myths of giants in most respects. They are often found in Jotunheim, of course, for that is their home. In addition, they seem to inhabit the wild spaces where man has not settled. This is how many modern heathens perceive the giants—they are distinct entities, but also akin to forces of nature, the wild vastness that we do not have any connection with. This does not, in and of itself, mean that the etin-kind are all unfriendly. Aegir, for instance, the master brewer whose abode is the ocean, is known to be an ally of the Aesir and Vanir, and he frequently hosts them in his hall. His wife, Ran, seems more distant, but she takes in the souls of sailors drowned at sea. Skadhi, when she comes seeking weregild from the gods to avenge her father Thiazi's murder, marries Njord. They later divorce, but Skadhi remains a friend to the gods and goddesses. Gerdh, the giantess, is persuaded—after many threats—to marry Frey. Even Odin, Vili, and Ve are from giant-stock. In other words, these giants, for whatever reasons, have chosen to ally themselves with the Aesir and Vanir, and are considered both friendly and part of the extended tribe. Most other etins are not in the same class, and it must be said that for many heathens this is nothing troubling—we do not know these jotnar, nor they us, and that is a fairly neutral thing to say. In fact, many heathens simply consider the jotnar who are not part of the Aesir/Vanir grouping to be utangardh. This will be discussed in more detail later, but the word translates to "out-yard," and refers essentially to anything not a part of a specific group.

On the other hand, there are the thursar (singular thurs) or thurses. This class of giant is bent on violence, chaos, and, ultimately, the destruction of Midgard. The thurs Surt, for instance, lives in Muspelheim. He has a flaming sword and, when Ragnarok comes, not only kills the god Frey but burns all nine worlds to the ground. The thurs Hrym is the captain of Naglfari, the ship made of human fingernails that the thursar ride in to attack Asgard, shattering the rainbow bridge, Bifrost. The majority of the giants in Muspelheim and Niflheim—fire and ice giants, respectively—are considered enemies of Midgard and join in the destruction of the nine worlds. The giant Vafthrúthnir is willing to kill Odin in their riddle-game. If we consider the jotnar to be akin to natural forces, the thursar are those forces which can be catastrophic. Similar to a Category 5 hurricane, they leave destruction in their wake. A hurricane cannot be considered "good" nor "evil" in and of itself, but its havoc underscores its impact on the world of men. No one wants a hurricane to strike in their backyard, nor their neighbor's. This is similar to the heathen concept regarding the thursar—they are either deliberately destructive or leave destruction in their wake.

In addition to the thursar, there are monsters in Norse mythology. Fenris, the bound wolf, will break free and swallow Odin whole. Jormungandr, the Midgard serpent, rises from the seas and poisons Thor with his breath. Troll-wives like Angrboda give birth to these monsters and are themselves considered monsters. The eagle whose wing-buffets create the north wind is called Hræsvelgr, translating roughly as "corpse-greedy." While not technically thursar, per se, these monsters are just as destructive. When taken together, the thursar and the monsters are in no way friends of mankind or the gods and goddesses. They are definitely utangardh to heathens, since heathens consider themselves the allies of the Aesir and Vanir. They do not question the existence of the thursar. There is little to no evidence that these beings were ever worshipped in the Viking Age. Since these beings are hostile by nature and either unconsciously or deliberately destructive, the thursar and monsters are classified as the enemies not only of the gods and goddesses, but by extension, of all of mankind. Modern heathens do not worship the thursar or the monsters for this reason, nor do they leave them offerings of any kind.

Offerings to the Vaettir

Folklore provides us with a great number of offerings appropriate to the wights of house and land. Whole milk, or raw if you can obtain it, is always welcome. Honey is a good gift, particularly when mixed with milk. Oats, barley, and other grains are left out for the landvaettir along with fresh-churned butter (organic butter or locally made butter, if available, are good substitutes). Beer and mead are acceptable as well as fresh cider for people who do not drink alcohol nor allow it into their homes. Fresh fruits, herbs, and vegetables, particularly during their respective harvesting seasons, are also welcome.

One way to ask the landvaettir to guard your homestead is to mix up milk, honey, and oats into a bowl. Then walk your property and, at every corner, offer out some of the mixture to the wights, thanking them for their presence and asking them for their help. This is a similar practice to a landtaking, which can be found in Part Two. Another traditional folkloric way is to leave a bowl of milk, whey, oats, or butter out on your porch, usually when the moon is out. Apartment dwellers can do similar things, leaving the offering on an altar or table space for several hours or overnight before pouring it out onto the ground outside.

You may want to build a wight-home for your house-spirits to live in. The simplest way to do this is to go out and find a rock about the size of a grapefruit. Ask the wights of the rock if they want to move in with you and yours, and leave an offering in place of the rock. Take it home and put it in a windowsill, near a doorway, or on your hearth if you have a fireplace. Make offerings directly to the alf-home, since they are in residence there.

A note on wights in general. Remember that animals are considered wights. Ibn Fadlan laughed at the Rus when he saw that the dogs ate the offerings they left out—in his opinion, the Rus were foolish to believe the spirits took the food they had offered, since everyone knew it was really the dogs. Well, dogs, cats, and other animals are landvaettir, so to the modern heathen sensibility it only makes sense that they would partake in the offering just as the invisible wights do. That said, when you are making offerings, do your best to ensure they are not toxic to animals, particularly if you plan on leaving them out overnight. If possible and necessary, keep an eye out for errant cats, dogs, or other house pets who might eat the offerings and then get sick. When outdoors, place the offerings far enough from your house that the local raccoons, skunks, or even rats do not think of your house as something they should investigate and potentially live in. If you are leaving offerings on a porch, wait a few hours and then place the offering further from the house. Remember that the idea of offering is to make the item/food sacred, then offer it to the invisible ones. They partake of the essence of the offering, and then the offering can be poured out on the ground, in the case of liquid, or safely discarded in a compost pile, recycled trash, or other container. Under no circumstances should food be left out to rot. Consider how you would feel if someone offered you a plate of rotten fruits, mold-infused grains, or curdled milk. We want to offer the best of what we have to the landvaettir, and that is what to keep in mind. Spoiled offerings are often considered offensive.

A Ritual for Apartment-Wights

Many of us live in apartments or condominiums, yet we seldom hear about rituals specific to those settings. This rite should work for hus-vaettir as well; the point of the ritual is to honor the vaettir who live with you, in your dwelling, whatever its kind.

The first thing you want to do is clean. Clean in the mundane sense, with dusters, mops, and brooms. Do the dishes. If you think about it, the apartment-wights are your roommates, and as a respectful "roomie" you want to show that you care for the space you're all living in. In particular, clean the room where you plan to perform the ritual and the kitchen before making anything for the vaettir to eat.

Items Needed:

An offering bowl or other container

An altar, if you have one, or a cleared table space

A candle; white or red preferred, in a candle holder

Offering of milk, butter, or bread

Set up your altar or table space with the offering bowl in the center and the candle either behind it or to one side. It does not matter which. Focus your mind on what you are doing—making an offering of welcome and thanks for those spirits who live in your apartment with you, both seen and unseen. Take a few deep breaths if you need to, to center yourself and help you focus on the ritual.

Light the candle. Pick it up and walk to your front door. Lift the candle high and make a hammer sign with it.

SAY: May the light of this candle ward the ways. Welcome the wealful wights of this place.

Moving clockwise, proceed throughout the apartment, repeating this at all windows and doors. When you are finished, return to your altar/ table and set the candle down. Make the sign of the hammer over the offering with your hand, the candle, or your hammer, if you have one. Ask that the offering be made sacred.

Present the sacred offering into the offering bowl. If possible, do this three times. Each time you make the offering, say words to this effect:

SAY: Spirits of this place, apartment-wights, I welcome you. Thank you for sharing your space with me. I offer this to you in welcome and thanks.

This ends the ritual. Leave the candle burning (under your supervision, of course!) and leave the offering in the bowl. If possible, let the candle burn itself out and leave the offering in its place overnight. If not, at least wait a few hours so that the gift can be shared.

The next day, or after a few hours, it is fine to blow out the candle and pour the offering out. If you can, pour the offering outside near a tree. If you can't, the offering remnants can be discarded in the proper trash containers or down your sink. Remember that the spirits partake of the essence of the offering; once they have done so, it is fine to discard it.

Another, less formal thing you can do is set up a small altar or space near your wight-rock or wight-home. Have a small container—using a shotglass is fine—where you can leave offerings. Every so often, leave some milk, or grain, hard alcohol, mead, or something similar in the small container and thank the spirits for warding and keeping the apartment safe. Again, leave it for a few hours or overnight, and then discard or libate it onto the ground. If you have land, or access to land, you may work a similar ritual for the land-vaettir as well; remember that they live on the property as well.

Notes on Chapter Five

1. Gundarsson, et al, *Our Troth Volume One: History and Lore* (North Charleston, SC: Booksurge, 2006), 455.

2. KveldulfR Gundarsson, *Elves, Wights, and Trolls* (New York: iUniverse, 2007), 2–3.

3. Gundarsson, et al, *Our Troth Volume One: History and Lore* (North Charleston, SC: Booksurge, 2006), 458.

4. KveldulfR Gundarsson, *Elves, Wights, and Trolls* (New York: iUniverse, 2007), 3–5. As a general note, KveldulfR Gundarsson published *Elves, Wights, and Trolls* in 2007. Any practitioner looking for in-depth research on the landvaettir should pick this book up and read it. Gundarsson goes into great detail, including charms to attract and send away various entities, small rituals that can be done, and other pragmatic ways of dealing with this subject.

5. KveldulfR Gundarsson, *Elves, Wights, and Trolls* (New York: iUniverse, 2007), 65.

6. KveldulfR Gundarsson, *Elves, Wights, and Trolls* (New York: iUniverse, 2007), 66.

7. Stephen Flowers, *The Galdrabók: An Icelandic Book of Magic* (Smithville, TX: Runa-Raven Press, 2005), 53.

8. Reimund Kvideland and Henning J. Sehmsdorf, *Scandinavian Folk Belief and Legend* (Minneapolis, MN: University of Minnesota Press, 1998), 223–4.

9. Reimund Kvideland and Henning J. Sehmsdorf, *Scandinavian Folk Belief and Legend* (Minneapolis, MN: University of Minnesota Press, 1998), 230–1

10. Reimund Kvideland and Henning J. Sehmsdorf, *Scandinavian Folk Belief and Legend* (Minneapolis, MN: University of Minnesota Press, 1998), 474.

11. Carolyne Larrington, trans., The *Poetic Edda* (Oxford: Oxford University Press, 1996), 52. Specifically, *Grimnir's sayings*, verse 5.

12. Carolyne Larrington, trans., The *Poetic Edda* (Oxford: Oxford University Press, 1996), 5–6. Specifically, *The Seeress's Prophesy,* verses 10-16.

13. Snorri Sturluson, The *Prose Edda*, Anthony Faulkes, trans. (London: Everyman, 1987), 96–7.

At the same time, [the] otherworld is never something wholly
other. It intersects with the empirical world of time and space
and is imminent within the here-and-now of reality.
—Michael York, *Pagan Theology*

Six

Creation and Cosmology

Heathenry is relatively new, culturally speaking, and coincides with the Postmodern Era; roughly, its beginning occurred when Asatru was formally recognized by Iceland in the 1970s. However we define ourselves, it is important to remember and not underestimate such events as the Industrial Revolution and its impact on modern society. It is equally impossible to disregard the scientific method and the spirit of inquiry it walks hand-in-hand with. In short, we cannot go backwards and we cannot erase our own past. Therefore, while the ancient ways are important to heathens, and they do their best to understand and reconstruct them, they must also remember their places in the modern world.

In this chapter we will discuss the creation myths and what can be known of heathen cosmology. Much of this comes from Norse mythology and can be found in both the *Poetic* and the *Prose Eddas*. As you will see, there are nine worlds in the Norse universe. There is some scholarly disagreement on precisely which nine worlds compose the "Nine Worlds," but overall they can be listed as follows:

Muspelheim	Midgard	Svartalfheim
Niflheim	Vanaheim	Jotunheim
Asgard	Ljosalfheim	Helheim

The World Cosmos of the North

In the beginning, the stories tell us, there was nothingness, and chaos. Muspelheim, a world of fire, heat, and ash, existed in the south, and Niflheim, the realm of ice, frost, and glaciers, existed in the north. Heathens place their emphasis on the north, which is ice, and on the south, which is fire. These are the two directions and elements most important to the modern heathen.

Between Muspelheim and Niflheim yawned the chasm known as Ginnungagap. This is one key to understanding the heathen cosmology— Ginnungagap is a word worth translating. *Ginn* does mean "gap," but it also means "vast" or "wide." *Ginnungagap*, however, translates most directly as "a chaotic or formless void." It seems rational to assume, then, that Ginnungagap was more a void than a "mere" gap or chasm; that it had no form also speaks to how things were at the beginnings of the mythic Norse world. Some heathens have speculated that Ginnungagap could also be considered a realm of potential—out of the formlessness and chaos rise the worlds that are "in order," including our own Midgard. When the magma of Muspelheim and the icy waters from Niflheim's churning well, Hvergelmir, met with a great hissing noise, rime formed. A cow named Audhumla licked at the rime until her licking freed the first being, the creature Ymir.

No one knows where Audhumla and Ymir came from. They simply did not exist, and then they did. This could well be history at work; there may be an older creation myth, dating back to Proto-Indo-European times, which shows its remnants here. The same can be said for Yggdrasil—the tree is not specifically formed in the creation myth; it is simply present. As *axis mundi*, it makes the most sense for it to have been there as Muspelheim and Niflheim were; it would give shape to the becoming universe if there were fire on the one side, ice on the other, and the great tree rising up through the yawning void of Ginnungagap, with its roots extending below the metaphysical lowest point and its branches up through the metaphysical upmost level. It has to be said, that's an interpretation of this author's own; the *axis mundi* historically, across cultures, seems to be the center-pole on which everything else revolves.

When Ymir sleeps, beings emerge from his armpits, his knees, and his feet. These are most often referred to as the ice giants, but may also have been fire giants. Both were considered etins, another word for giant, but thursar also. The thursar, the giants dedicated to chaos and destruction, are not friends of mankind. The giants rule the world within Ginnungagap for some time. When the etins Bor and Bestla give birth to Odin, Vili, and Ve (also Odin, Hoenir, and Lodur,[1] depending on one's mythological material), actions are set into motion. The three gods murder Ymir and use his body to create Midgard, or Middle-Yard. His skull is the vault of the sky and it is held up by four dwarves—Austri (East), Sudri (South), Vestri (West), and Nordri (North). His bones make the mountains, and the stones are his teeth. His eyebrows form the boundary around Midgard, and his blood drowns almost all of the giant-kin; Odin, Vili, and Ve's parents, the giants Bor and Bestla, escape in a boat, and the giants go to Jotunheim, or "Giant-Land," to live their lives from that point on. Odin, Vili, and Ve create the sun and moon, the worlds and everything in them. It is only after all of this that they come across the driftwood pieces fated to become the first humans.

Heathens agree, for the most part, that there are nine worlds in the heathen cosmology. The myths also refer to the nine worlds. Nine is a sacred number. One could very well argue that there are nine worlds because, at its essence, nine is the sacred number and that's how many the skalds used. That said, nine is mythologically significant; across cultures you will find that, whatever number is important to a given culture, it will repeat, appear, and reappear. In the Norse worldview, nine is one of the sacred numbers, as are twelve, three, and four. On the other hand, "nine" could very well be something similar to "many." "How many worlds are there?" the six-year-old asks. "Many," her grandfather answers. "How many?" "Lots." "How many is lots?" "Nine." This seems far too mundane to be considered the only reason for there to be nine worlds, but it is a possibility. Remember, these myths were the province of skalds, scops, and other traveling performers.

Poets recited the songs, stories, myths, and sagas well before they were ever written down. We should always remember that when a poet is reciting, he or she will change things around in order to conform to rhythm, meter, rhyme, alliteration, and artistic merit. Remember, too, that in stories, factual, able-to-be-proven accuracy need not be necessary. It's nice if poets make sense, and it adds an air of cohesion if the facts stated in a poem fit with what we know in the rest of the world, but it is not necessary. When the composers of the lays, poems, and songs that made up the *Poetic Edda* were writing things down, they were, first of all, writing down myths that were already in place and had been part of the oral tradition for several hundred years. Stories have a way of shifting over time, and while there are some great linguistic ways to track the cores of myths across time and culture, the truth is that things change. There might have been three worlds originally—we "know" (in the mythic sense) that, before the gods existed, there was Niflheim to the North, Muspelheim to the South, and a great yawning gap full of potential—Ginnungagap—between them. There may have been an infinite number of worlds, and we only remember the names of nine. We do not really know, nor can we, but it seems safe to assume that the nine worlds exist within the heathen mythological paradigm.

Present from the start are two of the nine worlds, Muspelheim and Niflheim. Both are most often considered as chaotic in form, with very little order to them. Niflheim is in the north, so they say, and is the land of frozen things. Ice, snow, frozen wastes, tundra, glaciers . . . it makes sense, if you think about it, that heathen ancestors decided this world existed where it did; geographically speaking, from Scandinavia to the north your next stop is the North Pole. There are not a lot of records as to what entities live in Niflheim; frost giants, one assumes. There is a well present in Niflheim. It is called Hvergelmir, and from it rise many rivers.

Muspelheim existing in the south also makes sense, geographically speaking, because as our ancestors traveled south through Europe, it certainly got warmer. Keep in mind, too, that Iceland in particular is a land of ice and fire to this day; formed of active volcanoes, carved by glaciers, its terrain is beautiful and deadly. We know that Surt lives in Muspelheim. In the myths, he will come forth from there with his flaming sword during Ragnarok, kill Frey, and set fire to the nine worlds. There are, most likely, denizens of Muspelheim as well—fire giants. We know from chapter 5 that the denizens of these worlds, often called thurses, or thursar, are either uncaring or hostile toward mankind. It is easy to see this connection. Anyone who has been in the desert sunshine or outside in a blizzard can tell you these are not friendly places to be. In a pragmatic sense, a volcanic fury may be fascinating to watch on television, but no one wants one to erupt in his backyard.

Midgard, which literally means "middle-yard," is the creation of the gods. Ginnungagap is not considered one of the nine worlds; it exists, or existed, and when the fire and sparks from Muspelheim met the icy winds and waters of Niflheim, they formed a rime. From that rime came the primal beings Ymir and Audhumla. But Midgard was not Midgard until after Odin, Vili, and Ve killed Ymir, because they created our world from his bones, teeth, flesh, eyebrows, and skull, among other parts.

We live in Midgard. Right here. This planet, the one we're walking on, is Midgard. Its denizens are all of us—humans, animals, reptiles, birds, rocks, trees, all of the vaettir. It seems a bit repetitive to define Midgard, since we're so intimately familiar with it. Still, here it is, the creation of the gods, placed at the center of everything. This kind of mythic thinking has been deemed false by the scientific record, of course. We are a planet rotating around a sun in a galaxy, part of a greater universe. In mythical terms, however, we can still say we are the center of everything. Midgard itself can be considered both mundane and sacred at the same time. There are certain locations in Midgard, such as groves, wells, springs, and so forth, that are recorded as holy, or which are, our senses tell us, more sacred than mundane. We can see traces of this in the archeological record as well, where sacrifices were known to occur.

Now, as Ymir died, the *jotnar* (singular form: *jotun*) who lived through the great flood of his blood floated away on its surface and went to live in Jotunheim. We are also not sure where Jotunheim came from. We have no idea. It was just there, when the etins—a class of giants, or jotnar—needed homes. The jotnar had a place to call their own. It seems that Jotunheim was initially defined specifically as a "place where the giants live." It is outside of Midgard. Thor and other gods travel to it from time to time—Thor mostly to destroy what giants he finds there—but it is not cited as being in any one particular direction over another. Some heathens place Jotunheim in the north, while others place it opposite Vanaheim, to balance the two. It is best to consider Jotunheim "over there." Where, no one really knows, but over there, somewhere.

Asgard is next, and it is the home of the gods and goddesses, the Aesir and the Vanir Njord, Frey, and Freyja. It is described as "above" Midgard, reachable by traveling the rainbow bridge named Bifrost. The bridge itself, like all the worlds, is guarded by the god Heimdal, whose senses are so acute he can see the wool growing on a sheep. The Aesir, the Vanir who were a part of a hostage exchange, their husbands and wives, and their children all live in Asgard, and most have their own halls there. It is important to pause here and discuss the Vanir who live in Asgard. Early on in the mythic past, the Aesir and the Vanir were at war with one another. After a time they decided to end the war and combine their forces. In the Iron Age and Viking Age, many disputes were settled by an exchange of hostages, and the same thing happened at the end of this mythic war. The Aesir Hoenir and Mimir went to live in Vanaheim. It is said that Njord and Frey were the two hostages the Vanir exchanged. Frey and Njord leave Vanaheim to live in Asgard. Frey is not only in Asgard but is the Lord of Ljosalfheim (also called Alfheim). Freyja, Njord's daughter and Frey's sister, also came to live at Asgard. We do not know why; she was not listed as part of the hostage exchange. They are the only three Vanir who live in Asgard. By association Frey's wife Gerdh is both an etin-bride and a Van by marriage, and lives in Asgard with Frey. Freyja is said to have a daughter, Hnoss, and one imagines that she, too may reside in Asgard—nothing is said one way or another, but it seems logical to assume a mother would keep her daughter close by.

Each god and many of the goddesses have their own halls—Valhalla is perhaps the most famous, but Frigga has Fensalir, Freyja has Sessrumnir, Njord has Noatun, and so forth. Vingolf is the hall of the goddesses in general, and Gladsheim is known as the abode of the gods. There are also at least two plains, Folkvang (which is Freyja's), and Vigrid, the plain where the final battle at Ragnarok takes place. At one point there was a wall surrounding Asgard; it was destroyed in the Aesir/Vanir war. The Aesir and Vanir hired a giant to repair it, but ultimately reneged on the bargain and sent Loki, in the form of a mare, to draw away the giant's magical stallion. We do not know if the wall was ever completed; there's nothing to say it was.

The next world heathens acknowledge as one of the nine is Vanaheim. This is the original home of Njord, Frey, and Freyja. We don't know a whole lot about Vanaheim. We know Njord returns home when Ragnarok comes. We know that it is probably in the west. The Vanir themselves we do not know a great deal about. There are some who speculate that Nerthus and Gullveig, the gold-greedy prophetess, are counted among the Vanir. Nerthus may well have been a Van. While there is no evidence for this, since we know that Nerthus and Njord are related, it seems logical. Many heathens consider Gullveig to be Freyja in disguise and therefore Vanic. Others see Gullveig as an entity all to herself, and while there is no evidence to say which type of being she is, the myths seem to relate that she comes from Vanaheim. Most modern heathens see the Vanir—most of the denizens of Vanaheim—as similar to nature-spirits. Some are willing to deal with mankind, as Njord, Frey, and Freyja are, others are fairly neutral, and some are very remote.

Frey is given Ljosalfheim as a "tooth gift," or as a gift due to him as an important son and a ruling Prince in his own right. Cosmologically speaking, most heathens agree that Ljosalfheim is one of the nine worlds, and exists somewhere in the east. There are records of Frey coming from the east, or from dawn's direction. *Ljos* means "light," referring to color/shade as well as brightness/daylight. In Norse mythology, as we have seen, among the groupings of alfar are the ljosalf, literally the "light" elf, and the svartalf, or "dark" elf. That each group has its own world speaks to their relative importance in the cosmology as a whole, but we do not know much of the ljosalfar. Many modern heathens consider them land-vaettir similar to the Vanir. Classification of entities can be very confusing. Sometimes the landvaettir are called Vanir, sometimes the Vanir are called landvaettir, and yet they are all considered distinct entities. For now, Frey is the Lord of Ljosalfheim, and the light-elves live there. The one thing to remember is that *ljos*—refers to color, or brightness, and not to "good," or necessarily even "positive."

Then we have Svartalfheim. *Svart* means "dark" and "black," and, as with *ljos*-, can mean both color and brightness. The Svartalfar, who as you might expect inhabit Svartalfheim, are also called dwarves. Odin, Vili, and Ve created the dwarves from maggots found feeding on Ymir's flesh; this description often colors our image of the svartalfar as generally small, living in the dark places, and a bit nasty in aspect. The dwarf Alvis is tricked by Thor to stay and recite his knowledge until dawn, when he is promptly vanquished; the sun enters the hall and he is turned to stone.[2] Dwarves tend to be found underground or in caves, so one might say they live in dark, or svart, places. If we stretch that analogy, and many do, then the ljos, referred to above, can also be above ground, or in the daylight. Generally speaking, many heathens tend to place Ljosalfheim and Svartalfheim opposite one another. Sometimes that means one is above the other, and sometimes it means one is to the east, and the other to the west. The point is one of cosmological and mythological balance more than it is one of literal direction.

The ninth world... gets interesting. We know that Hel, or Hella, the child of Loki, is sent to be the lady of the dead. This world is called Hel-heim, or Hel, and it's not a bad place. Hel is where the ancestors live on after they die. At least, most of the ancestors are there; a chosen few go to Valhalla, or Sessrumnir, some go to Ran's hall, which is under the ocean, and some heathens speculate that those who were in fulltrui relationship with specific gods or goddesses go to their hall. The fulltrui relationship is the closest example we have of heathens dedicated to one entity above others; fulltrui roughly translates as "friend of." The heathen afterlife is complicated; remember that there are multiple halls the dead go to, and if heathens have multiple soul-parts, it may be that heathens also have multiple afterlives. As an example, a woman might end up simultaneously residing in Hel (as the ancestral soul) and traveling with the family line as a dis (protecting the hamingja, another soul-part, also with links to the ancestral soul). Still, most ancestral dead end up in Helheim. Some think that Hel is the land, and Helheim the hall Hella keeps. This, then, would make Hel the ninth world. Some consider Helheim to be the ninth world, believing that Hel is the goddess and Helheim her world, much as Frey has Ljosalfheim. Others think that Helheim is not a world at all, but a subsection, as it were, of Nifhelheim, which would mean it is not the ninth world after all. There is also a Nifhel within Helheim—it is the place where murderers, rapists, and oath-breakers are punished for their transgressions. Some relate Nifhel to Nifhelheim, which muddies the waters even further. So what do we call the ninth world? Most modern heathens refer to Helheim, since it is important for ancestor worshippers to acknowledge where their ancestors, the honored dead, live eternally. There are some hints that Helheim might be "below" Midgard, giving it a rough cosmological location. Remember that the distinctions and directions of the various worlds are often blurred, or not given at all.

Now, from a pragmatic standpoint, it is important to remember not only that mythology is flexible, but also that it is not necessarily reflective of what we refer to as "consensual reality." As we know, Midgard is not the literal center of the universe. Remember, there is no inherent conflict between "myth" and "science." None whatsoever. It is, mythically speaking, entirely possible that both exist simultaneously. We are, in short, *both* humans who have evolved through genetic mutation on this planet called Earth, in its orbit in space, *and* the creatures the gods created out of driftwood shortly after they made Midgard. Modern human cultures tend to be binary—*either* something is one thing *or* is another. Mythology doesn't work that way. It works to explain the why of what we do, and provides the meaning for our particular culture. When a mythology no longer gives meaning to a given culture, it stagnates and dies. Life moves on, and a new set of myths rises to replace the old. The cosmology of the Norse mythological system forms the basis of our mythic reality, and there is no conflict between that mythic reality and the consensual reality all around us.

Creation of Humans in Norse Mythology

Heathens tend to be a world-accepting group of people. Unlike some members of the major world religions, very few heathens choose "religion" over "science." Mundane reality is what it is, and for heathens there is no inherent problem with this fact. They accept that there is also a more sacred, or mythic reality as well; they believe the Earth has a soul. That belief exists alongside the accepted science about our planet. Heathens do not discount the findings of science. Evolutionary theory, for instance, is something they believe in wholeheartedly. Creation myths are often seen as allegories, or sacred teachings, but are very seldom seen as "factual," in scientific terms, even by the most literal interpreters of our mythology.

In the Norse creation myth, Odin, Vili, and Ve were walking along a shoreline when they came to two pieces of driftwood, an ash and an elm. They gave the driftwood pieces three gifts, and the combination transformed the wood into two humans. When asked things like "Do you really believe Odin, Vili, and Ve created humans out of driftwood?" the modern heathen is most likely to say something along the lines of "Well, no, I believe we're mammals, and if you go back far enough we started from the primordial slime." At the same time, the modern heathen will say something like "However, what Odin, Vili, and Ve gave us is what makes us human." Heathens don't feel conflicted about this at all. The three gifts, *önd, oð,* and *lá,*[3] refer to far more than their literal translations.

Stanza 18 from *Voluspá* reads:

Ǫnd gaf Óðinn,
Óð gaf Hœnir
Lá gaf Lóðurr
Ok lito góða.[4]

Önd Odin gave them
Ód Hoenir gave them
Lá gave Lodur
and fine complexion. (author trans.)

Heathens tend to look at the meanings of words to glean their importance. They also tend to seek more than one source, if possible, for these words. The Cleasby-Vigfusson dictionary defines *önd* as "the breath, breath/life, the soul."[5] Ursula Dronke refers to the word's definition as "life and breath."[6] *Oð*, on the other hand refers to the "…divine inspiration and the immortal intellect."[7] Finally, we have *lá* and the phrase "*lito góða.*" Cleasby-Vigfusson gives us this: "of fine complexion, countenance, complexion, color, hue, a stain (as in a dye)."[8] Ursula Dronke explains more fully, saying that "The physical gifts—the covering of flesh and blood—*lá*—on the wooden bones, the graces of manners and utterance—*læti*—and the wholesome colouring and countenance of humanity—*lito góða*—come last."[9] *Góða* generally means "gods," or refers to the gods, which may mean that this gift, *lá*, is not merely our flesh and our blood, but also a divine gift of the gods.

These three gifts—breath, spirit, and "flesh and blood" or "comely hue"—are the three elements that make us human. So while we breathe as an autonomic response, we also have that which is breath (*önd* can also mean soul), and it is this "that which is breath" that gives us our life. Breath, then, becomes not only the literal process of breathing but is also sacred in and of itself, because our breath is the essence of our souls. Coupled with *oð*, we have not only our breath but our inspiration making us human; we are inspired not only by the world around us, but by the divine gift of inspiration itself. It is *lá* which gives us form, and shape. *Lá* makes us look the way we do. However, *lá* is also the gift of the gods, which can mean that *önd* and *oð* are contained within *lá*. We are, in essence, three different elements, and only when the three are taken as one are we human. Naturally humans wind up becoming more than the sum of their parts, which leads us to a discussion of *wyrd* and *örlög*.

Önd, Óð, and Lá–a Meditation

The most simple way to "get in touch" with the gifts that heathens believe were given to us by the gods is to simply meditate. While breathing quietly, relaxed, focus on the intake and exhalation of breath. Feel your body's warmth as you breathe, and listen for any insights or inspirations that may come to you while you are meditating. Taken together, these are, in order, önd, lá, and óð.

Another way to go about this involves focus, intent, and chanting. Once relaxed and focused, chant önd three times, each as one single exhalation. While doing this, focus on not only your physical breathing but the spirit, that which is breath, entering and leaving your body.

When finished, switch the chant to "óð." Again, do this three times, each with one long exhalation of breath. This time, focus on your inspiration, your imagination, the little wild thing that dances in your mind. This time it is neither entering nor leaving; this is a part of you. It may ebb and it may flow, but it is always there.

Finally, chant "lá" three times. Focus on your physical body, your bones, your hair, your skin. Relax your muscles, and be aware of the entity that you are.

Meditation on the World Tree

Go to a quiet place where you can be safe; indoors or outdoors is fine. Sit or stand comfortably. Take a few deep, calming breaths. Relax your muscles as you continue to breathe.

When you are ready, picture in your mind's eye your favorite place in nature. Be as specific and detailed as possible—locate the rocks and the ground, the trees and the skies, any water nearby, even what is smells like.

Find a tree within that space and focus on it. Visualize that you are standing directly in front of that tree. As you watch, it slowly gets larger, longer, and bigger around. Its three roots are gnarled and ancient, thrust into the ground to support a trunk you cannot get your hands around. Far above you the tree branches out, and upward. This tree has become the mighty ash.

Spend time leaning against Yggdrasil, the mighty World Tree. You can sense the pulse of sap flowing through it, and you can hear the whispering of its branches as the breezes pass through it. Every so often the trunk creaks or groans, in the way trees do. Imagine your place here, in sacred Midgard, and contemplate the other eight worlds and their connection to Yggdrasil. You may look around and catch glimpses of them, the same way you catch a glimpse of a rainbow in the skies just after a rainstorm.

When you are finished, rise and thank the World Tree for letting you spend time nearby. Watch as Yggdrasil slowly shrinks and fades from focus, leaving only the tree you initially saw. Focus on your breathing as the visualization fades. Wiggle your toes. Roll your neck. Look about you and remember the world you are in, this Midgard, this reality.

Notes on Chapter Six

1. In the *Poetic Edda*, "Voluspa 17" mentions only that there were three gods, and names them Odin, Hoenir, and Lodur (Verse 18). Snorri Sturluson's *Prose Edda* names the same three gods Odin, Vili, and Ve.

2. Carolyne Larrington, trans., The *Poetic Edda* (Oxford: Oxford University Press, 1996), 109–13. For the entire myth, see the *Poetic Edda*'s "Alvismal" (Larrington calls this "All-Wise's Sayings."). *Alvis* means "all-wise," and Thor asks a series of questions and riddles to "test" the dwarf's knowledge. What he is really doing is distracting Alvis from the passing of time, so that he can be trapped at dawn. When dawn breaks, Alvis is turned to stone.

3. Ursula Dronke, trans., The *Poetic Edda, Volume II: Mythological Poems* (Oxford: Clarendon Press, 1997), 11, 39-40. Dronke's notes on the sequence of ideas in "Voluspa" are particularly relevant, and worth exploring at length.

4. Ursula Dronke, trans., The *Poetic Edda, Volume II: Mythological Poems* (Oxford: Clarendon Press, 1997), 11.

5. Richard Cleasby and Gudbrand Vigfusson, *An Icelandic-English Dictionary* (Http://www.ling.upenn.edu/~kurisuto/germanic/oc_cleasbyvigfusson_about.html. Accessed March 16, 2011).

6. Ursula Dronke, trans., The *Poetic Edda, Volume II: Mythological Poems* (Oxford: Clarendon Press, 1997), 39.

7. Ursula Dronke, trans., The *Poetic Edda, Volume II: Mythological Poems* (Oxford: Clarendon Press, 1997), 30.

8. Richard Cleasby and Gudbrand Vigfusson, *An Icelandic-English Dictionary* (Http://www.ling.upenn.edu/~kurisuto/germanic/oc_cleasbyvigfusson_about.html. Accessed March 16, 2011).

9. Usrula Dronke, trans., The *Poetic Edda, Volume II: Mythological Poems* (Oxford: Clarendon Press, 1997), 30.

Do you still seek to know? And what?
—Voluspa

Seven

Wyrd and Örlög

Taken together, wyrd and örlög are similar to a tapestry—one set of fibers is horizontal, the other vertical, and they are so interwoven that they form a larger picture. This tapestry, if you will, has a beginning, but is constantly being woven at the other end. *Örlög*, which translates as "ur-law," is the point at which all things begin. *Ur* roughly equates to "first," or "primal," and means precisely that—ur-law, then, means the first or primal law by which we all are bound.

In Norse mythology, there are three Norns named Urdh, Verdandi, and Skuld. They feed and otherwise care for the World Tree, Yggdrasil. In some ways, we could argue that Yggdrasil has as much to do with örlög as anything else. The Norns reside at the base of the tree near the Well of Urdh (Urdh is the same word as Wyrd) and use its waters along with the white, rich mud at the tree's base to nourish Yggdrasil. We will discuss the Norns in terms of the heathen sense of time in the next chapter, but for now, if we see the Well of Urdh as the symbolic repository of all things that make up the past, we can imagine the unseen base of the Well as the first-moment, that which precipitated all the acts which have become layers in the water over time. That moment, layered deep in the abyss, is the örlög of everything.

Yes, everything. The Norse creation myth is the opposite of creation *ex nihilo*, or creation from nothingness. In ex nihilo myths, a god is there before the beginning of everything, and it is he/she who creates it all. Norse mythology states that first there were Niflheim, a land of ice, frost, and frozen things, and Muspelheim, a land of fire and magma. Ginnungagap stood separating them; it is from the union of fire and ice in Ginnungagap that the nine worlds formed. The gods came quite a long time later; well after Audhumla the cow licked Ymir clear of the rime, after he took nourishment from her, and even after the birth of Ymir's children, the first beings, the etins and thursar. Our gods, particularly Odin, Vili, and Ve, are definitely creator gods. However, we know that something existed well before they did. Heathens know that their gods will die. Presumably something will exist long after they are gone.

In addition to the örlög that came just after the moment of creation, or which might be creation itself, each of us has his or her individual örlög. It is that which defines us at the deepest unconscious and physical levels. As we work out the wyrd—or urdh, the permanent past—of our lives, the paths of our lives change. However, they can only change up to a point, because none of us can change our örlög. Some people have a stronger örlög to begin with—lines of heroes, for instance, tend to beget heroes, and heroes have a hard time living "normal, average lives." It works in the other direction, too; normal, average people have a hard time living to heroic standards. Like our gods, we were born and we live, and in time we will die. This is the natural span of life, and while it sounds fatalistic, it is ultimately realistic. Our gods are as bound by örlög as we are. Our ancestors were nothing if not pragmatic people; it makes more sense to assume that everything lives and dies than to ponder the immortality of a deity.

This is a complex subject, and one which heathens contemplate throughout their lives. At its simplest, think about a caterpillar. A caterpillar, should it grow, eat enough, develop its chrysalis properly, and then be able to cut itself out, will emerge as a butterfly. Unless, of course, it is a moth. There is nothing in the world that can change this—a Blue Morpho butterfly comes from a Blue Morpho caterpillar. A Gypsy Moth comes from a Gypsy Moth caterpillar. One can never be the other. In fact, they come from a long line of caterpillars and butterflies and have evolved from the caterpillars and butterflies before them. Örlög, then, for us, was originally laid down by the first of our ancestors, and we cannot change it. A mundane example would be the families we are born into—we cannot escape our DNA, no matter how much we may wish to.

We are bound by our örlög—we will become what we are destined to become—but our wyrd can change. Wyrd as a concept can be related to limited free will. All beings, including the gods, have choices. All choices are limited by our örlög—we cannot be what we are not—but within that boundary we can act as we wish. Continuing the caterpillar analogy, a Blue Morpho caterpillar must eat what is nutritious and safe for it to eat. It must live out its normal lifespan—so long as nothing interrupts it. The caterpillar might veer to the left, or the right, or even directly up a tree. It might eat right and be a healthy and fat little caterpillar indeed. All of these are actions that create a part of wyrd. In other words, the caterpillar has choices. It's still a Blue Morpho, but it can change the specifics of its life.

As another image, consider in this case a river like the Mississippi, which has a general flow but a large floodplain. For the most part, the Mississippi will stay within its current banks. However, should a powerful event occur, the Mississippi can change its course. It will remain within the boundaries of its floodplain, but it can, and does, shift. Örlög is the floodplain, and wyrd is the movement of the river. Both are continually in effect. Our past, our örlög, informs us because it creates us. However, what we do in our lives becomes our wyrd, and matters a great deal in terms of what our lives will eventually become. As we interact with the world around us, with humans, animals, gods, or whatever other entities we find out there, what develops is something resembling a tapestry; an ongoing pattern that is our life. Remember that creation occurred before the gods and goddesses existed. This means that they, too, have their own örlög. They, too, create their wyrd as they go along. In this they are no different from us and, as a matter of fact, in the end our gods die, just as we will.

Things start to get really interesting when our individual patterns interact with the patterns of others. Wyrd is often described as a large, infinitely long, yet unfinished tapestry. Örlög and wyrd work together in order to create the pattern itself, but wyrd is more than just the warp of the loom; it is the finished product as well. We cannot excise a piece of the interconnected pattern of existence any more than a weaver can pull out a thread already woven into the cloth; it leaves a hole, where fraying can occur. In caterpillar terms, every entity that the caterpillar encounters has the potential to change its wyrd. The caterpillar may encounter a bird. That bird might eat it, or might drop it. The caterpillar might be toxic to birds, in which case the caterpillar has impacted the wyrd of the bird. Our lives work in the same ways, and it is vital to remember that wyrd impacts every entity, both seen and unseen.

Every moment we encounter people, pets, rocks, trees, ancestors, descendants, and even gods. Every time any encounter happens, it changes all of the entities involved. In pragmatic terms, let's consider a grandfather. The granddaughter comes to him, upset because she is undergoing a divorce. He says to her: "All you can do is make the best decision you can make, and go on from there." Now she is comforted by those words and goes forth keeping them in mind; thus her grandfather has changed her wyrd. At the same time, perhaps the grandfather is comforted by the fact that she came to him for advice, and goes forward feeling more confident and more loved. This way, the granddaughter has changed his wyrd. This is a small example. Sometimes the winds of wyrd are strong. A hero who finally regains his father's sword to avenge his family will have a difficult time doing anything other than achieve that vengeance. That said, wyrd is made up of the small moments as well as the larger ones.

As vast as it is, the great fabric that is wyrd is not infinite. Just because it is beyond our limited human comprehension doesn't mean it has no end.

Everything that has a beginning ends. Therefore it makes sense that wyrd, too, will end someday. We see this in the myth of Ragnarok, when the nine worlds are consumed by the fires Surt sets when he waves his sword. All beings, including the gods, are destroyed in the conflagration save a precious few—two humans, and some of the gods' descendants. Baldur and, we assume, his wife Nanna return from the realm of the dead to help lead the new generation. In this way, we can also see wyrd and örlög at work. After a time, wyrd is completed and reaches its natural end. Örlög, however, remains. It is from örlög that the next generation forms its wyrd, and so on into the future.

Placing Yourself in Your Wyrd

This common practice will help you realize your own position in the world. Get out a few pieces of blank paper and a pen/pencil. Sit where you can write and not be disturbed. On the first piece of paper, write down everything that is good about you, from the most mundane to your best skill. Anything you can think of that you feel positive about, write down. Then, turn the paper over and write everything bad about yourself, all your bad habits, things about you that you dislike, and so on. Compare the front and back and see which outweighs the other. Then ask yourself—are you being too self-critical or too arrogant? Shift things around as best you can until you wind up roughly even, if possible.

On the second piece of paper you will do the same thing. This time, however, you are writing down specific actions you have taken. Remember, this is only about *you* and not anyone else. Write down every positive thing you have ever done on one side and every negative thing on the other. Make no excuses for yourself—you are the only one who will see this.

Look at the balance of your actions. It is that balance of the past which determines our present. Avoid self-blame or self-judgment—the point of the exercise is to understand where you are in the present moment, nothing more nor less. The odds are that you are a better person than you may think—writing down your positive actions will help you remember that. If done with honesty and personal strength, this exercise will be emotionally draining but, at the same time, very clarifying for you, letting you know where you stand right now in the present moment. Remember that, at any point you need to, you can do this exercise again to trace where you are. If you choose to keep these papers for yourself, you will also begin to see where you have been.

When things happen is as
important as how things happened.

Eight

Concepts of Time

In order to understand how our ancestors viewed time, it is important to spend a little bit of space examining language theory. Proto-Indo-European and other linguistic scholars have argued, more or less successfully, that we can determine culture based on the words ancient people used. The Proto-Indo-Europeans had no word for "palm tree," but they did distinguish between a number of other trees native to central Europe—firs, oaks, yews, etc. This implies just what you might think it does—that our ancestors had never seen a palm tree, which means they probably didn't live in a land where palm trees grew. They did have words for cart, cow, and horse, suggesting that they did have these things in their lives.

Remember that at no point in the evolution of human history was there one moment when people "stopped" speaking one language and "started" speaking another—no one ever went to bed one night able to understand their neighbor only to wake up the next day and not understand a word he's saying. Language evolves over time, just like everything else. That said, in Germanic languages we see something fascinating. Grammatically speaking, there is no future tense. We have a past tense (I did that). We have a present tense (I do that). But we have to construct a future tense out of the present tense. We add present-tense words to create an entirely different meaning (I will do that). This has led some scholars to assume that, for Germanic speaking peoples, the concept of "future" did not exist.

There was a sense of the future, but it was directly influenced by the permanence of the past and the fluidity of the present.[1] This attitude led to what early researchers and ethnographers called "Viking fatalism." The "Hávamál" itself advises that a person might as well get a good night's sleep, because there's nothing you can do about the future:

The foolish man lays awake all night
and worries about things;
He's tired out when the morning comes
and everything's just as bad as it was.
—*Sayings of the High One*, Stanza 23[2]

There's more to it than that, though, because a fluid present equates to a certain amount of free will—what we do now is up to us, and it will change the course of our lives. Free will and fate don't go hand in hand, generally. A person either has free will and can do anything, or is fated to live and die a certain way. However, it's this kind of dualistic thinking that gets us in trouble. We have a finite number of decisions and actions we can take in any given situation, and we have to choose between those decisions and actions when we're in the moment. Those choices then determine the next set of choices we will face. Taken together, we have a smaller and more limited amount of choices as we grow older. This limits our free will and creates a "conditional future" which can change moment to moment, depending on our choices. Let's unwrap this a little further. First, we need to understand the past.

Urdh, or *urð,* is the name of one of the three principal wells in Norse cosmology—named Urdh, Mimir, and Hvergelmir—each located in different places. Hvergelmir is the eldest of the wells; it is listed as existing in Niflheim, the land of frost and ice, which existed before the first being,

Ymir, and certainly before the gods. We can picture Hvergelmir as having seething, roiling water representing an icy but dynamic source for creation. Mimir's Well is named for the god Mimir; Odin sacrificed an eye to that well, so he could see the wisdom hidden within it. Urdh, on the other hand, is the well set at the base of the World Tree, Yggdrasil. Urdh (meaning "had become") is also the name given to one of the Norns, entities who sit at the base of Yggdrasil, feed it with mud, and who see and say the *örlög* (often mistranslated as "fate" rather than a law) of all mankind. In language theory, *urdh* is also the past participle form. The past participle is a specific type of verb, one that indicates an action that has happened, and ended, before another action. "She had been in graduate school" means that she—whoever she is—used to be in graduate school but is not in school anymore. We don't know if she achieved a degree or not, all we know is that she used to do something and doesn't do it anymore.

"Urdh," therefore, indicates a past action that is permanent. It has a beginning, middle, and end. It's not an ongoing event, and it cannot be changed. It may help to remember that the word "urdh" is the same as the word "wyrd." As we saw in the previous section, wyrd is a series of discrete, finite items, and so is our sense of the past—a series of discrete, finite events. That our ancestors named both a Norn and a well "Urdh" speaks to the importance of the past in the heathen worldview. Wyrd is the pattern of our individual existence, and the pattern of all existence. The Well of Wyrd, then, is the repository of all things past. The Norns feed Yggdrasil the white mud, which is itself made from the water of that well. In this sense we can say that Yggdrasil, the World Tree—the *axis mundi*— exists on its own but, at the same time, is dependent on the nourishment it receives from the past.

Taking the past into its context, we can better understand the present. Verdandi ("becoming") is the Norn most concerned with the present. In the heathen worldview, the present is what can be changed. The present occurs as a permanent state of "becoming," a liminal space between the past and the future. It may seem as though heathens believe the present is in a constant state of flux. In many ways, that is absolutely true. The present acts, every moment of every day. Action is the key—the present tense is an active tense, and the present moment in the heathen worldview is one of right action. In every circumstance, a heathen strives to do the right things in the moment. We also need to remember that even non-action is an action; the present is made of an entire moment—what is said or unsaid, witnessed or solitary, between a person and the environment he is standing in as the present happens. It is everything.

This is where the concept of limited free will comes back into play. Theoretically, we could argue all or nothing might happen in that moment just between the past and the present action. Indeed, at first blush the opportunities seem infinite. However, our choices do have limits. The permanence of the past directly influences, and limits, the action of the present. You are the actor, the precipitator of your own life and your own present. You can, in point of fact, choose your present for yourself. However, you are limited in your choices, and that limitation comes directly from your own past. Örlög limits everything; remember that a Blue Morpho caterpillar will never become a Gypsy moth. Wyrd also constrains our free will; if we consider all of what we have done, or has been done with us, or to us, it makes sense that these things would limit our actual choices. In a simplistic example, a person on the Atlantic Coast simply cannot look to the west and see the Rocky Mountains. She can go visit the Rockies, and there are any number of ways to get there, but she cannot physically see them from where she is standing. In order to see them, she first has to make the choice to travel to them. Let us assume she buys an airplane ticket—this is another choice, and one which limits her travel options. Each of these moments is a present action, which then limits her next set of choices. The intersection of past and present is subtle and often one of those things that we have no real words to explain properly.

The present changes; it is a constant flow, not a fixed point. As soon as the present becomes fixed by an action, it slides into the past. The past influences the present by its very presence—nothing in the past can be changed, and so it forms a kind of permeable boundary within which the present can occur. If the past can be seen as contained in the Well of Wyrd, we can imagine the present as the surface of the water. At its surface, water is mutable; it shifts with every motion. Sometimes water's stillness is barely broken—the exhalation of breath over the water will cause only a soft movement. At the same time, a hurricane's winds can cause the water to overflow its normal restrictions and even cause destruction on a massive scale. Our actions are the movements on the surface of the water, subtly or dramatically altering what is there. This is the permeable present—an instantaneous response to what actions we have taken. Just as the past limits the present by giving it a shape, the present impacts the future.

In heathen thinking, there is, at most, a conditional future. Remember that in Germanic languages the only future tense is a tense formed from conditionally modifying the present. The Norn Skuld ("will become") is the Norn most influencing the future, such as it is. Many modern heathens speculate that Skuld is the youngest of the Norns, and Urdh the oldest; this is modern time flipped on its head. One pagan philosophy sees the goddess as archetypal; in this philosophy the goddess exists as three archetypes—a maiden, a mother, and a crone. The maiden is youthful, full of promise, and much like the dawn of a day, while the crone represents the age of things, the darkest points of the night, and the wisdom that comes at the end of life. The heathen worldview is the opposite. There are no tripartite goddess figures. Heathens believe that they come from the past, and look toward the past as the source of information and wisdom. Their lives, in many ways, are lived backward. The permanence of the past is created in the present moment. A fatalistic worldview suggests that the future is fixed, and we cannot change it; the heathen worldview is that only the past is permanent, and any future is entirely determined by one's past.

This is why heathens consider the future conditional. Örlög fixes wyrd into its pattern, creating a "most likely" series of events leading to a fixed point. The future also depends entirely on the permanence of past action. The present is dynamic and changing—every decision made in the present will impact which of several potential futures will occur. That's all the future can ever be, to the heathen worldview—a set of most likely outcomes. A heathen is very much centered on the present moment, the here-and-now. No one knows his or her precise moment of death, and the heathen worldview is not concerned about that moment. Heathens don't focus on the afterlife, because there's not a thing they can do about that. Heathens don't even know what will happen tomorrow, really. As we've seen, the "Hávamál" advises its readers not to worry about such things.

What heathens can do is use the past and the present to alter the future. In a pragmatic way, let's say that a person wants to be a doctor when she grows up. There are certain steps which must occur. Every time she crosses an educational milestone—high school graduation, undergraduate studies, internships, and so on—she gets that much closer to becoming a doctor. The events in her past—all those milestones—bring her closer to her desired future. They are still no guarantee, however; any number of things might lead her to give up her chosen career for another one. This is why we speak in terms of most likely outcomes—if we do the work we need to do here, and now, in the present, we develop layers of the past which will make our desired future more likely to occur. This is also why heathens tend to be so focused on action and the present—if we want an outcome, we can only work for it here, and now. Present action will shape the permanent record of the past in our lives, which in turn shapes our future.

Considering Time

It is difficult to create a single ritual incorporating the whole of time. The following is more of an exercise. It can be done meditatively or literally, using pen and paper. At the end of the preceding chapter, we spoke of ways in which one can center oneself within wyrd and örlög. This is a similar exercise that can be done in a couple of different ways.

1. Trace an action in your past to its impact on your present. This can be a positive or negative act; it is your choice. I recommend beginning with something positive, because it will be less fraught with emotions than a negative action. Write the action down. Give it all the detail you can recall —the act itself, what brought the action about, how you

felt and perceived the action, and what consequences came from it. Now look to your present. How did that action change you? What are you, now, that you were not before the action happened?

2. Now, take a look at your present situation. Again, be as detailed as possible. Include your mood in the moment, specifics about your work, vocation, living situation, spirituality, and health. Choose one of these items and consider it in terms of your future. How is your present moment impacting your future choices? Keep your future choices as broad as possible, but notice the limitations your present is also placing on your future. As a simplistic example, perhaps you have a cold right now. You feel awful—you're sneezing, coughing, nauseous, what have you. Write all of the symptoms down on your paper. What are some of the future actions you may take based on the present situation of having a cold? Buying tissues, clear liquids, and chicken soup involves a trip to the grocery store—that is one potential future. You can stay home and wait it out—that is a second potential future. However, going to work tomorrow may not be a potential future at all, if you are sick enough. Going skydiving may also be out, thus eliminating another, perhaps more extreme, future. Look at what is possible, and what is not. The possibilities are not endless, but they can provide a sense of what the future is going to be.

Notes on Chapter Eight

1. Paul C. Bauschatz, *The Well and the Tree: World and Time in Early Germanic Culture* (Amherst: The University of Massachusetts Press, 1982). Bauschatz's excellent work,

The Well and The Tree: World and Time in Early Germanic Culture, takes apart the Germanic sense of time. Many, if not most, modern heathens ascribe to his point of view; I am one of them. However, it must be said that this is the only work on the Germanic sense of time; it has not at this date been corroborated with further research.

2. Carolyne Larrington, trans., The *Poetic Edda* (Oxford: Oxford University Press, 1996), 43.

Who are they, and why do they look so much like us?

Nine

Innangardh and Utangardh

It is with these important understandings—örlög, wyrd, and our sense of time—that we can turn to the cultural beliefs of the modern heathen. A key concept to heathen thinking involves what are known as *innangardh* and *utangardh*. The words literally translate as "in-yard" and "out-yard," and they are used to delineate not only the boundaries of land but social structures as well. Family, friends, kindred—these make up one's innangardh. We will discuss just what makes up a "kindred" in a moment, because "kindred" can include both chosen family and literal family members. There are certain obligations toward one's innangardh. These can be as simple as helping a close friend move into her apartment—again—or as complex as being willing to hear and help uphold an oath made by a member of your kindred.

Acquaintances and strangers are considered utangardh, because we do not know them and they are not closely related to us. It is important to note here that being in the utangardh is not a moral position, nor one of enmity, per se. They are simply strangers, we don't know them, and so they cannot be in our innangardh. Once they become better friends, or join the kindred, they enter the innangardh. Note here that there are no obligations to one's utangardh. This also makes sense—you probably do not feel obliged to help a stranger move, and heathens will often refuse to hear the oaths of strangers, because they cannot know if the oath will ever be fulfilled. We go over oaths more specifically in later chapters, but for now note that, for a heathen, taking an oath is one of the single most important tangible and spiritual things that one can do.

The concept of innangardh and utangardh is carried through to the consideration of the gods and goddesses as well. Generally speaking, the Aesir, the Vanir who have allied with them, and the giants associated with them are considered part of a heathen's innangardh—there are many heathens who believe the gods are also our ancestors, so they qualify as family. Neutral parties such as the unnamed Vanir and Jotnar more generally are considered utangardh, although here this is because they are simply strangers to us. The enemies of the gods—the thursar and others—are utangardh as well, because the Aesir and Vanir, a heathen's natural allies and potential ancestors, are for the most part enemies of the thursar. The vast majority of heathens will not blót to the thursar, because they are both in the utangardh and enemies to our innangardh.

The simplest way to understand innangardh and utangardh is by considering a Venn diagram. The smallest possible circle, and the point at which all other circles coincide, is the self. You are the center of your personal world, your own innangardh. Your family is also a circle. You are a member of your family and therefore your family is innangardh to you. A chosen group of heathens can take many forms; one of them is called a "kindred." Kindreds are made up of members who have chosen to ally themselves with one another, and who are often considered akin to family. You will hear heathens refer to other kindred members as "kindred-brother," or "kin-sister," which indicates how the kindred feels about one another. This is a simplistic example of what can be a complicated relationship model, but the understanding is that kindred may, or may not, be actual family, but they are all innangardh to one another. Other types of groups can form, as well. Some heathens are more tribal in their structure, and others practice a brand of heathenry called Theodism, where a group with a hierarchic structure is called a theod. In addition, there are also fellowships where typically no oaths are sworn to one another, yet the sense of family remains solid. Your chosen kindred or other group is a Venn circle that contains you, but it may not be the same circle as your family. Now there are three innangardhs—you, your family, and your kindred.

Everyone not in your family—which includes far-flung relatives, both past and present—is utangardh to your family. Family members are those people with a genetic or adoptive link to your family line. Your kindred-sister, since she is not directly related to you, is utangardh to everyone in your family except you—which means you have two separate innangardhs. There may be overlap—your children are your family in the literal sense, and may also be part of your kindred—and the edges can seem a little blurry as time goes on. Still, there is a distinct difference between the two sets of innangardhs. Does this make your family enemies to your kindred? Certainly not. The two sets are merely relative strangers to one another, or possibly friends.

Your friends, particularly your good, close friends, are innangardh to you. Some may be in your family, and some in your kindred. However, there is another set of friends who are neither family nor kindred, yet remain very close to you, personally. This is your fourth circle of innangardh. The best friend you grew up with and have known for thirty-three years is certainly connected to you and part of your innangardh. However, she may not be a member of your kindred, and that separates the two circles. The next circle might be those friends who are more distant to you. The next might be your local community, the next an organization you belong to, and another circle might be the country you live in. As you can see, the Venn diagram can be very complex, and there are those who argue that our world itself, in essence, is a type of innangardh in that we all live on it and care for it.

Everything else is utangardh. It's as simple as that. In a national sense, American citizens are not necessarily British citizens. This is not a problematic issue but a pragmatic one; we share a great many similarities, and our two nations are allies, but we remain distinct from one another. It is this distinctness which creates the innangardh/utangardh balance. This is why heathens consider the gods and goddesses, and those related to them, as part of our innangardh. This is also why those outside of that pantheon are considered utangardh. The other pantheons do exist. Polytheistic logic suggests that there is more than one everything, so it only makes sense that every other god and goddess exists just as ours do. That said, heathen worship is for the Norse gods and goddesses, among others, and not generally given to those not in our pantheon. Does that make another pantheon "less than" or "better than" ours? No—it simply means "different."

Innangardh and Utangardh Meditation

The first thing you need to do in order to prepare for this meditation is to spend time considering the various circles you belong to. It may be that your personal innangardh is tighter and smaller; it may be that you do not consider "Americans" in general as your innangardh, for instance. It may be that even your regional community is not your innangardh—heathen religion is community-based, but your community may not include anyone outside of your group, kindred or otherwise. It may be helpful to write down lists of people whom you consider innangardh and whom you consider utangardh. Remember, again, that utangardh does not necessarily mean enmity, for strangers are considered utangardh.

Sit or lie down comfortably. Focus on your breathing, and as your breathing deepens, feel your body relax. Picture a place in nature that you know well, and then place yourself within that picture. As you continue to meditate, imagine that your family is with you. Note all the members, and think about your relationships to them. In most cases, these will be positive or neutral relationships. Negative relationships can create a sense of utangardh between yourself and that person; this, too, is natural. Avoid focusing on the negative relationships, for now is the time to reinforce your innangardh.

Next, imagine your friends and consider them in the same ways you did with your family. If you are in a kindred, tribe, fellowship, or any other kind of heathen grouping, do the same with them. Note in your mind any connections between these three groups; chances are, for instance, that you are friends with your kindred members as well as considering them chosen family. Spend some time focused on these connections, these members of your innangardh, and how they relate to you. Imagine, for instance, lines extending out from the center of yourself to each member of these groups, family, friends, and kindred, connecting them all to you. Now imagine lines connecting some of them to each other. Some lines may form—your kindred has chosen to connect itself to each member, for instance—and some may not. See where those connective lines meet, intersect, and connect back to you. This is your innangardh.

When you are finished, take a few deep breaths. Leave the place in nature, and return to Midgard by focusing on your breath, your physical body, and the space around you. Listen for noises, take in any familiar smells, wiggle your toes, and open your eyes. Remain conscious of your innangardh as you move forward in your life.

*Written language can be considered
magical by those who cannot read.*

Ten

Runes, Charms, and Magic

eathenry has its own system of what can be called the esoteric arts. Two
prominent practices are using the runes and working seidh. There were
other forms of magic as well, including charms, herbal practices, and in-
cantations, but detailed discussions of these are beyond the scope of this
book. Still, any introduction to the heathen religious folkway should spend
some time discussing these runes and seidh. (Seidworking will be discussed in chapter 11.)

Runes were originally nothing more than a method of writing. Later,
magical uses of the runes can be found in both the Eddic and saga records
showing that the runes had magical uses. Tacitus mentions the casting of
lots, saying that the Germanic tribes have the "highest regard"[1] for omens
and lot casting. He goes into great detail discussing the method he witnesses, which we will discuss more fully later in this chapter.[2] We have no
other record of the runes being used for divination. Modern heathens do
practice runic divination, but it is worth noting that, as far as we can tell, it
may or may not have been a traditional use of the runes.

Historically speaking, there are varied theories regarding the exact origins of the runes. Runes, or runic inscriptions, have been found dating to 200 BCE.[3] Runes are found among the Scandinavians, the Icelanders, Anglo-Saxons, Frisians, and other Germanic speaking peoples at one time or another. They were used on everything from merchant's ownership tags to recording the deeds of a hero on a stone monument. Some inscriptions simply indicated ownership—one sample reads, "Domnal Seal's-Head owns this sword."[4] Some were clearly graffiti. Ellis Davidson points out the "effrontery" of traveling Vikings, citing the "runic inscriptions on ancient tombs like Maeshowe in Orkney."[5]

Cleasby-Vigfusson defines the word *rún* as "to enquire," and "writing," and the dictionary goes on to refer to the word as "magical characters," "a secret, hidden lore," and "mystery."[6] In his book, *Runes*, Ralph Elliott discusses the word and its adoption into Celtic, as *rūn*, where it meant "secret,"[7] and into the Finnish *runo* with the meaning "song."[8] Edred Thorsson provides us with the Proto-Indo-European root **reu-*, meaning "to roar,[9] while Maurine Halsall points to cognate words, such as the Old Saxon *runon*, meaning "to whisper."[10] It seems clear that the word itself was a complicated one, and one which changed meanings over time. We see that the runes are "secret," and can mean "mystery," and definitions like these can point us to more esoteric meanings.

Mythologically speaking, Odin is the father of the runes. In the Hávamál, Odin speaks of hanging from a windswept tree with no food or water for nine nights. He looks below him, takes up the runes, and cries out before falling back again.[11] We do not know why he screams; it is often assumed that the power of the runes is so great even Odin has some trouble gathering them up. Odin then goes on to recite numerous uses of the runes that he has mastered, including help-runes and runes against fire.[12] Odin also gives us clear insight into the runes and appropriate care of them. Hávamál stanza 144 has Odin's instructions, in question form:

Know'st how to write,	know'st how to read,
know'st how to stain,	how to understand,
know'st how to ask,	know'st how to offer,
know'st how to supplicate	know'st how to sacrifice? [13]

It seems clear that the first two verses are about the runes and how to work with them. The runes were both carved and written. "Stain" in both cases refers to using blood to redden the runes. The other two verses seem to be more about blót as a ritual, but imply the same thing. On the one hand, a solid heathen should have a grasp of what these things are and how to perform them properly. On the other hand, if you do not know how to do all of these rituals, do not do them.

As an example, we hear from *Egil's Saga* that Egil Skallagrimsson was proficient in runes. Egil sees that Helga, daughter of Thorfinn, has taken ill. Egil asks if anyone had found a reason for the sickness. Thorfinn replies, saying: "We had some runes carved…and since then she's been much worse." [14] Egil decides to try to heal Helga. When going through her room, he finds a whale bone with runes carved on it. Egil reads the runes, scratches them out, and has the whalebone burned. He says:

No man should carve runes
unless he can read them well;
many a man goes astray
around those dark letters. [15]

Egil cuts runes of his own and puts them under her pillow. Helga awakens from her delirium, and is soon on the mend. [16] This can, and should, be taken as a warning for all those who decide to work with the runes; they can cause harm and illness if handled incorrectly, even if the runes are intended as a healing rite. In short, avoid doing the work unless you have a complete understanding of any unforeseen circumstances that may harm instead of heal.

There are two main sets of rune rows left to us, the so-called Younger and Elder Futharks. Futhark as a word is named for the first six of the runes—

fehu (f), *uruz* (u), *thurisaz* (th), *ansuz* (a), *raidho* (r), and *kenaz* (k). The Younger Futhark was used during the Viking Age, while the Elder furthak's origins are more controversial. At the same time, in modern heathenry the Elder Futhark is the one more commonly used, so we will focus on it.

As a form of writing, each rune has its own letter, or associated sound. *Inguz*, for example, is most often used to symbolize the diphthong "ng." Additionally, each has a single-word association, probably used as a mnemonic for skalds and others who wished to remember the runes and their meanings. *Inguz*, the sound "ng" (as in "banking"), is also referred to as Ing, one of the names of the god Frey. Finally, there are three sets of rune poems most often used for interpretative purposes. They are the Anglo-Saxon (or Old English), the Norwegian (Old Norse), and the Icelandic rune poems. Carrying through on our rune inguz, the Old English rune poem is translated as: "Ing was first seen by men along the East-Danes, until he at last departed eastward over the wave, he ran after the wagon; thus the warriors named the hero."[17] All of these considerations must be taken into account when considering *inguz* and what it might have meant for our ancestors, and what it might mean for us today.

Focusing on the rune poems themselves provides a great deal of insight, particularly when taken from a heathen point of view. In studying *inguz*, then, we need to remember that Ing (Frey) was a hero-god who visited the Danes and then left toward the east, or the rising sun. This tells us that Frey might have associations with the east, and some heathens speculate that this must be the direction of Alfheim; Frey is departing from the East-Danes to his home further in the east. A complete translation of all three rune poems is beyond the scope of this book. That said, in general, the meanings taken from the rune poems of the Elder Futhark are as follows:

ᚠ Fehu: wealth and general distribution of wealth, gold causing strife between kin, and the brightness of the flood-tide

ᚢ Uruz: the aurochs, slag from bad iron, drizzle as the enemy of a sheep herder

Þ Thurisaz: a severe thorn, the ailment of women, thursar

ᚠ Ansuz: god, wisdom, a scabbard for swords, the chief of Asgard (Odin)

ᚱ Raido: blissful for the traveler but rough for the horse

< Kenaz: torch as a bright light, the curse of children, misfortune

X Gebo: a gift as a benefit and source of survival

ᚹ Wunjo: joy, prosperity, and bliss

ᚺ Hagalaz: hail, the whitest grain, the coldest grain, a mighty snowstorm

ᚾ Nauthiz: need can become oppressive, helpful if caught early, and hard labor

| Isa: ice, a danger to men, an unexpected bridge

ᛃ Jera: year, good harvest, a ripe field

ᛇ Eiwaz: the yew tree

ᛈ Perthro: dice cup, sport, and laughter

ᛉ Algiz: the elk-sedge (grass) cuts deep wounds

ᛋ Sowilo: the sun, victory, glory

↑ Teiwaz: Tyr, a good omen

ᛒ Berkana: the birch tree, devoid of fruit but youthful

ᛖ Ehwaz: a horse, the delight of noblemen

ᛗ Mannaz: man increasing on earth, dear to his friends

ᛚ Laguz: the sea, water, a waterfall, the swirling stream

ᛜ Inguz (Ingwaz): Frey, first seen by the East-Danes, the hero

ᛞ Dagaz: day, a benefit to all

ᛟ Othila (Othala): native/ancestral lands, valuable to any man

These are generalizations based on the rune poems, but the basic meanings of each rune can be gleaned. In terms of writing, spelling was not solidified until the coming of the printing press, and many of the ancient peoples spelled phonetically. *Jera*, for instance, is the "j" or "y" sound. Spelling out Freyja using the runes, there is no need to use both the y and the j—a single *jera* rune suffices as the sound. Freyja written into runes would be *fehu, raido, ehwaz, jera, ansuz*. Looking slightly deeper, the meanings of those runes, in short, are wealth, journey, horse, year, God/Odin (also mouth). What we can decide about those meanings, if anything can be decided, will vary according to the reader.

The interpretation of the runes can be highly personal. Studying the runes from a more mystical point of view involves meditation, study, and developing habits that allow one to connect with the runes in similar ways that one connects to the tarot or other divination systems. Tacitus does mention the casting of lots, and it is worth quoting him at more length here:

> For omens and the casting of lots, they have the highest
> regard. Their procedure in casting the lots is always the same.
> They cut off a branch of a nut-bearing tree and slice it into
> strips; these they mark with different signs and throw them
> completely at random onto a white cloth. Then the priest of
> the state, if the consultation is a public one, or the father of the
> family if it is private, offers a prayer to the gods, and looking
> up at the sky picks up three strips, one at a time, and reads
> their meaning from the signs previously scored on them.[18]

If we look at this passage from an esoteric point of view, we can reconstruct some practices and incorporate them into our runic divinations. There is the use of a white cloth and wood from nut-bearing trees to cut the runes into. There is a prayer of some sort to the gods, presumably to help the divination be accurate. The method of casting is described thoroughly, and reconstructionist-minded people can use it as a means of getting information. Each of the runes itself will have a meaning based on the rune poems, and can be interpreted inspirationally as well. All of these things can be used in conjunction with the runes, either the Elder or Younger Futhark, and may well yield answers.

This is where UPG, (unsubstantiated or unverifiable personal gnosis—the spiritual information gained solely from subjective personal experience), comes into play. Take, for instance, *isa*, which is the letter *i*. This may be all there is to it. But according to the rune poem, *isa* is a danger for men. This also makes sense, considering ice storms, the slipperiness and instability of ice, and how much ice our Northern European ancestors encountered during winter. There is another, more subtle line in the poems though, discussing a bridge. When we think of ice and consider a frozen river or other body of water, an ice road can form, which men and women can then use as a bridge to cross over. Again, this is fairly understandable when we look at the nature of ice. Here we can use our gnosis to glean something about the meaning of the bridge. An ice bridge is not there for long. It is not permanent, and can be treacherous to cross. That said, a person looking from a divinatory perspective may think that there is a road otherwise unavailable to the querent, if that person can see it and is brave enough to use it. If we consider *isa* as an ice bridge in more magical terms, it could possibly create an opportunity for a different direction to form in one's life. Again, this all falls into the realm of unsubstantiated gnosis—none of this appears in the rune poems regarding *isa*—but it seems that a logical, if inspirational, extrapolation can exist for those using the runes for more magical or divinatory purposes.

One use of the runes that has not yet been discussed is galdr. Galdr is an invocation of the runes as sound. We are not certain precisely where galdr comes from, but it is defined by *Cleasby-Vigfusson* as a "song" which is combined with "the notion of a charm or spell."[19] Often described as atonal, or "harsh" to the ear, galdr is a ritual incantation that Odin hints at in the "Hávamál," when he asks if the reader knows how to speak the runes. There seem to be two main methods when it comes to galdr. One uses only the sound of the rune in question. "Fe" of fehu, for instance, is chanted as one large exhalation of breath. The second uses the entire rune name, in this case fehu, chanted again along one exhalation of breath. Runes can be combined with galdr either as separate breaths—ah, la, oo— or as one single breath—ahhhhlahhhooo. These three sounds correspond to *ansuz, laguz,* and *uruz.* Taken together, they spell "alu," or "ale," which appears to have been a word used for blessings as well as to indicate the beverage. One could even galdr the entire word—ahhhhlllooo—as well.

When it comes to magic, galdr, divination, and other uses of the runes, an understanding of the heathen mindset is invaluable. In terms of world-view, knowing the mythology and some of the saga record surrounding the runes gives us an idea of not only why they were used, but how and to what purpose. The mythology also gives us a framework for under-standing—knowing that alu was used as a blessing word also indicates the sacred nature of ale. At the same time, heathens are, by and large, an in-dustrious, self-reliant people. Generally, heathen views on the metaphysi-cal aspects of the faith are similar to those of prayer. Both are intercessors that will have one impact or another on the world around us. However, working runes, charms, or prayers is not enough—one must go out and perform the hard, mundane work to achieve one's goals as well. Whether the spell or prayer simply eases the mind, or has a strong impact on the world is only relevant when one's determination and industriousness are also in play. As a brief example, imagine that you are unemployed. Using fehu for wealth and inguz for prosperity and good harvest, you invoke the powers that be and ask for help finding a job. That's all well and good. At the same time, however, you need to follow up your incantation with real-life work; you need to build a résumé, research jobs you may be qualified for, and apply for said positions. The common heathen thinking is that the metaphysical work can help by giving a kind of amplified effect on the mundane work. However, in order to be most effective, the magical work and the mundane work must go hand in hand.

Single Rune Cast

The single rune is the simplest overview of any situation. It can be used as a yes-no answer; the answer lies in the rune drawn. A rune like *sowilu*, indicating the sun and victory, is going to predict a positive/"yes" answer. A rune like *hagalaz*, the hail storm, is fairly clearly negative, or a "no" response. For a more complex look, see the meaning of the rune itself. *Berkana*, for instance, might connote an actual birth, or it might refer to a broader explanation dealing with the birch tree as a symbol. *Hagalaz* contains within it the destructive nature of a hail storm, which may indicate "storms" of a more spiritual nature.

Urdh—Verdandi—Skuld

It is important to remember the heathen mindset described in earlier chapters before performing this casting. Heathens believe the past is permanent, the present is ever-changing, and the future is conditional depending on the past and present actions. Therefore, when casting this rune row, do not think in fixed terms such as "past, present, and future." Instead, consider the runes as "that which has passed," "that which is becoming," and "that which shall become, given the current situation."

This is a simple three-rune cast. It is meant as a general overview of a situation that identifies the factors involved and the most likely outcome. The first rune drawn is the "urdh" rune—it points to the past which is directly related to the situation. The second rune drawn is "verdandi," the ever-changing present. It can often point to the right action that the querent should take, but it can also represent a more general course of action that needs to be taken. "Skuld," the third rune pulled, represents what is most likely to happen based on what has already happened and what actions are represented by the "verdandi" rune. Once all three runes are pulled, a sequence of events can be determined which should lead to the "skuld" rune.

This can be done in similar ways to the lot casting described by Tacitus. Use runes carved into wood from a fruit- or nut-bearing tree. Cast them all onto a white cloth. Looking upward, pull the three runes, one at a time. Divine as above in terms of the permanent past, the ever-changing present, and the conditional future.

Throwing or Casting Method

This method is good when seeking a more complex answer to any question. Reach into the bag or container you keep your runes in. Focus your mind on the issue at hand. Slowly stir the runes as you do so. When the moment feels right, grab whatever runes are in your hand and throw them onto a cloth or other area you are using to cast onto. These are the runes most relevant to the situation—leave the other runes in the bag. Look at the overall pattern of the runes that have fallen. Some will be closer together than others—these runes are, as one might imagine, influencing one another most directly. Take the picture in as a whole—divine each rune, but do so in terms of its placement in the overall pattern.

A Note on Murkstaves

Sometimes a rune will come out upside down. Sometimes it will be face down instead of face up. In some cases, especially when the runes are tossed, the rune might come out pointing sideways or at a strange angle. These situations can be referred to as "murk" staves because their meaning is more oblique. In the case of an upside-down rune, for instance, some readers see that as the reverse of the meaning of the rune; in this case things are read much like the tarot. Likewise, a rune that is facing down can be seen as the opposite of its typical meaning.

That said, another position to consider is that the runes mean what they mean, regardless of their appearance. In other words, *uruz* equates to the aurochs and the strength of that beast no matter no matter how it appears during the reading. What matters is its position in terms of the rune cast itself; if, for instance, it is closest to *sowilu*, meaning the sun or victory, *uruz* could indicate having the strength to attain that victory.

Ultimately it is up to the rune caster to determine how he or she feels about the runes and their positions in any given casting. I recommend choosing one method and sticking to it for best results.

A Note on Bind-Runes

In magical workings, the runes can be combined into bind-runes. Some bind-runes have a specific mention in the saga record. The so-called Helm of Awe that Sigurd takes from Fafnir after he kills the serpent was not a helmet, but a bind-rune often worn on helmets or as talismans on the forehead or neck. It made enemies neutral to you, and friends even closer.

Other bind-runes can be made based on intent. A fertility charm, pendant, or talisman could very well be made up of *inguz* (Frey is connected to fertility), *berkana* (the birch tree can also be associated with birth), and *jera* (good harvest). These three runes can be drawn individually, or combined together into a bind-rune. The talisman created could be worn by the person seeking fertility until pregnancy occurs, then discarded.

Remember, though, the warning we saw in Egil Skallagrimsson. Be careful that the runes you bind together are all for the same purpose, or something similar. Do not be too complex; three runes can suffice, or even four, but there is no need to throw every rune at an issue every time. Sometimes a single rune packs a focused "punch" and no bind-rune is necessary.

Notes on Chapter Ten

1. Tacitus, *The Agricola and the Germania* (London: Penguin Books, 1970), 109.

2. Tacitus, *The Agricola and the Germania* (London: Penguin Books, 1970), 109.

3. R. I. Page, *Runes: Reading the Past* (Berkeley: University of California Press, 1987), 6.

4. E. V. Gordon, *An Introduction to Old Norse* (Oxford: Clarendon Press, 1992), 186.

5. H. R. Ellis Davidson, *Gods and Myths of the Viking Age* (New York: Barnes and Noble Books, 1996), 13.

6. *Cleasby-Vigfusson*, accessed December 19, 2011.

7. Ralph W. V. Elliott, *Runes* (New York: Saint Martin's Press, 1959), 2.

8. Ralph W. V. Elliott, *Runes* (New York: Saint Martin's Press, 1959), 2.

9. Edred Thorsson, *Futhark: A Handbook of Rune Magic* (York Beach, ME: Samuel Weiser, Inc., 1984), 1.

10. Maureen Halsall, *The Old English Rune Poem: A Critical Edition* (Toronto: University of Toronto Press, 1981), 5.

11. Lee M. Hollander, trans., The *Poetic Edda* (Austin, TX: University of Texas Press, 1962), 36.

12. Lee M. Hollander, trans, The *Poetic Edda* (Austin, TX: University of Texas Press, 1962), 37–40. Not all of these runes has a direct translation to any Futhark. This has led some to speculate that these may be bind-runes, spoken of later in the chapter. The list includes eighteen runes Odin can use at will—help-runes, limb-runes, runes to unfetter him if he is held in chains or is otherwise bound, peace-making, fire-quelling, blessing-runes and runes to help bend women to his sway, among others.

13. Lee M. Hollander, trans., The *Poetic Edda* (Austin, TX: University of Texas Press, 1962), 37.

14. Örnólfur Thorsson, ed. *The Sagas of the Icelanders, Egil's Saga* (New York: Penguin Books, 2000), 68.

15. Örnólfur Thorsson, ed. *The Sagas of the Icelanders, Egil's Saga* (New York: Penguin Books, 2000), 68.

16. Örnólfur Thorsson, ed. *The Sagas of the Icelanders, Egil's Saga* (New York: Penguin Books, 2000), 68.

17. Stephen E. Flowers, *The Rune Poems Volume I: Introduction, Texts, Translations, and Glossary* (Smithville, TX: Runa-Raven Press, 2002), 19.

18. Tacitus, *The Agricola and the Germania* (London: Penguin Books, 1970), 109.

19. *Cleasby-Vigfusson*, accessed March 20, 2012.

Seidhworkers will say what they see.

Eleven

——

Seidh

Seidh, also seidhr or seið, is an umbrella term for a series of trance-style practices. Pre-Christian heathens in most locations did not have a shaman nor a shamanic culture. However, there are many scholars and heathens who consider seidhwork to be shamanistic in form if not in content. There are certainly some elements shared by both shamans and seidhworkers. Both enter some form of trance. Both intercede with the spirits/ wights while entranced. Both can "see" the outcomes of certain situations and sometimes even further into the future. Both can call protection on their people and curses on others. However, it is important to remember that these are two different practices, and seidh is the most relevant to heathenry past and present. It may be shamanic, it may not. It was something practiced by pre-Christian heathens, and it is something being reconstructed and practiced in the modern era.

The word *seidh* is defined in *Cleasby-Vigfusson* as "a spell, charm, enchantment, incantation,"[1] and also as "a kind of oracle, fortune-telling."[2] We are unsure of the word's precise etymology, but historian Stephen Pollington argues that "[o]ne interpretation of the Norse word *seidr* connects it to the root *sed—which lies behind English "sit," "sitting," and the French "séance."[3] Earlier scholars attempted to etymologically connect seidh with the modern "seethe," which comes from the Proto-Indo-European *seut-, meaning "to seethe, boil." Seidh as a practice does involve sitting of some kind. It could be via *utiseta* (sitting out, often on a mound at night) or by means of ascending to sit on a *seidhjallr* (a raised platform used especially for seidh). The word for "high seat" is also used in reference to seidh, and in this case it could be that the seidhworker is sitting in the local lord's seat to work her divining or other spells. On the other hand, there are times when a cauldron seemed to be boiled either directly in front of or beneath the *seidhjallr*, which some modern heathens think might connect the words seidh and seethe. The evidence linking seidh to seethe seems flimsy, and many scholars have argued that the two are from very different etymological places. As we have seen, the Proto-Indo-European root words for each are different, which certainly implies different meanings. Regardless, the link between seidh and sitting as part of its practices is clear.

We also have the word *spá*, which can be defined both as "to pry, look" and also to "prophesy" or "foretell."[4] Many modern heathens feel that spá, or spae, falls under the umbrella term "seidh" and is therefore only a part of a larger set of practices and just about as many others believe that spae is entirely different from seidh. It is best to consider this argument from several angles. Examining the source materials, we do see that both seidh and spá were often used interchangeably from text to text, and even from page to page. Therefore, to this author, at least, it seems that the practices are at the very least similar to one another, although seidh does seem to cover more ground in terms of its use to describe practices other than prophecy.

The *Elder* or *Poetic Edda* contains within it the "Voluspá." As we can see from the title, it is the spá of the Volva, and it does contain at least one prophecy within it. In "Voluspa 22," the character Heid performs seidh:

Seið hon, hvars hon kunni, seið hon hug leikken, which is, in nearly literal translation, something like: "(Performed) seid she, where she could, (performed) seid she (on) mind playfully."[5]

The word *playfully* presents its own difficulties. The word *leikken* is a form of *leika*, which means "to play sport," but also means "to delude, play a trick on."[6] Therefore the passage could also be translated as: "She performed seidh where she could, and performed seidh to delude the mind" (author's translation). This may be more to the point, since we know that seidh was used for nefarious purposes as well as good ones. *Ynglingasaga*, chapter 7, supports this. It is worth citing it at length here:

> Odin had the skill which gives great power and which he practiced himself. It is called seith [sorcery], and by means of it he could know the fate of men and predict events that had not yet come to pass; and by it he could also inflict death or misfortunes or sickness, or also deprive people of their wits or strength, and give them to others. But this sorcery is attended by much wickedness that manly men considered it shameful to practice it, and so it was taught to priestesses.[7]

As we can see, seidh was viewed with suspicion, and "manly men" did not practice it. This does not mean, however, that no males ever practiced seidh. In *Ynglingasaga*, chapter 22, we are told that King Hugleik "had with him sorcerers and all kinds of magicians."[8] The word translated as "sorcerers" is actually "seiðmenn" while the magicians are called "fjolkunnigr," implying that these two sets of men performed two different sets of magic for their king, one being seidh. As Pollington says:

> Females were considered especially gifted in prophecy and clairvoyance in Germanic tradition, as reported by Tacitus in *Germania*, but males could apparently compensate in some way.[9]

While "compensate" may not be the best word choice, the concept is a true one—men practiced seidh as well as women. This holds true in the modern era. Men and women perform seidh with equal effectiveness.

We do not know precisely what the practice looked like, nor how it was performed. In *The Vinland Sagas*, "Erik the Red's Saga" chronicles an encounter with a prophetess. A high seat is made for her; on the seat was a pillow made of hen feathers. The prophetess's appearance is also described in detail; she wears a blue mantle adorned with stones, a glass beaded necklace, a black lambskin hood, and so on down to the tips of her bootlaces, which were large tin buttons.[10] We are not sure why she is described in such detail, but for these items to be written down, some importance must have been attached to them. Perhaps it means simply that she is shown as a woman of means who can afford the best. Perhaps the reason is to record what might have been a final seidh practice in an effort to preserve it. We will never know. We do know that she carried a staff with a brass top of some sort. Some modern seidhworkers dress as closely to the above as they can. The explanation given for this is that the clothing triggers the mind and helps a person focus on the change between the mundane world and the world as seen in trance. Other seidhworkers wear whatever clothing they happen to have on; in other words, dressing as the seidhworker in Erik's Saga is not necessary to perform the work. By and large, most modern heathen seidhworkers do have a staff of some sort, which also helps them enter the trance by providing a trigger, and one that, at least in this seidhworker's experience, helps the entranced person remember where the mundane world is.

The ritual itself is not recorded anywhere. Erik's Saga, chapter 4, is the main source people use to reconstruct seidh, and it is only a basic outline of events. The seeress needed someone to sing specific songs for her to enter the trance; only one woman, Gudrid, remembers the words. The word used for the songs is *vardhlokkur*, or warding songs, and so many presume that some sort of warding, guarding, or other means of protection comes directly from the songs being sung. We have no record of the words used in the vardhlokkur, nor their tunes. After the songs are sung, the prophetess says that she can see the spirits present, and that they were "charmed by the singing,"[11] which could mean that the spirits were amused by the songs or, more likely, that they were magically enchanted and required to obey the seeress. In either event, from there she begins to tell prophecies. We do not know how the ritual ends, only that she is called away and goes to another farm.

There are a few other tantalizing clues in other sources. *Njal's Saga*, chapter 105, describes Thorgeir, the then-current lawspeaker. He is asked to tell, by law, if Iceland is Christian or not. He drapes a cloak over his head, and is left alone until he emerges with the decision, and states that Iceland will officially convert to Christianity as a whole, although heathen practices are tolerated in one's own home.[12] The description of this event has led many modern seidhworkers to pull the hood of their cloak, or some kind of fabric veil, over their heads prior to entering the trance.

That's all we really know about the seidh ritual itself—a woman agrees to enter a trance, someone sings songs for her, and then she prophesizes. A man goes under the cloak to gain wisdom and some sort of implied guidance, and emerges with an answer he takes to the Law Rock. In both of these cases, it seems that what is going on is better categorized as spae. Prophecy is involved more than magic, cursing, or otherwise binding people's minds. That said, since many modern heathens consider spae to be a part of seidh, reconstruction has come to focus on this ancient ritual we know so little about.

At the same time, the sagas are replete with spells, curses, and magic, many times being referred to as seidh. As an example, regarding Haraldr War-Tooth (also Blue-Tooth), it was said that:

> When he was young, it was determined that mighty sorcery (seiðr) would be worked, and it was enchanted (seidt) for King Haraldr such that iron would not bite him and so it was after that, and for this reason he did not carry a shield in battle and he was secure since no weapon could harm him.[13]

It seems clear that this is some kind of protective seidhworking. This is repeated in Thorstein's "Saga Vikingssonar," where Kolr Kroppinbakr does much the same kind of working so that his offspring cannot be hurt by weapons.[14] The opposite of this working is also in the saga evidence. In

"Gisli's Saga," a man named Bork pays Thorgrímr Nef, a known sorcerer, to make sure that there would be no help—no protection—and no rest for the murderer of Thorgrímr.[15]

Here is where the cautionary tales creep in. Seidh could do powerful, positive things—and equally powerful negative ones. It was viewed with suspicion then and now. Not all heathens practice seidh. Not all heathens should. There are many cases where modern heathens discard seidh as completely lost, or as never having existed at all. Some heathens will heap scorn on those claiming to practice seidh in any of its forms. Others are accepting of seidh as a practice, but are wary of those who practice it.

In any event, there are still those who attempt to reconstruct this practice and do so with varying degrees of success. It is a difficult art to work, and even more difficult to master. Seidh should be considered a lifelong discipline, and only the very basics can be taught in a weekend. A lot of variation exists in modern seidh and the way it is practiced. Some will only see for their own kindred, family, or tribe. Some travel to major festivals to perform the rite they have reconstructed. Most seidhworkers see their rituals as focused on the needs of the community at hand. This seems to have been especially true in the saga records—seidhworkers came at need, served the community, and then left again. The focus was on the community, for the most part, just as it is in modern seidh practice.

A Seidhworker's Look at Seidh

As a longtime seidhworker, I have personally come across many different shapes and styles when it comes to seidh. I considered carefully what, if any, rituals to include at the end of this chapter. As stated above, seidh cannot really be mastered in a weekend—although the basic edges of it can be grasped—and the sum total of any one seidhworker's experience cannot be boiled down to a few simple paragraphs in an introductory work of this kind.

Still, it seemed to me that this chapter I've written lacks what I call the "human touch." We talk about what seidh is and isn't. We discuss the derivation of the word and hint at what it could mean. We show tantalizing edges of practices long forgotten, but do not go into any depth regarding the modern rituals themselves. A part of this, in all honesty, is that seidh rituals vary a great deal from geographic area to geographic area, and from seidhworker to seidhworker. In 2012, Diana Paxson published a book called *The Way of the Oracle*. She spends a great deal of time looking at oracle work across varying cultures, and then moves into common practices involved in becoming a seer. She has included the seidh ritual she and others developed. I recommend the book as a good starting point for those who wish to enter the practice.

Across the board, as mentioned above, what we do see is a commonality of shape. Some sort of blessing and protecting begins the ritual. Many seidhworkers have written specific songs they use as invocations and as modern *vardhlokkur*. The seer enters the trance, either by using her own techniques or by using the techniques he was trained in by another. At some point, a question-and-answer session begins. At this time the seer speaks directly with the wights, gains insight, and speaks the answer given. Different seers perform the trance differently. Some spiritually travel to Helheim and ask the dead their questions. Some speak directly with Hel herself. Some stay in sacred Midgard, entranced but speaking to the wights in the place at the moment, and some spiritually travel to the Well of Wyrd and gaze into its depths for answers. Some bring their audiences along on the journey, others require that the audience stay in the room—i.e., not travel anywhere, spiritually or otherwise—while the seer gets the answers needed and relays them. What we see is the general similarity—a trance entered, questions asked and answers given—while the specifics vary. At the end of the session, the seer exits the trance—again, there are many ways to do this, but often songs or chants are used. Sometimes offerings of thanks are given, sometimes not. The ritual is ended.

Speaking for myself, seidh has been a life-altering experience. It is difficult to put into words, and at times I think that it is better to remain silent than it is to blather on endlessly about events which, ultimately, are personal, deeply inspirational, and have a great deal to do with unverified personal gnosis more than, strictly speaking, a scholarly touch. I seldom attend seidh rituals where I am not actively engaged in part of the rite; I find it better to not know my fate than to question everything. I do small work weekly, and sometimes daily, to keep my skills sharp—I find that, much like a muscle, the ability to perform seidh needs to be "worked out" in order to stay in shape. I do perform seidh at public events, a practice that others sometimes find objectionable. I absolutely see my work as an extension of service to the community. Perhaps not the entire community, but those members who are in need are often helped by the work. I have taken on a few students in my time, and my first "lesson" tends to be: learn to breathe and call me in a year. I say this as much to determine who is willing to do the work as I do to underscore the importance of breath to a heathen mindset. Breathing, as I have explained earlier, is not merely the autonomic response; there is sacredness to the breath itself as the gift of Odin.

Therefore, here is a bit on how to breathe:

Sit in a quiet place. It can be indoors or outdoors. It can be in a specific high seat, a camp chair, or on the floor. I recommend having something to lean your back against because sometimes, when spiritually journeying, your physical body can slump or even fall over. This has happened to me and a few other seidhworkers I know, and we have all agreed that trying to perform seidh while crumpled up is, at best, undignified. More seriously, sudden movements of the body can pull one out of the trance state.

Close your eyes and focus on your breath. Slowly start to lengthen your breaths, and slow your breathing. Try to develop a rhythmic breath that inhales for four counts, pauses for two counts, exhales for four counts, pauses for two counts. Repeat this pattern. For some, staying in this pattern the entire time one is in trance is invaluable. Personally, because I have asthma, it's better for my lungs to use this pattern to focus, then let go and let my body breathe naturally. While breathing, focus your mind on a single object. It can be any object you choose—an apple, a tree, a piece of art—but it should be a more or less still object, or an object at rest. Keep your focus up until you can view the object in three dimensions; rotate the image in your mind in order to do this. Try to touch and feel the object. Try to smell it. Everyone has different dominant senses; figure out which yours is by seeing which of these techniques works for you. It may be that you can work with multiple senses at once.

When the image "breaks"—your mind typically wanders—return to focusing on your breath in the 4-2-4-2 pattern. Slowly let your breathing return to normal. Feel your body, what it is touching, where you are in the room or other space you're in. Open your eyes and take in as many visual cues as you can to remind yourself that you are in the mundane world.

Practice this when you are compelled to do so. Daily, or at the same time every day. Weekly, perhaps on the same day each time. Monthly, even. At first you may want to do this often. It will be harder than you think to hold your focus on one item, let alone use all your senses to experience it. It can be done, over time and with practice.

This is only the first step on a long path. Remember to be patient with yourself.

Notes on Chapter Eleven

1. *Cleasby-Vigfusson*, accessed November 2, 2012.

2. *Cleasby-Vigfusson*, accessed November 2, 2012.

3. Stephen Pollington, *Leechcraft: Early English Charms, Plantlore, and Healing* (Swaffham, Norfolk, England: Anglo-Saxon Books, 2000), 64.

4. *Cleasby-Vigfusson*, accessed November 2, 2012.

5. Dan Campbell and Anna Wiggins, trans., *Völuspá: A Dual-Language Edition with Complete Glossary* (Hillsborough, NC: Iðavelli Hof, 2011), 32.

6. *Cleasby-Vigfusson*, accessed November 2, 2012.

7. Snorri Sturluson, *Heimskringla: History of the Kings of Norway* (Austin, TX: University of Texas Press, 1964), 11.

8. Snorri Sturluson, *Heimskringla: History of the Kings of Norway* (Austin: University of Texas Press, 1964), 25.

9. Stephen Pollington, *Leechcraft: Early English Charms, Plantlore, and Healing* (Swaffham, Norfolk, England: Anglo-Saxon Books, 2000), 64.

10. Magnus Magnusson, trans., *The Vinland Sagas: The Norse Discovery of America* (London: Penguin Books, 1965), 81–82.

11. Magnus Magnusson, trans., *The Vinland Sagas: The Norse Discovery of America* (London: Penguin Books 1965) 82–83.

12. Robert Cook, trans., *Njal's Saga* (London: Penguin Books 1997) 181.

13. Stephen Flowers and James Chisholm, trans., *A Source-Book of Seid* (Smithville, TX: Runa-Raven Press, 2002), 20.

14. Stephen Flowers and James Chisholm, trans., *A Source-Book of Seid* (Smithville, TX: Runa-Raven Press, 2002), 20.

15. Stephen Flowers and James Chisholm, trans., *A Source-Book of Seid* (Smithville, TX: Runa-Raven Press, 2002), 8.

"An age which took its gods seriously
would not be likely to treat an oath lightly." [1]

Twelve

Ethics, Hospitality, and Oaths

In order to understand heathenry, we need to understand the worldview of heathens both traditionally and in the modern world. Nowhere is that as important as it is in understanding heathen ethics. A monotheist world-view, for the most part, is what one could call "world-rejecting."[2] A world-rejecting perspective views everything on this plane as temporary, and also fairly irrelevant, because the goal is to ascend to a "better" world after death.

Heathenism, on the other hand, is considered a "world-accepting" religion. Heathens live in the here and now, and typically are not at all focused on the afterlife. There are multiple afterlives in heathen thinking—Valhalla for the chosen slain, Ran's hall for those drowned at sea, Helheim for the majority of heathens and their ancestors, and others—but there is no focus on where a heathen will go, nor does heathen behavior stem from a desire have a better afterlife. No one knows precisely where we will go after we die, so it is better to live in the active present than it is to worry about the future. This makes the most sense when considering the heathen ethical system from the Germanic perception of time. The past is fixed and we cannot change it. The future is entirely dependent on the past and the active present. It is simpler, more logical, and in many ways, easier to spend our time and energy focused on our actions in the present.

This does not mean we can do anything we want. The past binds us, as we have seen, and it is only in the present that we can shape the future. Under the auspices of limited free will, the more choices we make, and the more actions form our pasts, the fewer "real" options we have for our present. The longer we live, the fewer choices we really have, and thus the future becomes narrower and narrower until we can accurately predict the "most likely outcome" of everything that comes next. Heathen ethics reflect this. Logically, positive actions now will lead to a more positive series of outcomes for the future. Therefore action is important, and this includes ethical action as well.

Traditional tribal peoples across the world tend to have, as a central tenet of their cultures, a belief in the intricate connections between different states of being. Modern peoples tend to refer to this as a "holistic" approach; in fact, most people agree that the mind, the body, and the spirit are all components of the same, whole being. Science supports this way of thinking—multiple studies have been undertaken regarding issues like how meditation and stress affect the physical body, how mental disorders can cause physiological damage, and so on. The next logical extension of this is that the mundane world and the other worlds connect with one another in similar ways. Michael York sums this up as follows: "A fundamental pagan attitude…is one that considers the possibility of active exchange between this world and the otherworld."[3] In heathenry, what is done in Midgard has a resonance on a mundane and sacred level as well.

By and large, heathens believe that there is no "real" future, only a series of most likely outcomes. They believe that everything is interconnected through the Well of Wyrd—and by "everything" heathens mean not just the average, everyday motions of their lives, but every act, sacred or profane, physical or spiritual. Heathen ethical systems, therefore, are based on the actions taken in the here and now, because only through those actions can they make an impact on the world around them. What this can mean is that the heathen ethical system is situational. In situational ethics, the actions of the people involved depend on the complexities of the situation, and will vary depending on circumstances, people involved, location, and other factors. While it is true that our responses will change according to any given situation, there are those who take situational ethics to imply that heathens have no ethical system at all. In other words, if heathens can do anything they want, given the situation, then they have no moral compass. Nothing could be further from the case. Heathen ethics may be situational, but they are also virtue-driven.

The Germanic tribes tend to fall under what sociologists, anthropologists, historians, and other scholars refer to as "warrior cultures." A warrior culture tends to be focused on battle and preparing for battle. Warrior cultures tend to form in marginal environments, where resources are scarce—food and water are not abundant, the weather is harsh or extreme, and resources are limited. This is not to say that every person was a warrior, and this was definitely not the case with the Germanic tribes, who had farmers, traders, settlers, and other groups of people as well as seasoned warriors. What it does say is that the set of virtue-driven ethics warrior cultures develop is shared by all members of that culture. Here is one example, taken from the *Hávamál*:

From his weapons on the open road
no man should step one pace away.[4]

This should be taken literally, and in a warrior culture one should keep one's weapons close at hand. Those of the culture who did not fight in battles or blood feuds could also see preparedness in this stanza. A traditional warrior culture woman, for instance, would keep her keys nearby, or on her belt, so that she was always prepared. We can speculate that she might also keep weapons close at hand in case she needed to defend her property when her husband was out trading, or if she herself went to war.

In a warrior culture, reputation matters and is seen in every aspect of life. It is important to have a good reputation. The Hávamál says that our good names will live on after our deaths. The only way to have a good reputation is to build it over time, and then maintain it. Bad behavior weakens one's reputation. Good behavior increases it. A pattern of good behavior will build up one's reputation more favorably; therefore, heathen actions in the present tend to be ones that maintain or build reputation. Let's take honesty as an example. If a person is honest, he tells the truth, particularly with his friends. A pattern of behavior forms over time. In this case, an honest man has the reputation he has built as an honest man. If that person is caught in a lie, it is all the more shocking because he is known to be truthful; this means a loss in reputation. Those who are liars have reputations as well. The liar cannot be trusted and is more likely to be shunned by other heathens because he has proven to be untrustworthy.

The polytheist Greek philosopher Aristotle examined virtue-driven ethics in great detail throughout his life. He wrote *Nicomachean Ethics* to explore ethics in terms of ancient Greece, and argues that it is the pursuit of virtue that makes mankind "happy"—for only the virtuous can be happy. It is important to note that the Greek system and the Germanic one were very different from one another. For instance, Aristotle believed that the "virtuous man" was a man committed to the state. Most Northern European tribal peoples, while highly organized within themselves and in their contacts with others, did not organize into anything resembling a "state" system as we understand it until after the Conversion Period. At the same time, if we as polytheists want to catch a glimpse at what a polytheist culture looked like, it's a fairly good idea to study Aristotle; he was, at least, a polytheist, and his philosophies more closely match modern polytheist thinking.

According to Aristotle, every virtue had its opposite vice. Courage, for example, was considered virtuous, while its opposite, cowardice, was a vice.[5] However, every virtue taken too far became a vice in and of itself. Cowardice was a vice, but so was foolhardiness. A man who ran headlong into danger with no consideration for his own life or those of his allies was foolhardy, and that was a vice. Therefore, according to Aristotle, the best thing a man (or woman) could do was be courageous while at the same time avoiding the excesses of vice that came from both cowardliness and foolhardiness. Living a virtuous life meant working actively on maintaining the balance found in the virtue itself. Passivity, or "doing nothing," was not virtuous, because being passive meant never engaging in the acts themselves. In other words, the virtuous man engaged in action, and through that action determined where the proper, virtuous, "middle-ground" of any virtue existed. Courage is a value many warrior cultures share, and we can see that it should be tempered by striving to be courageous without being foolhardy or cowardly. In heathen terms, the reputation of a woman's courage will precede her, and she will be known as a courageous woman due to her actions. If she is cowardly, or foolhardy, her reputation will suffer. If, on the other hand, she maintains courage by finding the middle ground between the two, and actively strives to maintain that virtue, her reputation will increase. We can see several stanzas in the Hávamál which encourage this kind of moderation. Stanza 64 discusses moderation concerning wisdom:

Every man wise in counsel
should use his power in moderation.[6]

In addition to guarding reputations, heathens tend to build relationships of reciprocity. There is a sense of give and take among heathen communities. In this they are akin to small towns—perhaps one day you give your neighbor gas to mow his lawn, and a few weeks or so later he gives you sugar when you're out and in the middle of baking cookies. The value of the items exchanged does not really matter, as long as a reciprocal balance is maintained. What matters more is that the exchange has been given and received. This give and take rises beyond mundane needs and into sacred ones; heathens consider their relationships with the gods to be reciprocal. This is why offerings are so important to heathens. There is little to no sense that a god may be angry and must be appeased. Instead, a person becomes something of a friend to the gods, giving back in exchange for all the gifts the gods have given.

Reciprocity runs like a gleaming thread through everything associated with heathenry. It does the same thing in most tribal cultures across the globe, and even down through time, so it should come as no surprise that, actually, it's not a word you see a lot of. Reciprocity is so deeply understood as to be nearly subconscious; people do it without even thinking about it. When someone gives you a present during the "holiday season," you feel an urge to give them something in return. That feeling of obligation, that moment of necessity, is the learned behavior of centuries speaking to you. It is the essence of reciprocity. We hear its echo in the Hávamál:

> "'Tis better unasked than offered overmuch;
> For ay doth a gift look for gain."[7]

In other words, when we give gifts, heathens tend to expect some kind of gift in exchange. As already said, by and large, heathens do not remind one another of their reciprocal duties. No polite person says something like, "Hey, remember that time ten years ago when I gave you a dollar? You never paid me back." Instead, it is assumed that the dollar, or some other equivalent, will make its way to the original giver. Reciprocity is not about tit for tat any more than it is meant to be taken advantage of. It is simply an unconscious system found within heathenry which echoes through the majority of heathen ethical behavior.

There are checks and balances to every system, including ethical ones, and in reciprocity the concept of virtue maintains a "middle-ground" series of actions. It is better, so we have seen, to offer nothing than to offer too much. While the stanza above is specifically speaking about blót, it applies to mundane lives as well. Hard feelings can arise when one person gives too much and is taken advantage of. Hard feelings can also arise when the person gives too much and his actions cannot be balanced by the reciprocity of others. In short, reciprocity is not about the monetary value of a gift, nor a "one-upmanship" contest where each seeks to outdo the other in terms of lavishness or expense. The balance of the virtue must be considered at all times. Give willingly, but also receive willingly. Be open with one another, and maintain your reciprocity with one another not merely by gift-giving, but also by using the intangibles—being there for a friend in need, knowing that she will later be there for you. This is reciprocity in action.

Hospitality

Blessed be the givers! A guest has come in,
Where is he going to sit?[8]

Hospitality is another central tenet of heathen practice. If we look at marginal habitats, we can see where food, drink, and a warm place by the fire may be a survival issue. Warrior cultures tend to prize hospitality in general, and once under a host's roof, a guest expects not only to be cared for, but also to be protected by the host. A good host builds a good reputation and, given hospitality's crucial position on the ethical ladder, can be assured of his or her reputation. Reciprocity is in play as well. A guest has certain expectations of his host. A host has certain expectations of her guest. The Hávamál contains several stanzas regarding hospitality. We see that:

Fire is needful for someone who's come in
And who's chilled to the knee;
Food and clothing are necessary for the man
Who's journeyed over the mountains.[9]

The Hávamál is replete with stanza after stanza speaking not just about the responsibilities of a host, but also the requirements of a guest—don't overstay your welcome, Hár urges. Don't come late to a feast, don't abuse your guest-right. In other words, it's not just about being a good host, it is also about being a good guest. This is where we can see reciprocity come into play as part of the virtue of hospitality. Hospitality is not unique to heathenry—it is found as a central ethic among warrior cultures throughout the world. This, again, relates to reputation and to safety. If a person is alone, he is, in essence, in a dangerous situation. Once he has asked for, and received, hospitality, then the host is responsible for his safety. In traditional tribal cultures, this is taken literally. In modern terms, we do not find much violence—blood feud has been replaced by more civil means of confrontation. Still, a host is expected to see to the protection of her guests; in fact, her reputation is increased by her ability to be a good host and provide for her guests. Once she has the reputation of a good hostess, she can be seen as virtuous.

As a cautionary tale, though, it is important to remember Aristotle's point of view regarding virtue as an active working toward the balance between vices. The vice associated with hospitality can be most easily defined as "miserliness"—not sharing resources, hoarding them for one's self, or giving the barest minimum are all examples of this. In *Njal's Saga*, one of the sharpest insults Hallgerd throws at her first husband is "miser." He slaps her for this insult to his character. Hallgerd, being Hallgerd, then has him killed.[10] In *The Saga of the Icelanders*, Egil Skallagrimsson is served too much ale by his host. Drunk, Egil pushes his host up against a post in the hall and vomits on him.[11] He then accuses the host of vomiting on him first. As amusing—and repulsive—as both these examples are, they both underscore the importance of being a good host. Taking that too far, though, is equally problematic—a host who gives everything away without concern will soon find himself dependent on others or unable to provide for his future guests. In saga after saga, we read about a good-natured person who shows hospitality and takes in an outlaw only to have his hall burned down and his property destroyed—all because he took in the wrong person.

Finally, let's fold in the holistic approach—a hospitable person will take in people and offer them his or her home, food, and shelter. Heathens believe that this hospitality involves nonhumans, as well. Winternights, one of the traditional heathen holy days, involved inviting all the "wealful wights" (or, in modern English, "helpful beings") indoors to stay the winter. It involved leaving out the last sheath of grain for the horses of the Wild Hunt to feed on. It involved offerings indoors as well, sharing portions of food and drink to the wights who were wintering with the host and hostess. Winternights was a time when hospitality was offered, and accepted, and that involved sacred and mundane ideas of hospitality.

When heathens practice blót, they are giving to the gods or other wights out of a sense of gratitude for the gifts they have, in their turn, given to heathens. Hospitality among fellow humans, then, should be seen as a form of reciprocity. At the most mundane levels, that is precisely what hospitality is all about. A great deal goes on between host and guest that is assumed, or unconscious—if a host says "Help yourself to what's in the fridge," he is assuming the guest will know what that really means is "Grab a can of Coke and a snack," not "Take the contents of my refrigerator and run away with it all." A guest can expect that, if a sudden rainstorm drives everyone inside, she can say "Hey, do you have a towel so I can dry off?" and the host will offer people towels to dry off with, even if he doesn't have sets of clothes for people to change into. In turn, he's probably going to assume his guests will sit on their towels and not drip all over his good furniture.

Oaths

At this point, we have discussed the importance of the heathen conception of time and have also discussed how heathen ethics in most cases are situational and based on behaviors found in many warrior cultures around the world. Reputation, reciprocity, and hospitality are, by and large, the three most important principles heathens live by. They are taken together and blend into one another—no one is distinct from the others. Given that heathens have at best a foggy sense of the future, and see the past as permanent, we can see how behavior directly impacts the here and now. Since behavior falls from the present into the past and becomes permanent, heathens can also say that any action or nonaction they perform falls directly into the Well of Wyrd. This in its turn impacts wyrd itself, changing the paths of their lives through present behavior. Nowhere can this be better seen than in oath-taking.

The taking of an oath is serious business for heathens. They believe that a combination of oaths and action help to solidify a community. Words spoken in general terms fall into one's wyrd, but an oath taken with an oath ring in hand transcends the mundane and takes on a nearly sacred significance. An oath can be taken in private or with a gathered community of people. Generally speaking, particularly in terms of marriage, the heathen mindset tends to agree with Sanford Levinson's study of oaths. According to Levinson, "[t]he seriousness of a commitment was measured by the degree of publicity that attended it. Promises made in private were regarded as having little worth as compared to those before witnesses."[12] This related especially to marriages, where witnesses were required in order to seal the oath, but in modern heathen terms the sentiment is true for almost every oath made. For many heathens, the taking of an oath does not merely bind the person speaking the oath, but it also binds any witnesses. By their presence, and their willingness to hear the oath, they are bound to see it take a positive outcome. While it is up to the individual to perform the actions that will ensure his oath is met, the heathens who heard the oath are going to support him and help him keep on track.

The utmost importance of the oath and its keeping, or breaking, falls upon the person/people who took the oath, but any witnesses are involved, albeit to a lesser extent. At the same time, reputation is in play—a person who sees her oath through has a greater reputation than one who does not. A person who regularly breaks his oaths will often not be allowed to take an oath in front of other people. Any oath broken has a negative impact on a person's wyrd. There are times when an oath must be broken, perhaps for the sake of someone's health, or in cases of divorce, but these are still considered oaths broken. The person who holds the oath, even when it is broken by another, is often seen as having little to no impact levied on his reputation or wyrd. We will discuss this in more detail later in this chapter, but for now it is also important to note that there are several different kinds of oaths, and each has its own outcome.

Most oaths taken throughout life are situational. An assertory oath, for instance, is in evidence at a court of law, when the witness swears to tell the truth. Here, the oath is for the moment only; once off the stand the witness is no longer compelled to fill the assertory oath. A promissory oath is typically between one person and another, or sometimes between a group of people. A promise is made that needs to be fulfille, and once it is fulfilled, the oath ends. A promissory oath can also involve the witnessing of a promise; a person might swear that he heard another person promise to do such-and-such a thing by a certain date. Fealty oaths cover marriage and also the fidelity of the oath-taker to an individual person in general.

Oaths can also have an impact on the broader community. Some branches of heathenry require that every member of a tribe swear loyalty to one leader, or chieftain; this is an oath of fealty. Allegiance or loyalty oaths, on the other hand, tend to imply fidelity to the state, or, in a heathen case, to a kindred as a whole. When we pledge allegiance to the flag in America, what we are really doing is offering an allegiance oath to the United States as a nation. There are judicial oaths, where a set formula might be used to settle a difference between two people. These were particularly prevalent in the ancient world, where a specific format was adhered to for each judicial act. The failure to follow these set procedures in any sense was met with scorn and derision. Credal oaths include the religious affirmation of belief or certain tenets of faith. Many heathens choose to make credal oaths when they convert to heathenry, basically stating that they now hold to the new religion and its tenets. Abjuration oaths renounce a former belief, loyalty, or practice. These are also taken by many heathens, often in turn with the credal oath. One simple example of this combination would be something like: "I deny my former allegiance to God and my service to Him; I am now heathen and owe my loyalty to the gods and goddesses of Northern Europe."

If the making of an oath is a serious business, the breaking of an oath is at least equally so. The main consequence of breaking an oath is a loss of honor and prestige. In other words, breaking an oath lessens one's reputation and, potentially, position in the community. This can be a small community—maybe only the witnesses of the oath lose their faith in the person breaking it. It can be larger and, as the length of one's reputation grows, a person should remember the various communities he belongs to and come to terms with the oath's breaking. At the least, ridicule should probably be expected. In fact, calling someone an "oath-breaker" is considered a serious insult.

There are a few ways to mitigate the issues surrounding oath-breaking. Remember, first, that one's reputation matters. A person who normally fulfills every oath to the letter will probably be treated better than a constant oath-breaker. She will still lose prestige, but it will be mitigated by her reputation overall. Another way of lessening the impact of a broken oath is by providing assurances beforehand. This often comes as the oath itself is taken, and can stand as a sort of capital against any breaking. Each case will be different. Let's say a person vows to become fulltrui to Frey. The gathered community screeches to a metaphorical halt and, before the person can utter the words, collectively asks "What happens if you don't?" This is where the assurances happen. These are typically set by the community and not the potential oath-taker. Let's suggest that the community decides that, as an ascribed penalty, if this person should not fulfill their oath, he or she has to blót a boar to honor Frey, and invite everyone to the feast. At this point, the potential oath-taker can step back and not take the oath at all. This is met with no ill will, and might be the wisest course. On the other hand, if he or she accepts that assurance, then the expectation is set. The community will be watching. If the oath is met, there is no problem. If the oath is not, the community is going to start wondering when the feast will be. Failure to blót the boar and have a feast is doubly problematic; at this point the oath will effectively be broken twice. Sometimes the ascribed penalties can literally be "capital"—promises of monetary recompense, goods and services to be provided, and so forth can be assurances as well.

High Stakes Oath-taking

Blood feud was common within Viking Age society, and the sagas are full of examples where an oath is made to set the peace, and later broken. Breaking the oath was seen as tantamount to a declaration of war, and the violence would begin. In an effort to keep the peace, compurgation began to replace blood feud. In compurgation, a person could be acquitted of all charges based on the sworn statements of his/her neighbors, friends, or others willing to speak in his behalf. Additionally, hostages were exchanged to ensure the keeping of peace. Perhaps the most famous example of this in Norse materials is the exchange of hostages ending the battle between the Aesir and the Vanir. So long as the hostages were well-treated, the peace was kept. Killing a hostage was an act of war and a violation of the peace oath. People who continually broke their oaths were often shunned by the community at large. At the time, this practice had serious repercussions, because the person could not expect help if she needed it. This was akin to a conviction of lesser outlawry. Greater outlawry meant the person could be killed by anyone who saw him, and no negative consequences would be given to the killer.

No part of ethics can be taken to exist in a vacuum. An oath can be seen as situational, and over once the situation is resolved. It can be seen as semipermanent or permanent, depending upon its wording. In any case, the oath is a serious matter and not taken on lightly by any heathen. Remember, too, that an individual's behavior matters a great deal—but so does the reputation of his tribe or kindred. The idea is akin to a group being better than the sum of its parts. A kindred made of strong, honest, courageous people develops a reputation of its own; the kindred itself is seen as being strong, honest, and courageous. All its members, then, must be the same kind of people, and saying "I am a member of Kindred X" carries weight in the larger community. Breaking an oath threatens the individual's reputation, but it also negatively impacts the prestige of the kindred as a whole.

What if You Need to Break an Oath?

There are times when an oath must be broken. These are typically not easy times for anyone involved. After all, keeping an oath in good times is easy; the challenge rises with the level of difficulty during harder times. First and foremost, a heathen will urge you to keep your oath, and perhaps even offer help so that you can do so. That said, sometimes breaking an oath is for the greater good. In the case of a divorce, for instance, one or both partners may have broken the marriage oath, and the marriage is irretrievable. It is better for the two to part than it is to remain together;

thus the broken oath is mitigated by the circumstances. If there is a case of domestic violence or other abuse, getting away is clearly the better action, even if it technically requires the breaking of the marriage or other oath to do so. Sometimes an oath simply cannot be met, no matter its parameters. Here are some practical pieces of advice:

- If any kind of assurances were made at the time of the oath, be sure to fulfill those obligations. It may be financially or emotionally difficult, but remember that the impact to your reputation will be lessened by maintaining the promises you made as part of the process.

- Discuss the oath-breaking with your kindred, tribe, or community. Talk about why the oath was broken, and be honest about your role in it. This is an exceptionally difficult thing to do. Let them listen and weigh in on what they think and feel. They may want you to pledge something, or do something to help maintain your, and the group's, reputation. Be fair and honest about your capabilities so they can make an appropriate choice. Do what is asked of you.

- Consider the circumstances of leaving an oath-bound kindred. This may involve the return of a kindred symbol, or of having a sumble or other ritual to officially break the ties that bound you. Participate in these as openly and honestly as possible.

- Asking for forgiveness is a touchy thing. Heathens don't necessarily forgive; after all, what is layered in the Well of Wyrd is already permanent. Ask instead how you can help retain your reputation. Sincere apologies are often accepted, but they must be sincere, and not simply a means to an end.

- Remember, all past actions are permanent. You cannot change an oath once it has been made. You can, however, act in the present moment in order to add a more positive layer to your wyrd.

• Go forward with positive action. The better your actions are, the better your reputation will be. Try not to dwell on the situation; pay your dues as required and then do not break any oaths again. That is the best way to keep your reputation intact in the long run.

Notes on Chapter Twelve

1. John A. Widson, "The Oath in Ancient Egypt" (*Journal of Western Studies* 7:3, 1948), 155.

2. James C. Russell, *The Germanization of Early Medieval Christianity* (Oxford: Oxford University Press, 1994). This book speaks at length about world-accepting versus world-rejecting faiths. Russell's position is that this is one of the key elements of pre-Christian paganism that needed to be altered in order for the conversion to Christianity to occur. This was especially difficult when it came to the Germanic tribes, who were not focused on afterlife matters to start with. In fact, he argues that a great deal of Germanic tribal thought had to be adapted into Christianity to make it acceptable in the first place. I cannot recommend this book enough to any reader thinking about the Conversion process or pre-Christian Germanic ethical ideals.

3. Michael York, *Pagan Theology: Paganism as a World Religion* (New York: New York University Press, 2003), 21.

4. Carolyne Larrington, trans., The *Poetic Edda* (Oxford: Oxford University Press, 1996) Stanza 38, 19.

5. Aristotle. W. D. Ross, trans. *Nicomachean Ethics* Book III (Chicago: William Benton, 1953), Ch. 6, 361. Aristotle

discusses various virtues at length, to reveal their extremes and the balance between them which produced virtue. His argument ran that the virtuous person was also a happy person, simply because she was happiest in the pursuit of virtue. This may seem a circular argument at first, but when you consider that a world-accepting religion is focused on present action and not an afterlife, the message becomes clearer. Chapter 6 is dedicated entirely to the virtue of courage.

6. Carolyne Larrington, trans., The *Poetic Edda* (Oxford: Oxford University Press, 1996), 23.

7. Carolyne Larrington, trans., The *Poetic Edda* (Oxford: Oxford University Press, 1996), 14.

8. Carolyne Larrington, trans., The *Poetic Edda* (Oxford: Oxford University Press, 1996), 14.

9. Lee M. Hollander, trans., The *Poetic Edda* (Austin, TX: The University of Austin Press, 2004), 37.

10. Robert Cook, trans., *Njal's Saga* (London: Penguin Books, 2001), 21.

11. Ornolfur Thorsson, ed., *The Sagas of the Icelanders* (New York: Penguin Books, 2000) "Egil's Saga," 139.

12. Sanford Levinson, "Constituting Communities Through Words that Bind: Reflections on Loyalty Oaths" (*Michigan Law Review* 84–7, 1986), 1456–57.

PART TWO

Thirteen

Heathen Rituals, Heathen Ways

Heathen rituals tend to fall into two classes: blót and sumble. At a blót, an offering of some kind is always made. Heathens believe that the exchanges of gifts—in the form of offerings—are ways to develop long-term relationships with the gods, ancestors, or landvaettir. The word blót connects to the modern word "blood," and is used to refer exclusively to animal sacrifice. Votive offerings—mead, fabric, weapons, carvings, pretty much anything other than an animal—were more closely considered "rituals." In the majority of modern heathen practice, the word blót is used interchangeably with either animal or votive offerings. It can be confusing, so it is always worth asking which one is meant before attending the ritual. Remember that heathens do not give offerings to "appease" or "prevent the wrath of" any entity. Instead, blóts are an occasion to reflect on what the god, goddess, ancestor, or wight being honored means to you and to build on relationships with them. In blót, heathens stand shoulder-to-shoulder with their community, their ancestors, and their gods and goddesses to give specific honor to an entity. Some sit, and yes, some kneel, but the point is that in a blót, heathens are in sacred space and standing on hallowed ground, in the presence of the holy.

Sumble, on the other hand, is about building relationships within the community itself. A sumble is a sacred ritual form of drinking, and it must be said here that, if someone for any reason does not drink alcohol, they do not need to do so at a sumble. Cider or other nonalcoholic drinks can be used to good effect. In a sumble, there are typically at least three rounds. The first goes to the gods and goddesses. The second pass of the horn is to toast our ancestors and deceased heroes. The third—and subsequent—rounds tend to be "open." An open round allows for boasting, toasting, reciting poetry, singing songs, and so forth. As you can see, that third round can lead to a fourth, or fifth… which is why a great many outsiders believe that the Asatru are heavy drinkers. Typically speaking, being drunk at sumble is actually frowned upon and many heathens only take sips as the horn passes by. This is not always the case, naturally, and sometimes sumble can be a rollicking fun time. Still, the sumble is considered a sacred act that connects the community to itself, so it should not be taken lightly.

Husel is the word for feast. At most heathen events, the order of proceedings goes as follows: blót, husel, and then sumble. A husel could—and in this case should—be a feast of the blót animal's meat; portions are given to the gods as burnt offerings, and the rest is ritually consumed at husel. In the case of votive offerings, the feast can be put on by the host and hostess of the day, or can be a potluck affair where everyone brings a dish. Sumble might, or might not, follow husel.

Other important rituals involve life-markers such as marriage, the naming of infants, man- and woman-making ceremonies (similar to the bar and bat mitzvahs), funerals, and the like. These tend to be broader in terms of their formats, and I will give some examples. At this point, know that they are equally important to heathens and are treated with due solemnity.

Writing Your Own Rituals

The first question we need to ask ourselves is a thorny one—do heathens even need clergy? In many other faiths, clergy are the ones who construct, write, and perform religious rituals, or tend to holy places and are even assigned to churches. Heathenry, on the other hand, is primarily home—and community—based. Rather than focus holiness on one person or group of people, we all act in our homes, alone and with family, friends, and kin. In other words, the person officiating the ritual becomes the *godhi* (the ritual leader) or *gythja* (feminine form) for that moment in time.

This has, indeed, made many heathens think. There are certainly those—including myself, as a gythja—who see a need for trained clergy to help out where they're needed. Others feel no need for clergy at all. The pro- (or anti-) clergy argument has a lot of complexities, which are beyond the scope of this book. The reality, regardless of which side you happen to fall on, is that you will probably be called on to officiate a ritual at some point. You may even be called to do several. At least two large heathen organizations do have clergy programs that you may enroll in to learn the details. Remember, though, there are no set "divinity schools" for heathenry, no set liturgy, and not very many books to comb through to find out why and how heathens do what they do, let alone discuss what it is they're doing. Eventually, you are going to get to a point where you need to write, and officiate, your own ritual. Don't panic. It happens to all of us.

I'm going to start off by listing a few of the behind-the-scenes issues that surround ritual. This is the kind of stuff people don't automatically think about, and it may seem "obvious" once you have thought of it. It's true, this is fairly pragmatic information; anyone who has ever thrown a party for more than about twenty people will probably recognize some of this behind-the-scenes planning. In any event, here we go:

First off, know your audience—if you are hosting a ritual in your living room with you and your five kindred mates, that's one thing. If you are officiating at a ritual scheduled during a large pan-pagan festival, that's another. Some rituals are so public that literally anyone might wander in at any point, which means you might have to spend some time, either beforehand or as part of the ritual, explaining the significance of what you're doing, and you will have to do more to establish a feeling of group unity for the ritual to proceed successfully. If you have a "mixed bag" of heathens and non-heathens present, it is helpful to consider the ritual in terms of "speaking the same language"—in other words, you might have to do things a little differently than you would at home, so that everyone present can understand what is going on. You also might have to explain a lot more than you would for an all-heathen audience.

Secondly, you need to ask yourself how many people are coming. Include adults and children in your list of attendees. The larger the group of people, the more work you as the officiant will have to do to establish sacred space, form cohesive group unity, and manage the ritual's progress. If there are children coming, ask how old they are. One fourteen-month-old can easily take over and dominate any room. Imagine five fourteen-month-old children. Or, perhaps more terrifying, five fourteen-year-olds! You would do well to ask how many of the children will be participating in the ritual—if none of them are, you may need to find out who is going to keep an eye on them while the adults are performing blót. Remember that the more people you have present, the longer the ritual will be. If you have a limited amount of time—for instance, if you have a one-hour slot booked in a festival setting—then the number of people present might mean having to simplify the ritual in order to stay within the time constraints.

Third, you need to consider where you are holding the ritual. If you are going to host a blót in your living room, then you can only invite as many people as the living room can comfortably hold; if you have too many people crowded in, the atmosphere can be more about "not elbowing your neighbor," which can negatively impact the ritual. On the other hand, if you are holding your ritual outside, while you have more room, you will also have to project your voice in order to be heard. Heathens, as a general rule, tend to be stoic about weather, and you can probably have your outdoor ritual even if the weather isn't cooperative, but if you are planning on having a fire, you will need to remember things like keeping the wood dry, having a properly set fire in a safe fire-ring or outdoor fireplace, and making sure the fire is lit before the ritual. In hot conditions, you might want to consider shade, and you definitely want to provide more water prior to and after the ritual. These considerations, when handled beforehand, will make it easier on the day of the blót, simply because you will know you have your bases covered.

As a matter of politeness and good hospitality, always do your best to have some consideration for people with any kind of disability. If you have a blind person present, be sure someone is there to guide him safely through the ritual and any movement that might be required. If a deaf person attends, be sure to face her so that she can read your lips. For those who cannot stand up for very long, be sure to identify them and provide seating. Be willing to consider limited mobility issues as well.

Fourth, make sure you have all of your ritual tools present. This includes whatever offerings might be part of the ritual—grain, wood carvings, mead, cider, vegetables, etc.—as well as the tools themselves. If you are planning to open with a hammer-hallowing, for instance, make sure the hammer you are going to use is on the altar table. If you are using mead, or wine, or beer, make sure you have a corkscrew or bottle opener placed where you can put your hands on it—maybe not on the altar, but in your pocket or next to the bottles. On that note, you might want to open those bottles before the ritual starts—it will make things smoother and avoid potential liquid explosions. Remember that the more people you have, the more mead/cider you will need. If you are going to make burnt offerings, be sure that they're flammable, but avoid any items with varnishes, paint, or other potentially toxic chemicals.

Timing and ritual complexity should be taken into account. Modern Euro-Western audiences don't habitually attend rituals that take all day. As a rule of thumb, anything less than fifteen minutes feels "too short" for a group, and anything longer than about an hour or an hour and a half feels "like forever." Mind you, if the ritual is good, and the groove is in everyone's hearts, the time will pass without notice. But as an officiant, the very last thing you want is shuffling feet, fidgety bottoms, and people looking at their watches. At the same time, a shorter ritual should not need a lot of detail and complexity while larger ones may require more, depending on the circumstances. Longer rituals tend to require more components to keep the sacredness present and at the forefront of people's hearts and minds.

Ritual Roles and Participation

Now we can move into more specific blót details. One involves a single officiant—one person performs all the roles during the ritual. While this makes for a straightforward, coordinated ritual, but decreases the amount of active participation. However, if multiple people are sharing the ritual structure, they need to define roles so that everyone has a chance to perform something. Furthermore, heathen rituals tend to be fairly participative, meaning that everyone gathered will have at least a small, personal role to play. That said, there still needs to be a focused center. This means that no matter how many "assistants" you have, there should be one clear officiant—this is especially true in larger, more populated rituals, which need more focus in general. Each person should have a designated role in the ritual that he or she "leads"—one might be in charge of the hammer hallowing, one in charge of blessing the mead, one in charge of invoking the gods and goddesess, and so forth.

The blót should be designed clearly around its central purpose. If, for instance, you decide to write a blót to Thor, thanking him for protecting Midgard, then everything should orbit that—soup to nuts, it should be about thanking Thor. You should also have some understanding of what is, and what is not, appropriate within ritual parameters. If you are thanking Thor for his protection, then it is most definitively not appropriate to, for instance, raise a toast to Jormungandr, the World Serpent and Thor's mortal enemy.

When it comes to speaking and performing the blót, some people memorize what they are going to say beforehand or use a book to stay focused and able to say the right words at the right times. Some people do not memorize a thing, preferring to speak from the depths of their hearts in the moment. Different people have different skills in this regard, and it is important to remember who is best at what. If you are the kind of person who gets choked up, for whatever reason, and just are not very good at verbal improvisation, then don't put yourself into that situation. At the same time, be flexible enough that you can "roll with the punches." If you skip a section, for instance, just let it go—stopping the entire ritual, saying "Wait, I forgot this bit," and starting over again ruins everything.

Remember that no plan survives first contact. Not one. Inevitably, the ritual you wrote, as sublime and holy as it may be on the page, will develop a life of its own as you perform it and as your audience interacts with it. Keep a sense of humor. When small things go awry, do not panic, but just give a bit of a wry smile and move on. Obviously, if things go so horribly that the ritual breaks down, it's better to just end it right then and there. (We'll be talking about that a little bit later.) For now, just remember that things will happen—unexpected things—and you might as well accept that right from the start. See every ritual you write and practice as a learning experience, and you will do fine.

Designing a Blót

First, let us strip down a ritual to its bare essentials. Typically, any ritual, in any tradition, religion, or folkway, contains the following elements:

- Creation of sacred space

- Invocation

- Blessing of offering

- Central point/focus/performance of ritual

- Sacrifice

- Closing of sacred space

It should go without saying, but heathen rituals fall within the heathen worldview. We do have some examples left to us about how blóts were performed, and they all boil down to the same characteristics listed above. You will find sample blóts scattered in this book, as well as the ones below. Heathens tend to use votive offerings, or representational objects, and they do tend to make a sacrifice—in their worldview what heathens are doing is engaging in an act of divine reciprocity. Therefore, whatever gifts are given, or offerings made, should be appropriate to the subject and be, at minimum, the best available items. We need to remember that our ancestors didn't head down to the local Walmart and hit the clearance section when they were looking for gifts to give our gods and ancestors; they gave the best of what they had. That might have been the first fruits of harvest, a particularly fine ell (a length roughly similar to an arm-length, or yard) of linen or wool, a well-forged weapon, a favorite necklace... or any of a number of things, each relevant to the particular subject. Thor wields Mjolnir, the short-handled hammer he uses to slay giants and other enemies of mankind; therefore, it stands to reason that a hammer might make an appropriate representational offering for Thor. In many modern heathen minds, the sacred mead itself is both symbolic of hospitality and reciprocity and a most appropriate gift. Many heathen rituals use the mead as the sacrificial offering itself.

In its simplest form, a blót can look something like this:

You can grab a bottle of beer from your fridge, pop the cap, go outside, make the hammer sign over the bottle's mouth, say "hail," drink a bit of the beer, pour the rest out onto the ground, and go back inside. That's a blót. It can be a very effective blót, for a solitary practitioner or even as a personal, private moment between you and your ancestors, or the landvaettir, or whomever you're sharing the gift with. At the more complex end, you can have a set of three actions to create the sacred space, do multiple invocations, have the blessing, spend a good deal of time developing the "center point," offer multiple sacrifices, spend time thanking everyone and everything you invoked, and then close with another set of prayers. Both—and all the grades in between—will still follow the same basic, bare-bones structure.

This is where the art of ritual creation comes in. You should plan to spend the majority of your creative and sacred efforts developing the "central focus" of your ritual. This is the "meat," as it were, the point at which the holy comes, and the gathered community share, and at this point the spiritual depth and calling should hit the hearts, minds, and souls of the people. This is where the divine inspiration happens. Again, the keys here are focus and intent—too little of either and the ritual will not go as well. What follows are some tips of the trade that heathens tend to use when writing blóts and other rituals.

Kennings and Alliteration

A *kenning* is a word or phrase that is used in place of a subject, in order to describe an aspect of that subject. Kennings differ from bynames, which are also used. Think of the difference as a descriptive phrase versus a nickname. Freyja, for instance, is also called Horn, Syr, and Mardoll; these are bynames, or alternate names, for Freyja—much like my name is Patricia, but I am also Patty, and also Ms. Lafayllve. Kennings for Freyja include things like "boar-rider," "bright gold weeper," or "Njord's daughter." These are descriptors that indicate who Freyja is, or aspects of her character. Pre-Christian heathen ancestors spent a great deal of time making up kennings to refer to everything from bread to ale to Valhalla and back again. Many of them can be found in Snorri Sturluson's *Edda*, also called the *Prose Edda*; he compiled a series of poetic devices into the *Skaldskaparmal* and the *Hattatal* within the *Edda*; they make for lovely, moving poetry. They also make excellent ritual invocations.

Another poetic device favored by the pre-Christian ancestors was alliteration. Icelandic poetry was a complex thing; there were different rhyme and rhythm patterns to indicate subjects, formality, and usage—a praise poem took on one form, a love poem a different one, and a saga-song a third form. Alliteration, however, is a fairly simple device—alliteration is all about repetition of sound. Which sound you use is your choice; consonant alliteration is the most common form and, in modern American English at least, usually happens in the first letter or syllable of each word in a series. "Whales wend the waters wide" is an example of a consonant alliteration, namely of the "w" sound.

Adding kennings, bynames, and alliteration to your ritual will increase its beauty. We can argue that any words will do, because in ritual it is the intent that matters, but what having these verbal structures in your ritual does is help increase the sense of sacredness and the sense of formality that often separates the mundane from the holy. They cue everyone to notice that something special is happening, something "out of the ordinary," and can help with setting the ritual mind and spirit into place.

Let's use an example to demonstrate what I am talking about. We'll keep it simple—the blessing of the mead in order to make it sacred. First of all, the reason we do this, religiously, is to separate average, everyday mead from sacred mead, the liquid of which metaphysically represents the water in the Well of Wyrd. In fact, one can imagine the tip of the drinking horn as touching the well itself, so that any words spoken over the horn and its sacred mead transmit themselves directly into wyrd's pattern. Mead is especially sacred when it is the offering being used in the ritual. You've poured the mead into the horn, held the horn, and prayed over it; now it's time to say something, so that the audience knows what is taking place. Here are some options:

- You can simply and silently make the sign of the hammer over the liquid.

- You lift the horn and say, "Let this mead be made sacred, so it can carry our words into the Well of Wyrd." You make the hammer sign over the surface.

- You can say, "Aegir, I ask that you bless this mead on our behalf." Another option might be something like "Bragi, bless this mead," since Aegir is the brewer-god, and Bragi, as a skald-god, is associated with mead as the gift of poetry. Another entity to call on is Kvasir, whose blood went into the first brew-pot to make mead. You can choose to combine two or three entities associated with mead in the invocation, as in: "The blood of Kvasir, brew of Aegir, now is made holy."

- You alliterate. "Bragi bless this brew." "We are grateful for this, the gift of Aegir."

- You use kennings. "Gift of Aegir" is one, "Kvasir's blood" is another; both refer to the mead itself.

- You combine a little bit of all of the above. My current favorite prayer at this time goes a little something like this: "Blessed boon of bees, blood of Kvasir, bountiful brew of Aegir, bear our wealful words into the Well of Wyrd."

Whichever you choose, remember that the point is to make the distinction between everyday mead and the mead being used in the ritual as an offering, reciprocal gift, and libation. In short, the vital piece here involves imbuing the drink with prayer and intent, and therefore making it holy. Each officiant should have his or her own style when it comes to liturgical expression, at the same time every ritual should be internally consistent. If you use kennings and alliteration in one place, use them throughout the blót for consistency. As a rule of thumb, larger rituals lend themselves to more formal patterns of speech, and smaller, more familiar ones make do with more simplistic patterns—again, the key is to consider which you have, and on what levels of comfort you, as the primary officiant, operate. You may want to consider memorizing a few phrases so that they flow more easily out of you when you are in the ritual itself. The phrases you memorize should be the kind you can carry around as a kind of ritual "toolkit," in case you are called upon to do an extemporaneous ritual.

Heathens consider the number three to be one of the holiest numbers; repetitions in threes (or sixes, nines, twelves, twenty-fours) reinforce the sacredness of that number and also help heathen audiences focus on our rituals. Four is another number heathens occasionally use. As an example, an invocation to Odin might repeat three of his kennings:

"Sleipnir's rider, whisperer and roarer of runes, inspiration-god, Odin, I call to you."

Repeating an action three times, too, reinforces its effect and the overall heathen worldview regarding patterns. We see this more subtly in the sumble, where there are three main toasting rounds with the drinking horn.

The cosmology of the Norse belief system has already been discussed in Part One. Most commonly, heathens tend to set their altars up in the north, because they face north and heathens come from the north—after all, they are the descendents of the northmen. However, that is not always the case, and often with good reason. A blót to honor Sunna, the goddess whose chariot holds the sun, might face east, since she rises from there. A ritual might focus on a particularly holy tree, or rock outcropping, or source of water; these may or may not be precisely "north," but are agreed upon as sacred by the community, and therefore become focal points.

As time goes on, you and your local community will end up developing specific ritual formats. This is in keeping with tribal traditions cross-culturally; there are the private practices, the tribal/clan practices, and the larger, public practices. An attentive person can recognize specific regional variations; for instance, in the American Northeast Asatru community, the habitual closing prayer goes as follows:

"From the gods to the earth to us, from us to the earth to the gods, a gift for a gift."

This is said by all the attendees of the ritual, and happens at the same time as the libation of mead is made. It comes from *Ravenbok*, created by Lou Stead and the original members of Raven Kindred. You might not find that prayer anywhere outside of the Northeast Asatru community, although it has spread significantly over the years. In the Northeast region of the United States, at any rate, you will hear it often. It's almost a hallmark of our geography.

Here's the thing about these sorts of habitual formats: they make the connection between the mundane and the sacred that much easier to discern, and that much more deeply rooted in the spirit of the community and its members. It's a little bit like muscle memory for athletes and dancers—once you perform an action often enough, it becomes lodged in your muscle memory. At that point, you no longer have to consciously think about an action: it is automatic. A quarterback does not have to think about grabbing the ball, stepping back, lining his fingers up on the seam, pulling his arm back, aiming, and throwing; he calls the play, sees the opportunity, and throws. So, too, do religious structures and formats become part of what we might call "spiritual memory"—we no longer have to focus on these details, they just happen. And therefore, we have more "room" to experience the spiritual growth and fellowship, the inspiration that happens in a good, well-written, well-performed ritual.

Now, here's another thing—these habits cannot be adopted wholesale. They have to develop over time, with the consent of the group. I can no more walk into, say, a kindred based in Sacramento, California, and make them do what I want and have it work, than a quarterback can walk onto a baseball team and have them know how to tackle. Kindreds should be encouraged to develop their own identities through their practices. Regional similarities are encouraging and will also develop as time progresses and the larger regional community begins to feel a sense of collective identity. Yes, the underlying structures that we started with are identifiable across cultures and across time, but it's the details of practice that infuse the religion with its own life force, and that process cannot be rushed.

Once you have begun the ritual, for the most part, you need to complete it. This might mean a lot of changing as you go along—as mentioned before, you might forget a section, or stumble over a kenning. The best thing to do is to smoothly go on. Do without that section or work it back in later if you can find a good spot for it on the fly. Clear your throat or apologize, and say the phrase again. Keep calm and don't panic.

We also need to pay attention to omens around us. Maybe a puff of cooling breeze will swirl through the sacred area, or it will stop raining long enough for your ritual to go off. Sometimes even a flock of birds can be a good omen. That said, there are also bad omens. If you find truly bad things happening—the horn gets dropped and breaks, the mead turns out to have gone off, or the altar tips over—you may want to consider ending the ritual. If that should happen, close quickly, thanking the gods, landvaettir, and ancestors present, and let that be the end of it.

The truth is that most blóts and rituals go off just fine. Some will be deeper and more emotionally stirring than others. Some might seem so simple that they're over before anyone can feel connected, while some wind on for so long that everyone breaks out of the ritual mindset. Every time you perform, or attend, a ritual, it will be different from the last. That is another thing the officiant should remember—every ritual you write will be different. And even if you perform the exact same blót twice, different things will happen within it. That is all part of the adventure.

Sample Blót to Frigga

First and foremost, we need to remember who Frigga is, and what items or offerings are most sacred to her. In this case, we know that she is the highest-ranking Asa goddess (remember that Freyja, her equal in rank, is a Van). She governs the household, is the keeper of the keys for that hall, and runs her own hall, Fensalir. We know that she weaves cloth, has many handmaidens who do various things, and can also sit at Odin's High Seat, Hlidskjalf. She sees the moving of wyrd but says nothing.

In general, Frigga also governs the frith. This was something that ranking women were known for. She calms turbulent social waters and ensures that no violence occurs in her halls. This is an important aspect of Frigga, particularly when warriors were known to fight one another openly in feast halls and where feuds could span generations. It is Frigga who is charged with the keeping of the house, and all things within it. Some say this includes children and childbirth as well as other tasks involving the home.

Therefore, the first thing to consider is the outcome of the blót. Most blóts are means of thanking the entity/deity in question for their gifts, but there can be other reasons to blót. In this case, we are going to ask Frigga to share her ability to maintain frith in our own homes, and to lead us by her example. I am going to break this blót down to its component parts so that people can see where each piece of the ritual "puzzle" exists and feel more confident in writing their own rituals. I am including kennings and alliteration, and also assuming this will be a blót with twelve people present. Finally, I am including many of the considerations mentioned in this chapter in order for the reader to see the thinking that can go on as part of ritual preparation.

Items Needed:

Altar table—large enough to hold all ritual items

Altar cloth—Hand-woven material would be best, but linen, as something woven by women in the Viking Age, would also be appropriate. Another option would be to use grandmother's table cloth, to connect the ancestors and their ways with Frigga and hers.

Offering bowl—large enough to contain the liquid offered as part of the blót. One option would be to use the same offering bowl in all blóts, which helps make the bowl itself sacred. Another option would be to use a bowl your family has handed down to you or a bowl commonly used in your kitchen to prepare food.

Frigga statue or representation of Frigga—This is optional, but if you have one or can make one, it would help signify the deity the blót is being held for.

Keys—These are generally held to be a symbol of Frigga, the mistress of the keys and ruler of the household. These can be used in place of a statue as representations of Frigga, or put on the altar on their own merit. Older-style keys, such as those found in antique stores, are lovely, but the keys to the household will do.

Hammer—If you plan on doing the hammer rite, have one present on the altar. I have an antique wooden mallet that I use for this purpose and specifically on altars to all household deities.

Mead—If you have or drink mead, have the libation open and ready to pour into a horn or other drinking vessel. Apple cider works as well, since the gods and goddesses feed on golden apples to maintain their youth and immortality.

Horn or other drinking vessel—This is to share the libation with the group. If you do not have a drinking horn, consider using an heirloom glass or other vessel that you only use for sacred purposes.

Any other gifts or offerings for Frigga—Some place fresh flowers on altars to Frigga as gifts for her. Others may place some hand-woven material on the altar, or a drop-spindle filled with woven yarn. If you are asking people to give offerings to Frigga, or to have items blessed by Frigga, have them place those offerings on the altar, or as near it as possible.

Creation of Sacred Space

Assemble the altar in advance. Many heathens place their altars in the north, but in this case an excellent place for Frigga's altar would be in the middle of the home itself. If people have brought offerings or items to be blessed be Frigga, be certain they are on the altar before beginning the ritual.

When everyone has gathered around the altar, start by asking everyone to take a deep breath or two, and to focus their minds on the outcome of the blót—to ask Frigga to share her ability to weave frith in the gathered community.

Stand facing the north.

SAY: Before there was time, before the stars were ordered in their places, there was a land, Niflheim hight. It was a land of ice and frozen things. Inside it roiled the great well Hvergelmir, and from this roiling well rose the icy waters, which formed rivers streaming about.

Stand facing the south.

SAY: In this time also was another land, Muspelheim hight. It was a realm of fire and all things molten and in flame. The magma, earth made fluid, poured from Muspelheim.

Stand in the center, facing either west or east. (The direction here does not matter.)

SAY: Between these lands lay a mighty gap, Ginnungagap, a place of roaring potential. From the north the rivers poured into the gap, and from the south the magma poured. When they met deep within Ginnungagap there rose a mighty hiss of steam, and as it cleared, the mighty ash, Yggdrasil, rose, its roots entwined with all things underground, and its branches reaching ever upward and over, covering all the worlds in its protection.

It was here, in Ginnungagap, in the sight of Yggdrasil, that the waters of Niflheim and the fires of Muspelheim met, and formed the rime that was to become our earth. Here we stand in sacred Midgard, the center of all things.

Invocation

There are two schools of thought regarding invocations. Either all the gods, wights, and ancestors are called, or only the deity being honored with blót is called. Here we combine the two. Frigga's invocation comes last because it is the most important, setting the focus for the blót itself.

Face the altar.

SAY: Shining ones, holy ones, gods and goddesses all. You Aesir and you Vanir, we ask that you join us as we honor Frigga, to share your presence with us this day. Hail the Aesir. Hail the Vanir. Hail the gods.

Those present should echo the hails, so leave space for the responsorial. Offer a small drink or offering of grain, placing it in the offering bowl.

SAY: Ancient ones. Those whose bones are our bones, whose blood runs in our veins. Alfar, disir, ancestors all, we ask that you join us as we honor Frigga. Share your wisdom with us as we work this rite. Hail the alfar. Hail the disir. Hail the ancestors.

Repeat the responsorial and the small offering of food or drink.

SAY: Those who crawl or swim or fly, those who seek the air or go on their bellies, all you seen and unseen, landvaettir all, we call to you. Please join us as we honor Frigga on this day. We ask your friendship with us as we perform this rite. Hail the landvaettir.

Repeat the responsorial and the small offering of food and drink.

Take a few calming breaths, and focus on Frigga. Think of what she represents to you, and to the gathered community as a whole. Consider also the working of the blót, its focus, and its outcome. Then look directly at the representation of Frigga on the altar.

SAY: Keeper of keys, mistress of Fensalir, beloved goddess, we call to you now. We work this blót today in your honor, wife of Odin, and we ask that you be present and witness us. Weaver who waits, seeress who sees but never speaks, lady of Asgard, we call to you. Hail Frigga.

Repeat the responsorial and the small offering of food and drink.

Blessing of Offering

If all the offerings are already on the altar, proceed immediately. If not, ask the gathered company to present their offerings now, and lay them on the altar. Fill the horn or other drinking vessel with mead/cider and lift it up. Make the sign of the hammer over the top of it.

SAY: Blessed boon of bees, bountiful brew of Aegir, blood of Kvasir. May this mead carry our words from here into the Well of Wyrd, where they will reside forever.

Assign someone to hold the horn, and give it to him/her. If the mead/cider is your only offering, move immediately into the central focus of the blót. If there are other offerings, face the altar.

SAY: Frigga, these offerings are gathered here for you. See them and know of our respect and love for you, Lady of Fensalir. Bless them, as they are yours.

Central Point/Focus of the Ritual

This ritual is focused on Frigga sharing frith in our homes and her continued leadership by example. There are two main ways to focus the ritual—either move directly to the passing of the horn, or spend time making offerings before passing the horn. Either way, it is the job of the person performing the ritual to be the strong center at this time, keeping the blót focused on its outcome.

SAY: Beloved of Odin, mother of Baldur, we call to you now. Times are troubled, and we notice strife even in our homes, and amongst the community. Weaver of linen, seeress, mistress of Fensalir, we make these offerings this day so that you may guide us. Help us to maintain the frith-bonds between us, that we might remember all the good we are to one another. Help us soothe the social waters, so that strife may fade away. Help us by continuing to be an example for us, that your ability to maintain frith among the gods will prove the ways we maintain frith with one another, and in our homes. Let the inviolable peace reign, and may your wisdom guide us.

Face the altar and place your hand over it.

SAY: Glad gifts are given rest on your good altar. Accept these as our thanks for your continued assistance to us. We offer them in honor of you.

Ask for the drinking horn containing the blessed mead. Raise the horn high.

SAY: Now we drink our toasts to you, keeper of keys. We raise this in your honor, and speak over the horn, that our words might reach your ears.

Pass the horn to the nearest person. At twelve people, there should only be one round of toasts to Frigga; more than that and the blót itself may fade away and become more like a sumble. All words should focus on Frigga and the purpose of the blót. You may want to gently remind people of this before passing the horn.

Each person says their own words to the goddess. Silent prayers are acceptable. After each person is finished, the group should echo "Hail"—this is a means by which the community accepts the toast made as a positive one. The person holding the horn should take a drink from it as well; this is a ritual sharing of liquid similar to that in the gods round of sumble, except with focus on the words themselves being taken to the goddess by means of the shared drink. When the horn returns to you, offer up your own words of prayer and thanks. Then place your hand over the horn.

SAY: Wealful words have been whispered over the waters of the Well, where they will form their own layer in wyrd. Wishes offered, thanks given, we share this drink now with Frigga.

Pour the liquid remaining into the blót bowl. Place the horn to one side. If only using the liquid in this part of the ritual, then this is the sacrifice as well, and you can proceed to the closing of sacred space.

Sacrifice

How you handle this section depends entirely on the substantive parts of the ritual. If, as seen above, the only sacrifice made is the liquid blessed in the drinking horn, libate it or proceed to the closing. If the gathered people have placed on the altar items they only want to have blessed, raise your hand over the altar.

SAY: Frigga, keeper of keys, wielder of wisdom, we ask that you bless this altar and all items on it. They will be physical representations of the frith we have asked you to share with us this day. Hail Frigga.

The gathered company should repeat the "Hail Frigga" after you. Then proceed to the closing of sacred space.

If, on the other hand, the votive offerings are to be given to Frigga, you need to offer them up at this time. They could be burned in a fire—which should be lit beforehand and tended to keep it from going out—and each person offers their item to the fire, one at a time. Since Fensalir refers to the fens, many think that Frigga's hall is on or near a swamp or bog. Given this thinking, you might want to dig a hole, place the offerings in it, pour water over it to create a "swamp," and then bury them. You may also want to wait until after the blót and then go to a swampy area to offer them out to Frigga. The point is this: all of these things should be thought about and planned for in advance of the ritual. If the offerings are to be destroyed, gather them.

SAY: Frigga, we give these gifts to thank you for the gain we have received from you.

Each person should go to the altar, retrieve his/her sacrificial item, and walk to the fire/burial hole in silence. Meditate on frith, and on thanking Frigga for sharing her insight with you. Offer the item, then step aside to make room for the next person.

Closing of Sacred Space

After the sacrifice/offering has been made, thank all the entities you spoke to in the invocation, leaving Frigga for last as she is the focus of the blót. If you did not pour out a drink or offer a food item at the invocation, it is important to do so here. In our belief system, a gift looks for a gift, so you need to leave something for the gods, wights, and ancestors. This completes the cycle of exchange.

SAY: Holy ones, shining ones, gods and goddesses all. We thank you for your presence here today. Hail the Aesir. Hail the Vanir. Hail the gods.

SAY: Ancient ones, ancestors, alfar and disir. We thank you for your presence here today. Hail the ancestors.

SAY: Wights of place, you here who have gathered with us, we thank you for your presence here today. Hail the landvaettir.

Lift the blót bowl and carry it outside to the nearest tree, rock, or holy ve, if you have created this kind of permanent sacred space. If there is a single special place where you can feel the gods, ancestors, and wights gathered, go there.

SAY: Offerings have been made, words have been spoken. Frigga, we thank you for your many gifts to us, and especially for helping us maintain frith in our homes and community.

If you need to remain indoors, leave the liquid in the bowl and on the altar for several hours before discarding, that the gods may gain their portion. If at all possible, go outside to the nearest tree, rock, or holy ve. You may go to one you have libated on in the past or move to the space in nature that you can sense is the most holy. Pour out the offering.

SAY: Well have we offered, and well have we thanked. We libate now to the gods, the ancestors, the wights, and most especially to Frigga, who we honor here today. Hail Frigga.

This ends the ritual. Traditionally, the next step is to eat together. This can be a potluck, where everyone brings a dish, or some meal cooked and presented by the host and hostess. Remember the purpose of the blót, and maintain the frith while you are all gathered together.

Sunna rises and Sunna falls,
marking the change of the season.

fourteen

Blóts for the Holy Tides

Blót (also spelled "blot") is one of the two main rituals found in heathenry. Blót is a way to connect ourselves to the gods, the ancestors, and the land-vaettir. We believe in forming positive relationships with all entities within the heathen worldview as a means of spiritual connection. Sample blóts of various kinds have appeared throughout this book, and writing ritual has been covered in chapter 1, above. Those blóts, which vary in complexity and focus, are meant to be used on their own and also to spur one's own ritual process. This section provides sample blóts for the main holy days, or "tides," as we call them.

The Hammer Rite

This is a brief ritual cleansing and hallowing of space. It is a modern invention, closely resembling the Lesser Banishing Ritual of the Pentagram, a ritual developed in the early twentieth century involving calling out to the directions to invoke protective spirits and create sacred space, in both form and purpose. Many modern heathens use this as an opening to their rituals, and just as many do not. Still, it is a useful way of clearing and creating sacred space.

Using either your ritual hammer or raising your hands to the skies, face north, and repeat the following:

SAY: Hammer in the north! Hallow and hold this holy stead!

> *Make the sign of the hammer toward the north. Turn and face the east.*

SAY: Hammer in the east! Hallow and hold this holy stead!

> *Make the hammer sign toward the east. Turn to face the south.*

SAY: Hammer in the south! Hallow and hold this holy stead!

> *Make the hammer sign toward the south. Turn to the west.*

SAY: Hammer in the west! Hallow and hold this holy stead!

> *Make the hammer sign toward the west. Raise the hammer directly above you.*

SAY: Hammer of Asgard! Hallow and hold this holy stead!

> *Make the hammer sign above you. Hold the hammer toward the ground.*

SAY: Hammer of Midgard! Hallow and hold this holy stead!

Two Variations of the Hammer Rite
Variation One:

> *Stand with the hammer raised, facing north.*

SAY: Hammer in the north! Hallow and hold this holy stead!

> *Then turn to face the south.*

SAY: Hammer in the south! Hallow and hold this holy stead!

Stand in the middle of the space, or directly in front of the altar.

SAY: Mjolnir, mighty hammer of Thor, hallow and hold this holy stead!

Variation Two:
This is short, sweet, and to the point. Stand with your hammer raised, or your hands to the skies.

SAY: Hammer of Asgard. Hammer of Midgard. Hallow and hold this holy stead.

Make the sign of the hammer over the altar or overhead.

Solitary Blót

Asatru, or heathenry, is at its essence a community-based religion. Blót and sumble are based on forming and continuing community bonds in a sacred way, and a community of one cannot stand. At the same time, however, it may be that there are no other heathens in your area, or that you are new to Asatru and have not formed any local community connections yet. Additionally, blót inside the home forms the basis of individual spiritual connection to the gods, the ancestors, and the local house or land spirits. Solitary blóts tend to be more simplified, but just as meaningful, as kindred- or community-led blóts.

At its simplest, blót does not even need to be spoken, but is heard in the heart. Find a bottle of your favorite beverage. Mead and ale are the most traditional offerings, but cider or any cherished drink works as well. The point is to offer something the gods, ancestors, or vaettir will appreciate. Never offer something you don't like—it comes off as something like "Hey, I hate this. You have it." Remember, be on your best behavior, and never be rude.

Stand in front of your altar or out in nature near a tree. Open the beverage. Take the time to consider what you want out of the offering. If you have a particular god or goddess in mind, focus on what you know about him or her and how you desire to form a connection or thank them for their gifts to you. If an ancestor, remember what you can of that person as they were in life. Once you have focused on these things, and you feel in your heart that it is time, lift the bottle/mug/horn in a silent toast. Take a sip, then share the rest by pouring it out into an offering bowl or directly at the tree's roots. Spend another silent moment thanking the god/person/wight you are honoring, and then walk away. The rite is over. If you are using an offering bowl and are in an apartment or other place where you cannot get outside, leave the offering in the bowl for at least half an hour—this gives the spirit time to take the essence of the offering—then pour the contents down a drain.

Yule Blóts

Yule is one of the two most sacred holidays in the heathen calendar. It begins on the solstice, after Mothers' Night, and runs for twelve nights. There are many ways to respect the season—decorating with fresh evergreen is traditional, as is having a Yule tree with presents under it. Yule is a season of giving and building community ties, and some give out one gift every night for the twelve nights of Yule. Others exchange gifts when they see one another, or as part of a Yule celebration. The specifics always vary, but overall, Yule is a time to build community through gift-giving and celebration through the darkest nights of winter.

A Yule log is traditionally burned through Yule. However, many modern heathens do not have access to outdoor bonfire spaces, fireplaces, or wood stoves to do this. A large, three-wicked candle can do just as well. Typically the candle is lit at sunset of the solstice night, and left to burn until everyone goes to sleep. (Never let any candle or open flame burn unattended.) The candle is lit as the sun sets every night for eleven more nights, symbolizing the twelve days of Yule.

Another part of Yule, of course, is the feast. Pork is a traditional food—try wild boar if you can get it. People can lay their hands over the pork and offer prayers, blessings, and good wishes over the meat before it is roasted. It is said that the prayers are born by the boar up to the ears of the gods and goddesses. Feasts can be potluck affairs as well.

What follows are a series of blóts most often found as part of Yule traditions among many heathens. Personal meditations, individual blóts, and private rituals are options for the season; not all heathens can be with their fellow heathens for all twelve nights of Yule. How and when they are performed can vary, with the exception of Mothers' Night.

Mothers' Night Blót

Mothers' Night blót often opens the Yule season, and it honors the disir. It was traditionally held on or about December 24, and is fine to celebrate then. The tradition seems to have been that Mothers' Night was held indoors. We are not certain why being indoors matters in this regard. It could simply be the case that Mothers' Night is held at the height of winter. Then again, staying indoors could be an indication that the disir ruled over hearth and home.

Items Needed:

Altar

Altar cloth

Items sacred specifically to the disir—
    mementos or photos are perfect for this.

Offering bowl

Mead/ale/cider

Hammer

Horn/cup

Use the mementos or photographs of your family's mothers to create the altar. Rest the offering bowl in the center, and place the hammer and the horn/cup onto the altar. If you like, you can also use flowers as offerings to the disir and as a means of decorating the altar. (To better set the mood on this winter evening, place candles on the altar is another option; light the candles as the opening to the ritual and let them burn throughout, blowing them out after the offering has been made and the ritual closed.)

Begin by raising the hammer and performing a version of the hammer rite, above. Then invoke the disir specifically:

SAY: Honored dead. Disir. You women who watch over us, guide us with your wisdom, and help maintain the family line, we call to you. We ask that you be present with us this Mothers' Night.

Put mead/cider in the horn or cup, and hold it high. Make the sign of the hammer over the liquid.

SAY: Aegir, this is your mighty brew. We ask that you make it sacred, so that our words may be carried through it into the Well of Wyrd.

Pass the horn either person-to-person or by asking for someone to be a designated horn-bearer and carry the cup from person to person. Each individual should take the time to speak of his/her specific disir before raising the horn, saying "Hail the disir!"

When the horn returns to the person officiating the blót, it should be held high again and the following words, or words like them, are spoken:

SAY: We hail you, mighty disir, on this Mothers' Night. We hear your stories. We remember you and keep you alive in our hearts. We listen for your wisdom. We offer this in thanks for the many gifts you have given us.

Pour the offering into the offering bowl. This can be done silently, with a simple "Hail the disir!" repeated by all present once the liquid has been emptied into the bowl. Libate the liquid onto a tree's roots.

Sunna Blót

There are heathens who hold an all-night vigil on the night of the solstice and blót to Sunna as she rises in the east. It can be difficult to stay awake for an entire evening, but with friends gathered the time passes more quickly. Finding the exact time of sunset and sunrise is a matter of a quick Internet search these days. Begin the vigil as the sun sets. This does not have to be a serious, formal occasion—in fact, the odds are that staying up all night can be a lot of fun. In any event, a sumble or blót may be held during the vigil, or burnt offerings made if a fire is available. This will vary depending on the person and the group hosting the vigil.

At dawn, everyone still awake should gather and go outside. Face the east. Bless a horn of mead.

SAY: Solstice night, Yulefire bright, waiting for the dawn. Solstice morn, Sunna reborn, the wheel goes on and on. (words by Michael Hicks)

Everyone present should take the time to toast to Sunna, and then the mead can be offered out directly onto the ground. Again, if indoors, pour the liquid into an offering bowl, wait at least half an hour to an hour, and then pour the remaining liquid either onto the ground outside or down the drain.

Odin Blót

In winter, the Wild Hunt streams across the skies. Odin leads the hunt, and folklore suggests that a final sheaf of grain would be left to stand in the field to feed Odin's horse, Sleipnir, as they rode by. Some heathens choose to honor Odin at Yule, either late at night during an all-night vigil or on one of the days of Yule. Yule is a time to receive omens for the year to come, and this also seems a good thing to do when honoring the Father of the Runes.

Items Needed:

Altar table

Altar cloth

Offering bowl

Small bowl or other container, holding at least
one full set of the Elder Futhark

Mead/cider

Horn/cup

Two candles in holders

Representation of Odin, if available

Build the altar so that it is in the north. The offering bowl should be centered on the table, with the candles to either side. The runes should be easily

available as well. Turn off all of the lights in the room or ritual area; if out-
side, wait until full dark to perform this ritual.

Begin in the dark. Invoke the gods and goddesses, the ancestors, and
the landwights.

SAY: Hail to the gods. Hail to the goddesses. Hail to all the Aesir and Vanir.
We ask that you be present with us as we perform this rite.

SAY: Hail to the ancestors. Those whose bones formed our bones, those
whose blood sings in our veins, we call to you. Alfar, disir, please be
with us and share your wisdom as we work this rite.

SAY: Hail the landvaettir. All you spirits of land and sky, water and stone,
you wealful wights, you are welcome as witnesses to this rite.

The officiant should then invoke Odin.

SAY: Whisperer, roarer, wise wanderer, we call to you. In the darkness we
ask that you come to us. All-Father, Rune-Father, Wish-Father, we ask that
you be with us this long winter's night. *Ansuz—ansuz—ansuz*, Odin. Share
your wisdom, your vision, your insight with us. Odin, we call to you.

SAY: As we walk through this longest night, we seek insight for the coming year. As we seek inspiration in the darkness, we come into the light.

Light the candles. Take up the container of runes and go to each per-
son. Have each person take a rune, look at it, and then either keep it for
the coming year or (if there is only one set of runes in the bowl) return
it. The officiant should take his/her rune last.

Lift the horn/cup and fill it with mead/cider. Raise it, and make the
sign of the hammer over it.

SAY: Blessed boon of bees, bountiful brew of Aegir, blood of Kvasir, carry
our words to the Well of Wyrd.

Pass the horn around in silence. Each person should take some time to think about the rune they have been given as an omen for the next year, then silently thank Odin for his wisdom. When the horn has been passed, return to the altar. Pour the liquid directly into the offering bowl.

SAY: Odin, we give this gift in thanks for your inspiration this evening.

Empty the bowl's contents outside on the ground or onto the roots of a tree. If indoors, keep the offering on the altar for several hours before pouring down the drain. Those people more familiar with the runes should offer to give people help with their meanings, if desired. The omen taken is often a quite personal thing, and it should be noted that there is no need to share unless one wants to.

Closing Yule

On the twelfth evening, the time has come to close the Yule season. This can be done with a minimum of ceremony or with a blót. If using a Yule candle, this is the last night you will light it and let it burn. My kindred's practice is to keep some of the evergreen used to decorate the home at Yule, along with the remnants of the Yule candle, to light the Midsummer fires. Other groups keep the maypole they raised on May Day and use it as the Yule log. The point of these sorts of mini-ritual practices is to form a connection with the cycle of winter and summer. Another simple mini-ritual is to be mindful when putting the Yule decorations away for the year; remember what they represent, how the twelve nights have gone, and how Sunna is returning once more.

Charming of the Plow/Disting

This blót is typically held in early February, near the time of the Celtic Imbolc. Both represent a turning point into the end of winter. Cows begin to give milk and chickens begin to lay eggs again around this time of year, so it is important to remember what the season meant—a return of milk and eggs signified the coming summer and meant fresh food in the larders. At the same time came the Disting, a ritual to honor the disir. Many heathens combine the Charming of the Plow with the Disting, since they come so close together at the beginning of the month. Others separate them into the Charming of the Plow and an ancestor ritual to honor the disir. Since a blót to one's ancestors already exists in this book, the following ritual is for the Charming of the Plow. Those of us who are farmers and own plows should use them in this ritual, but small-time gardeners can also use their implements, perhaps a spade or a small hoe.

Items Needed:

Altar table

Altar cloth

Offering bowl

Small evergreen branch or bundle of birch twigs

Hammer

Mead/cider

Horn/drinking vessel

Any farm or garden implements you use

Hallow the space however you wish, using a variation of the Hammer Rite or by other means.

Pour the mead/cider into your drinking vessel. Lift it into the air and make the hammer sign over it.

SAY: Blessed boon of bees, brew of Aegir, blood of Kvasir. I ask that this mead be blessed, so that its contents may carry our words into the Well of Wisdom.

Invoke the gods, the ancestors, and the wights. Remember to allow time for people to respond to the hails as you say them. As a variation, you can ask other people in the group to do these invocations. After each series of hails, pour some of the liquid from the horn into the blót bowl as offerings to the gods, ancestors, and wights.

SAY: All-mighty ones, shining ones, Aesir and Vanir, I call to you. We ask that you bless this ritual with your presence. Hail the Aesir. Hail the Vanir. Hail the gods and goddesses.

SAY: Ancient ones, those whose blood sings in our veins, and whose bones are our bones, I call to you. We ask that you bless this ritual with your wisdom. Hail the alfar. Hail the Vanir. Hail the ancestors.

SAY: Wealful ones, wights of earth and air, wights of fire and water, I call to you. We ask that you bless this ritual as witnesses. Hail the landvaettir.

Perform one round of toasts. The subject should deal with the blessings of tools before the spring thaw comes. Toasts to Sunna are also appropriate. After the toasts, pour all of the remaining liquid into the blót bowl.

Take the evergreen branch or birch twigs from the altar. Sprinkle a little of the liquid in the bowl onto everyone—softly touching their hands or the tops of their heads. This is called hlaut, and is another form of blessing.

SAY: Receive the blessings of the season.

After this has been completed, move to the various gardening and farm equipment gathered for the ritual. Sprinkle each liberally.

SAY: Be blessed with strength, power, and resilience as we turn the soil. Break not, falter not, jump not in our hands as we turn the soil. Be wielded well, be helpful, assist us as we turn the soil.

End the ritual by thanking the gods, ancestors, and landvaettir. Remember to wait for people to echo the hails at the end of each toast.

SAY: Shining ones, gods and goddesses, Aesir and Vanir, we thank you for your presence this day. Hail the gods. Hail the goddesses.

SAY: Ancient ones, ancestors, alfar and disir, we thank you for your wisdom this day. Hail the ancestors.

SAY: Those who live on this land, all you wealful ones, we thank you for your blessings this day. Hail the landvaettir.

Pour out the remaining liquid in the offering bowl. If possible, pour some onto each field or garden you plan on seeding and working on during the coming summer.

Ostara

Ostara celebrates the end of winter and the beginning of the planting season. In the pre-Christian times there were only two seasons—winter and summer. Ostara could then be used to mark the end of winter and the beginning of summer. Some heathens celebrate Ostara on the spring equinox for that reason. Others celebrate this event around or on the Christian Easter holiday. This makes some sense, considering that the Anglo-Saxon *Eostre* eventually became the modern word Easter. Still others host Ostara on the first Sunday after the first full moon after the spring equinox—this coincides with Easter, as the practice was adopted by Medieval Christianity. In any event, not much is known about Ostara. Her name means "east," and that is the direction she comes from. We know she travels in a cart. The Venerable Bede writes that there is an Eostre month, and says that feasts are held in her honor at that time.[1] Jacob Grimm points out that the month was most likely April or at the end of March.

There are some modern heathen "traditions" developing around Ostara. These are typically based on folkloric practices or the unverifiable personal gnosis (UPG) of the particular individual or group hosting the event. Here are a few:

- Colored eggs: hard-boil white eggs. Use a crayon or other wax marker to make decorative marks, runes, or other symbols of the season. If you wish, you can also choose to design marks that symbolize your own needs or desires. After the markings are done, color the eggs. You can use traditional, natural dyes such as beet juice, or you can use coloring kits available throughout the Easter season. Leave the eggs on the altar as you perform your Ostara ritual. Take your egg(s) home after the event. Be sure to eat the eggs before they go bad—the concept here is that you are "taking in" the blessings, prayers, etc., for that particular egg.

• Decorate a tree in your yard with ribbons and hanging eggs.

• Chase away Old Man Winter: This is a fun variation on a simpler ritual. A person is asked to represent Old Man Winter, or even an ice giant. He or she should have fun with this, putting on costuming if desired, "roaring," and otherwise running about as if Winter is still alive and well. People— especially children, if there are any present—chase Old Man Winter away. Ostara is then welcomed in. In this case, it might be fun to have a young woman, perhaps the horn-bearer, represent Ostara. Old Man Winter is chased away, and then Ostara appears. She is welcomed by one and all.

Items Needed:

Altar

Altar cloth

Hammer

Offering bowl

Horn

Mead (or other liquid)

Representation of Old Man Winter—this can be a bundle of sticks made to resemble a man, husks of corn, grain stalks, etc. The materials should be dry and flammable.

Representation of Ostara

Outdoor fire pit or fireplace

Create the altar in the east, the direction Ostara arrives from. Call on the gods and goddesses, the ancestors, and the landvaettir to witness your rite. Fill a horn with mead and bless it using the sign of the hammer.

SAY: Spring has come, and Ostara dawns in the east. We now say good-by to Old Man Winter, for the season is no longer his.

Have someone bring forth Old Man Winter.

SAY: Let us toast Old Man Winter as he leaves on his travels.

Ask a woman, preferably the youngest, to carry the horn from person to person. The horn gets taken, a toast to Old Man Winter is given, the person drinks, then hands the horn back to the horn-bearer. The horn-bearer makes sure that everyone is given time to toast and to drink from the horn.

SAY: Farewell to you, Old Man Winter.

Put Old Man Winter into the fireplace or fire pit. Light the fire and stand for a few moments in silence, watching the representation of winter burn away.

SAY: Now we welcome Ostara as she wends her way toward us. Let us toast in her honor.

Ask the horn-bearer to pass the horn. Every person should have time to hail Ostara in his or her own words, drink from the horn, and return it to the horn-bearer.

SAY: These are our wishes and hopes for the coming season. May they reach Ostara's ears, that she might bless and answer us with a healthy and fertile spring season.

Libate the mead into the offering bowl. If possible, pour the mead onto the open fire. Be aware that this may put the fire out, so be certain that Old Man Winter is over half burned, if not completely burned, before starting the ritual. Later, bury any remains from the fire.

Midsummer

Midsummer marks the halfway point of the year; it is the solstice opposite Yule, and should be seen as a summer celebration. Here we have the longest day instead of the longest night. Depending on geographical location, the first harvest happens right around Midsummer. Consider using the fruits and vegetables of the season—whether from your garden or a farmers' market—as offerings for a Midsummer blót.

Several folkloric traditions mention Midsummer fires, often bonfires, and the use of burning wheels. Some create large "wheels" made from dried wheat stalks, corn husks, or a variety of other materials. The wheels are then lit by the bonfire, and pushed off to roll down a hill. This can be a fire hazard, as can be imagined, and should not be performed without proper preparation, including notifying and gaining permission from local authorities. Instead, consider making small, hand-held sunwheels and burn them in your fireplace or outdoor fire pit. With some prior planning, you can use the dried-out greenery from your Yule celebrations to create the sunwheel to burn—which symbolically connects the two solstices.

Folklore has it that leaping the bonfires at Midsummer brings good luck. Consider having a safely contained open fire that people can jump over, if they wish, to ensure their own good fortune.

Midsummer can easily be related to Sunna, the sun. Consider a blót to Sunna as she sets in the western horizon. The exact time can be determined using the Internet, so this can be done at sunset regardless of the weather. Use a blót structure similar to the Sunna blót described above, during the Yule celebrations. The altar should be facing west instead of east, so that you can face Sunna as you thank her for the longest day.

Harvest

The harvest, again depending on geography, roughly surrounds the autumn equinox, the time when the day and night are the same length. This is when the final preparations are made for the coming winter—and remember, in Northern Europe winters were long. Above the Arctic Circle, winters lasted as long as six months, with the sun not even rising during the midst of the season. Careful preparations had to be made.

One way to connect with ancestral practice is to do precisely this—prepare for coming winter. If you brew, brew beer out of the grains harvested in autumn. Make mead from the honey that bees have produced. You can make pickles, sauerkraut, and even yogurt and cheese at home. Dry fruit or vegetables and can them. If you are a farmer already, these preparations come naturally. If you are a small gardener, the sense is the same—this is when you harvest those last vegetables and fruits, dry your herbs, and preserve whatever you can. These sorts of things remind us of our ancestors' practices and, while very practical, can help us keep in a sort of "spiritual touch" with the ways of the disir and alfar.

Harvest rituals often involved bonfires. They were not leapt at this time, but in some places people made a "dolly" out of corn husks, hay, or wheat stalks. This dolly was then danced with, often by a young woman symbolizing summer. The corn doll and the woman dance around the bonfire several times, and then the doll is burned in the fire. This can be done on a smaller scale, burning the doll in an outdoor fire pit or in a fireplace, if these are available. Often, the best of the harvest was also burned as an offering to the gods and goddesses, the ancestors, or the landvaettir.

Finally, offerings of food and drink were often left outside for the landvaettir or other wights to eat and drink from. It was once customary in some areas to leave the last sheath of wheat standing in the field. This was a gift for Sleipnir, Odin's horse, who got hungry while riding in the Wild Hunt. Milk, honey, butter, and other dairy products were left out for the beneficial wights, as were oats, other grains, and sometimes beer.

Harvest Blót

Items Needed:

Altar

Offering bowl

Horn or other drinking vessel

Ale or apple cider

Basket or other flammable container filled with seasonal,
    locally harvested fruits, vegetables, or grains

*Build a large, hot fire. Have someone tending the fire while the blót is going
on, so that it does not go out.*

    *Use the hammer rite or other words to bless and create sacred space.
Try words like these:*

SAY: We stand in sacred Midgard now, where the worlds meet. We stand
while the roots of the great tree expand below us. We stand while the
branches of Yggdrasil stretch out above us. We stand in sacred Midgard.

    *Invoke the gods and goddesses as you choose. You can also invoke
only the harvest gods, like Frey.*
    Invoke the ancestors.
    Invoke the landvaettir.

SAY: Today we celebrate the harvest. The day is equivalent to the night,
and from this point forward the night will grow colder and darker. The fire
warms us, protects us, and gives us light as we wend our way to winter. We
are fortunate this year. Our harvest has been plentiful, and we can feed our
people and the wealful wights throughout the coming season.

    Lift the basket up over your head.

SAY: Mighty ones. Shining Aesir and Vanir. Ancient ones. Alfar and disir.
Wise ones, land- and husvaettir. We offer you the best of our harvest, in
thanks for your many gifts this year. We offer you the best of our harvest,
that you might eat with us at table. We offer you the best of our harvest, in
welcome and in gratitude.

    *Place the basket on the fire. Watch in silence for a long moment, and
look to see that the basket, at least, has caught fire before continuing.*
    Lift up the horn. Fill it with ale, the brew of the season.

SAY: May the brewing gods bless this bold beer.

Pass the horn either with a horn bearer or from hand to hand. Each person should lift the horn and offer words relating to the harvest season. When it returns, say your own words and then lift the horn again.

SAY: May these words be welcomed. May the Aesir and Vanir, ancestors and vaettir, share with us. We offer this as your portion.

Pour the ale into the offering bowl. Place the horn down and lift the offering bowl.

SAY: We thank you for our good harvest.

Slowly pour the ale into the fire. Keep in mind that beer has a lower alcohol content than mead or hard alcohol—this means that the liquid can overwhelm the fire and put it out. That's not a desired outcome, so be careful with the pour. If the fire is small, consider offering some of the ale to the fire, and then pour the rest out around the fire's edges.

Stand for a long moment of silence. If desired, the rite can end precisely this way—offerings made, let the gathered people watch the fire and silently collect their own thoughts, impressions, omens, and so forth. Silence can be a powerful tool.

SAY: This rite is ended.

This ritual depends on a fire, and an outdoor fire at that. In a fireplace, the fires should be lit as above, and the offerings made—remember, though, the capacity of the fireplace and chimney, and adjust the size of the offerings as needed. If your rite is indoors, omit the fire and leave the basket on the altar along with the offering bowl. If at all possible, leave these offerings outdoors and pour the ale at the roots of a tree.

Winternights

Winternights officially begins winter. It is most often held at the end of autumn and after all the harvests have been brought in. In the Northern Hemisphere this typically happens in October or November; the opposite is the case in the Southern Hemisphere, which will be celebrating Ostara and the coming of spring at this time.

Winternights is about bringing everything indoors to survive the winter. The people gather in the long halls before the first snows fall, and all allies are welcome with them, especially the ancestors, the gods and goddesses, and the beneficial spirits of the land and home.

This blót can be held indoors. A fire can be lit if there is a fireplace, or consider lighting the room with candles. As is, this is a solitary blót. The blót can remain simple and to the point even with more than one person present. A more elaborate ritual can also be constructed, if you desire.

Items Needed:

Altar

Offering bowl

Horn or other drinking vessel

Ale or mead; apple cider or apple juice

Raise your hands over your head. Face north.

SAY: Hammer in the north, hallow and hold this holy stead.

Make the sign of the hammer. Face south and raise your hands in the air.

SAY: Hammer in the south, hallow and hold this holy stead.

Make the sign of the hammer. Lift the horn and fill it with mead. Make the sign of the hammer over it.

SAY: Mighty Mjolnir, bless this brew.

Take a single sip, then pour some of the mead into the offering bowl. Invoke the goodly/positive land and house spirits, the ancestors, the Aesir and the Vanir. After each invocation, take a sip from the horn and then pour some into the offering bowl.

SAY: Winternights comes when winter awakens. Welcome, wealful ones. Welcome, wights. Wend your way to this place of warmth. We welcome you with drink.

Take a deep sip of the mead, then offer the rest out to the wights. Pour it into the offering bowl.

SAY: A gift for a gift.

This ends the ritual. If at all possible, go outdoors and libate the liquid at the roots of a tree. If you cannot go outside, live in a city, or otherwise have no access, leave the liquid in the offering bowl overnight. Empty it into the drain the next day.

Remember to modify this depending upon your indoor pets—cats and dogs should not drink alcohol!

Notes on Chapter Fourteen

1. Bede, *The Ecclesiastical History of the English People,* trans. Leo Sherley-Price. (London: Penguin Books, 1990), 104.

fifteen

Sample Life Rituals

Life rituals are those rituals that mark change in a person's life. These are the special moments that govern the cycle of life itself—births, weddings, deaths, and so on—and their importance cannot be understated. As with many rituals, scant evidence of any specific ritual has survived into the modern era. Heathens have had to re-create these life rituals as they have had to do with many other traditional practices. The rituals written below should be seen as starting points or ways in which to look at heathen tradition.

Birth/Naming

In pre-Christian times, it seemed that a certain period of time needed to pass between actual birth and a naming ceremony, often nine days. At that point an infant was considered strong enough to survive, and was presented to his/her father by the mother. A father's acceptance of a child meant that the entire family would welcome and protect the child as he or she grew up. It also meant that inheritance rights applied to the child—a vital issue in the pre-Christian world.

In modern terms, a child is still presented by its mother to the father. The father still names and accepts the child as his and part of his family. These are often seen as mere formalities—very few if any parents refuse their children—but are still part of the vibrant practice that is heathenry. A name attaches the child to Midgard more formally, and sets his or her wyrd into motion. Naturally, names are decided by both parents and typically chosen before the ceremony. Naming ceremonies are a time for celebration, to welcome the new life into Midgard formally. Naming ceremonies can be public affairs or private, family-only events.

The use of a leek in this ceremony is more important than it may appear. We have some records of a horse's "wain"—a dried penis—being used to bless the new child. We modern heathens find that horse penises are quite rare. The leek, then, replaces the horse's wain as a symbol of life and fertility. Leeks were a popular plant in the Northern European areas, and provide a solid substitute.

Items Needed:

Altar

Altar cloth

Representations of the ancestors

Offering bowl

Leek

Mead/water

Horn/cup

Hammer

Assemble an altar holy to the ancestors, to have them present for the acceptance of a new member of the family. Gather whatever family members are present toward the front, and other invited people after them. The mother approaches with the infant in her arms.

Mother: I come here this day to name the child yours, and a part of the (surname or surnames) family.

Father: I see this child. Give him/her to me.

Mother passes child over to his or her father.

Father: This child is hale, whole, and healthy. I recognize him/her as part of my family, the (surname). This is the child of (mother's name) and mine, and is welcome to Midgard.

Father takes up the leek. Mother pours the mead/water into the offering bowl, then presents the bowl to the father. The father dips the leek into the bowl and then sprinkles some of the liquid onto the baby's head.

Father: With this blessing I name you (child's full name). Welcome and be blessed with our family's joy.

Mother: I name this child (child's full name) and welcome him/her to our families.

At this time, a horn can be filled with mead/water, blessed, and then passed to everyone present. People should toast the new baby by name, offer wisdom, blessings, or welcome, and then take a drink from the horn. When finished, empty it into the offering bowl, which will mingle it with the liquid used to name the baby. Libate the combined liquids onto a tree or other place in the yard. If indoors, let the liquid stay in the offering bowl throughout the rest of the celebration before pouring down the drain.

In the case of a single parent, an officiant can stand in and lead the ceremony, giving the child to the parent so that he/she can do the naming/blessing. If these are same-sex parents, simply choose who will perform which ritual role, and go from there. Some parents also have the officiant perform the entire rite, which is also perfectly acceptable. Some parents choose to do this alone, others with people present. Sometimes a parent will name the child as part of the open rounds of sumble. When this occurs, the next round is dedicated to the baby.

Man/Woman Making

A man or woman making marks the time when a child begins to take on adult responsibility for himself/herself. Traditionally, the boy would be sent on a hunt, to prove he could provide for his family. A girl's time to become a woman typically coincided with the onset of her menses. In both cases, there may or may not have been an official ceremony marking these events. In modern times, however, it has become fairly typical to do something to mark the specific time a child's responsibilities become the responsibilities of an adult.

In personal observation, one of the simplest and most profound ways to mark this time is for the child to hold some kind of vigil. The child goes into a quiet room, or outdoors, then waits with a horn and mead. One by one, adults—family, kindred, friends—come to the child. The adult shares whatever wisdom he/she wants to share. The child welcomes them, offers them a drink, then sits and listens to what the adult has to say. When all the adults are finished, the child contemplates all that has been said, then leaves the room or comes indoors to be welcomed by all gathered.

The specifics of this rite of passage can vary depending on the group's belief. It could remain a private, family affair, much as the naming ceremony. It could be that only men attend the boy's rite, and only women attend the girl's. Or both men and women may be in attendance. An officiant could lead the opening and closing of the ritual, or even be present throughout. More formality can be added, or less, depending on the needs of the gathered company.

Wedding

Weddings are joyous celebrations. They are also a formal, ritual way of combining two families into one, as represented by the married couple. Weddings in pre-Christian Northern Europe tended to involve things like peace treaties and land and inheritance issues, and had less to do with love, per se, than on contractual obligations. In modern times, the name of the game is love, and the love between two people being recognized by the family and friends of both partners.

Traditional weddings, as such, were not high on ceremony. An oath between the couple was spoken, usually on the lord of the household or the leader's oath ring, the band carried on the upper arm or held sacred in a special place. A feast was held in the couple's honor. The couple may, or may not, have been ritually sent to bed. We know that a representation of Thor's hammer, Mjolnir, was placed in a bride's lap to ensure her fertility.

In modern terms, several things should be kept in mind. First of all, the odds are that the family gathered for the wedding may not be heathen. While this should not change a heathen's wedding, it is often polite to add enough of a modern wedding ceremony so that a non-heathen will still recognize what is taking place. The officiant may want to speak a paragraph or two about what heathen weddings are, and what to expect. Next, the formality and length of the wedding depend on the decisions made by the couple. Some may want to include readings from the lore, others may not. The couple should have input into the ceremony, and can help shape it to fit their own sense of the occasion.

Finally, in the modern world, same-sex marriages exist and do not directly contradict anything in the heathen belief system. An officiant may feel comfortable performing a same-sex marriage; another officiant may not. It is the right of the officiant to accept or refuse to perform any ritual, for any reason—it is also the right of the same-sex partners to choose who to officiate their wedding. This is true for heterosexual partners as well. When choosing to marry, every consideration should be taken into account, and this includes who performs the ceremony. The officiant can be heathen clergy or a close friend. The officiant can be a Justice of the Peace or someone who specializes in performing wedding ceremonies. The main issue in any marriage is the legal one—consult your local state or county regarding who is, or is not, allowed to sign the marriage certificate.

In terms of the ceremony that follows, I have chosen to use the words "bride," "groom," and "officiant." This is mostly for the sake of clarity, and should not be taken as a "heterosexual only" position. As a person who has married both heterosexual and same-sex partners, I can say that the shape of the ceremony remains the same, as does its emotional and sacred impact. My general practice when writing wedding ceremonies is to use the first names of the couple involved instead of using the words "bride" or "groom."

The basic shape of a wedding ceremony can change depending on the couple's needs. The parts involved are as follows:

Processional

Opening

Sanctification of Space

Invocation

Reading

Swearing of vows

Exchanging of rings

Exchange of gifts

Reading

Presentation of couple

Closing

Recessional

Many of these can be seen as optional. A wedding could be as simple as: Opening, invocation, swearing of vows, exchanging of rings, and closing. Couples may desire to write their own oaths—or vows—and recite them as well as reciting the more modern "traditional" vows found in most modern weddings. They may want to only use their own vows. As you can see, weddings are very important ceremonies and should be geared to the needs of the couple.

Sample Wedding Ceremony
Processional
Opening

Officiant: Welcome. Please be seated. This wedding may be a bit different from those you have seen before. Groom and Bride are Asatru, and this ceremony reflects their religious beliefs. We call ourselves Asatru, heathen, or Theodish, and are polytheist reconstructionists, which is a fancy way of saying that we follow the gods and goddesses of Northern Europe—Thor, Sif, Odin, Frigga, Frey, Freyja, and others. In heathen tradition, a couple swears their oaths upon an oath ring, exchanges gifts with one another, and asks the ancestors, land spirits, and god and goddesses to look over their union. We place strong emphasis on families coming together through the couple because, as ancestor worshippers, we feel that the entire family—even those who have passed on—shares in the union of the couple we see before us this day.

We are gathered here today to bear witness to the wedding oaths of Bride and Groom. May the ancestors, the Aesir, the Vanir, and the land-spirits share this joyous time with us and this couple.

Invocation

Officiant: Shining ones—Aesir and Vanir—holy gods and goddesses, we ask that you be here today. Thor and Sif, Odin and Frigga, Frey and Frejya look down on this couple and bless them with your presence and your wisdom this day.

Officiant: Spirits of the land and spirits of the sky. Stone-spirits, water-spirits, all those seen and unseen, be with us this day as we witness the union of this couple.

Officiant: Ancient ones, ancestors, bear witness to this union. You of the (Groom's surname), welcome Bride into your family embrace. You of the (Bride's surname), welcome Groom into your family embrace. Whisper your wisdom to them both, wrap them in warmth, and share your weal with them always.

Officiant: Hail to Var, handmaiden of Frigga. You witness and care for the oaths of couples. We ask that you bear witness to the oaths sworn between Bride and Groom today, hold them close, and keep them so long as these two are wed.

Swearing of Oaths

Officiant: In older times, much like now, promises were often sworn on an oath ring. The ring remained as a powerful symbol of the oaths sworn upon it, and represented a tangible bond between the couple who have spoken the words from their hearts to one another. Bride, Groom, would you please take up the ring?

(Bride and Groom take the oath ring with their right hands.)

Officiant: Now shall you pledge your troth to one another. Your words will bind you, one to the other, in the presence of the gathered community.

Officiant: Bride, will you repeat after me: "I, (full name), take you (full name), to be my lawful wedded husband. I shall honor you and cherish you, respect you and love you. I shall cleave to you in good times and in bad, in sickness and in health, in joy and in sorrow. I promise to love you and support you for as long as our love shall last."

(Bride repeats words as they are spoken.)

Officiant: Groom, will you repeat after me: "I, (full name), take you, (full name), to be my lawful wedded wife. I shall honor you and cherish you, respect you and love you. I shall cleave to you in good times and in bad, in sickness and in health, in joy and in sorrow. I promise to love and support you for as long as our love shall last."

(Groom repeats words as they are spoken.)

Exchange of rings

Officiant: I have heard these words and they are good. May I please have the rings? *(The rings are handed to the officiant. Officiant holds them over the oath ring.)* In heathen traditions as in many modern ones, rings are a symbol of the union between couples. We also believe that rings are a visible replacement for the oath ring and the promises these two have sworn between them.

Officiant: Var, oath-keeper, you who govern the contracts between men and women, please bless these rings. May they provide this couple comfort in troubled times, strength in times of need, and a reminder of the two become one.

(Officiant removes oath ring and sets it upon the altar.)

Officiant: Groom, please place this ring on Bride's finger and repeat after me: "I give you this ring as a symbol of my love and my vow."

(Groom repeats the words and places the ring on Bride's finger.)

Officiant: Bride, please place this ring on Groom's finger and repeat after me: "I give you this ring as a symbol of my love and my vow."

(Bride repeats the words and places the ring on Groom's finger.)

Officiant: Please kiss one another as a symbol of your union.

(Bride and Groom kiss.)

Exchange of gifts

Officiant: In elder times, an exchange of gifts would occur at this point. Traditionally, a man would give the keys to his hall and his chests as a symbol of her position as the head of the household. A woman would give a man a well-crafted sword as a symbol of his position as protector of the family. Today, gifts are often also symbols of one another's ancestors, representing the two families becoming one. Bride, Groom, do you have gifts for one another?

(Bride presents her gift to Groom, explaining its significance. Groom presents his gift to Bride, explaining its significance.)

Presentation of Couple

Officiant: I have heard the oaths sworn and seen the gifts exchanged. Bride, Groom, will you turn to face the gathered company? *(They face the audience.)* By the power vested in me by (wherever you are certified to perform marriages) and in the presence of the gods and goddesses, the ancestors, and the landvaettir, I declare Bride and Groom a lawfully wedded couple.

Recessional

If the couple wishes, the hammer can be laid in the bride's lap either as part of the ceremony—after the oaths, rings, and gifts are exchanged—or as part of the reception festivities. If the couple does not desire children, this tradition can be skipped altogether.

Divorce

When we marry, few of us consider divorce. Love will last forever, or until death do us part. The married couple often feels that they are now acting as one unit and will be partners. They feel the strength of their commitment and their oaths binding one another, and are going to act in accordance with their oaths. As a matter of fact, many couples do end up together through the thick and the thin times, raise any children they may have, and remain successfully married for a very long time, often up to the death of one or the other partner.

At the same time, many couples divorce. I won't get into examples or divorce rates—my point is that there needs to be a realization that divorce is an outcome some of us experience. There are many reasons for divorce, some amicable and some considerably otherwise. There are mental and physical safety reasons, which should be handled as swiftly and thoroughly as possible. Some couples simply "grow apart," or find their lives taking separate directions for so long that they no longer feel they should be married. There are a host of reasons. What we seldom talk about is the sacral nature of divorce.

When we marry, we often do so in religious or other sacred ceremonies. Even a secular marriage has some exchange or promise spoken in it. Heathens value oaths as expressions of wyrd—and take oaths very seriously. What happens during a divorce? In addition to the tumult and chaos, the hard feelings or the grieving, the relief or the resignation, a divorce can be a very difficult thing to manage at the judicial level. Divorces are complicated things, and there are many changes to address. Among these is the dissolution of the marriage oaths.

Heathens take oaths seriously. Breaking an oath is also taken very seriously. This does not mean staying in a miserable situation, but it may mean counseling, or discussions by both parties as to what should be done. At the same time, sometimes one partner will not be interested in either of these things. Either way, a divorce is a breaking of the marriage oath. Some heathens take great comfort from a ritual, some are not interested, and some may have to perform a ritual on their own. A divorce ritual should be a means of gaining closure—a sacred acknowledgement that the marriage pact has been broken and is now dissolved.

There is no one way in which this should be done. Each person has his or her individual feelings on the matter, and in some cases it may be best not to see one's former partner at all. Some desire a great deal of ritual, others require none whatsoever. One may ask for a ritual to occur, and the ex-husband or wife may refuse. In short, any divorce ritual has to take a number of items into consideration, which means there will be a great deal of variety between rituals. Writing one's own divorce ritual can be extremely difficult, especially if a great deal of emotion is involved. Remember that a ritual, if needed, can occur at any time. Sometimes it may be easier to wait through some of the raw emotion—or it may be best to do it swiftly. This must be decided by the individual or the couple.

One way to accomplish the divorce ritual is to simply release the other person from their vows. Create sacred space, then fill a horn or other vessel with mead, cider, or any other liquid. Look at the person you are divorcing, and say words like:

"Once dear to my heart, once taken above all others, I now release you from your vows to me."

Have the person repeat the same thing to you. Drink together from the horn in acknowledgement of your words, and close the ritual. This can be done individually if the other person sees no need for a ritual to occur.

If personalized oaths were written for the marriage, those words can be used in a divorce ritual. Release the person you are divorcing line by line, or speak what you are doing by dissolving the oath. Words like "I release you from your oath to care for me above all others" can also be read as "I shall no longer care for you above all others." The latter words may be particularly effective if you are performing the ritual by yourself or in the company of your kindred or community.

You can also choose to destroy symbols of the marriage itself. Some people choose to cut their marriage rings into pieces and burn or bury them. A drinking horn carved especially for the wedding can be smashed and the pieces burned, buried, or otherwise removed from the household. These are symbolic ways of "breaking" the marriage and can be worked in alongside a releasing of the marriage oaths. Some people find it easier to ritually destroy an object than to form words relating to the divorce. This is why a specific ritual cannot be written—each is unique to itself, and reflective of the situation. If you cannot write one yourself because you are too close and your emotions too raw, consider either waiting until some of the emotional fallout has faded, or asking someone to write a ritual with you.

Funeral

The transition from life into death is often one of the most emotionally disruptive and moving times of life. The important thing to remember is that heathens believe that death makes the departed an ancestor, meaning that the person will still be part of their worship, and thus still a part of daily life. Additionally, as long as we remember the person, they remain "alive" in our hearts and our minds—and this is the closest thing heathens have to immortality.

Funerals can take on many shapes, with eulogies and readings that are often done by family members and close friends. The rough shape of a funeral is as follows:

Opening

Invocation (usually to the ancestors)

Opening remarks

Eulogy (eulogies—the number depends on the family's wishes)

Reading (the "Hávamál" verses below work well here)

Remembrance

Closing

What follows below should come before the remembrance but can be after the eulogy and reading.

Officiant: In ancient times, much like today, we Asatruar honor our dead by keeping their names, and their stories, alive in our hearts and in our minds. The "Hávamál," the wise sayings of Odin, teaches us that:

Cattle die and kinsmen die
One day you, too, shall die.
But I know one thing that never dies
and that is the fame we earn in life.

The "Hávamál" also says:

Cattle die and kinsmen die
One day you, too, shall die.
But I know one thing that shall not die
and that is the good reputation of a man.

Each of us earns our own fame in life. We have the careers we have chosen, our hobbies, and the things that we do well. It is these sorts of actions that build our reputations. We also have faith—faith in the gods, in our ancestors, and in the spirits of the land.

What we also have are our family, our friends, and our kin. As part of our faith, we venerate our ancestors—those who have come before us. We do this by remembering their fame and their reputations. We talk about them; we tell their stories, and it is this which keeps them alive in our hearts.

(Deceased) is with his/her ancestors now. They have welcomed him, given him a warm place by the fire, fed him, and provided comfort after his passing.

It is up to us now. We keep (deceased) alive in our hearts by remembering him, toasting him, and honoring him in his place among the honored dead. We tell his stories so that he will live forever. Let us share our memories of (deceased) with one another now. Please feel free to come forward and tell us a story, so that we may remember him.

Note: Depending on how many people want to tell stories, this can take up time. It is best to discreetly keep your eye on the time, and stop when the allotted time is up.

Here is another way to end a funeral service:

Officiant: Every person we meet in life touches us. A stranger passing in the street smiles, and we feel uplifted. A friend listens in a time of need. A partner knows just when to hold our hands. We take a part of them into us, as well. We might take a turn of phrase and make it ours. We learn from our teachers, and also from our friends, then take that wisdom into our hearts. Our parents raise us, and we take a great deal from them. Let us take a moment of silence to reflect on what (deceased) was in our lives, what she gave to us, and what small portion of her we have taken into ourselves.

(Moment of silence should be approximately 30-60 seconds.)

Officiant: May we always remember (deceased) in this way.

Change is chaos.

Appendix:
The Problem of Loki

One of the main issues found in heathenry today deals with the god Loki. Put plainly, there are those who will worship him, and those who will not. Some heathens refuse to use his name in order to avoid attracting his attention. Others welcome his attention and invoke him often. For many, there stands a sort of "mutual non-aggression pact." The feeling here is that if the person leaves Loki alone, Loki will in turn leave that person alone. In this sense there is not, by and large, any enmity. It is simply a matter of wanting to be left alone, and avoiding action that will attract Loki's attention. By and large, a majority of heathens do not worship Loki. This does not bother his followers; they are loyal to him regardless.

In terms of mythology, Loki's motives are complex and often revolve around his giving recompense for a problem he caused. For instance, he is the mother of Odin's eight-legged horse, Sleipnir. This is a great gift, as Sleipnir is among the only animals able to travel throughout all the nine worlds, including the realms of the living and the dead. Lokeans will point this out as a positive outcome. That said, the rest of the myth must be considered. After the mighty war between the Aesir and the Vanir, the walls around Asgard had fallen. A giant builder came along and said he would rebuild the walls within three seasons. His price was the sun, the moon, and a marriage to the goddess Freyja. When the giant asked if he could have his horse to help him, Loki agreed. The horse was clearly magical and the work neared completion in no time at all. Three days before summer, the gods determined that Loki, whose idea it was to hire the giant in the first place, was "responsible for the most evil … and declared he would deserve an evil death"[1] if he did not find a way to stop the builder from completing his work. Loki swears oaths that he will fix things, and then transforms himself into a mare to lure the stallion away. We are then told "Loki had such dealings with [the stallion] that somewhat later he gave birth to a foal."[2] This foal is Sleipnir. Lokeans often argue that all the gods made a collective decision and later punished Loki as a kind of fall guy, but a close reading of the myth shows that, indeed, it was Loki who made that promise to the builder in the first place.

In another myth we see Loki as the primary instigator of the trouble. It is said that Odin, Loki, and Hoenir are traveling together when they decide to cook an ox they found. An eagle comes and says the ox meat will cook only if he gets his portion first. Loki, angry at this, strikes the eagle with a long pole. The eagle flies off with Loki stuck hanging on to the other end of the pole. The eagle is the giant Thiazi in disguise, and he says he will free Loki only if Loki brings him Idunna and her apples. Loki promises to do so. He does this by luring Idunna into a forest, where Thiazi, in eagle form, snatches her away. When the gods investigate, they learn that the last time she was seen, Idunna was being led into the forest by Loki. They arrest Loki and, again, threaten him with death. Loki swears to get her back, borrows Freyja's falcon cloak, and flies to Thiazi's home, Thrymheim. He transforms Idunna into a nut and flies as swiftly as he can back to Asgard.[3] Again, it can be said that Loki returned Idunna to the Aesir and Vanir, which is a good thing—Idunna's apples keep the gods young and fit. However, it is clear from this story that Loki got himself into trouble and was willing to steal Idunna away to get himself out. It is only when the gods discover what he has done and threaten to torture and kill him that Loki swears to get Idunna back. This can be seen as rather self-serving: Loki does not want to die, after all, and it seems the easiest way to avoid death is to return Idunna. We see this behavior in myth after myth—Loki gets himself in trouble, does something worse to get out of trouble, and then recompenses the gods when they discover that he is to blame.

Found in the *Poetic Edda*, "Lokasenna" is also called "the flyting of Loki." Flyting was a kind of ritualized insult contest that often involved using truth to point out another person's weakness. In this case, Loki is the one doing the flyting at a sumble. Here, the gods and goddesses have entered Aegir's hall as allies to Aegir. Outside, Loki murders one of Frey's servants. He then enters the feast hall, and challenges—or flytes—each of the gods and goddesses in turn. He insults them in the worst ways he can think of, mainly accusing the goddeses of promiscuity and sleeping with him and calling the gods cowards or accusing them of "unmanliness." The more the gods and goddesses defend one another, the more he attacks them with taunts and insults. Ultimately Loki breaks the frith of the hall, first by murder and second by boasting that he was among those who killed Thiazi, Skadhi's father. She swears her vengeance on Loki and soon has it. Loki flees, transforming himself into a salmon, but the gods catch him. His son is killed and his entrails used to bind Loki to a rock. Skadhi sets a poisonous serpent above Loki's face, where its venom drips down and tortures him. Loki's wife, Sigyn, holds a bowl over his face to capture as much poison as she can, but eventually the bowl fills and, as she emp-ties it, Loki writhes in agony. Lokeans will often cite this myth as the Aesir and Vanir going too far; naturally Loki wants vengeance after these events. The argument goes that these punishments are out of the natural social order—Loki's son is murdered in front of him, Skadhi's vengeance is too tortuous for anyone to endure, and it is these things that ultimately cause Loki's break with the gods. It is clear that the events of the Lokas-enna drive Loki away from the Aesir. On the other hand, it could be that the gods and goddesses are fed up with his behavior and punishing him for these final transgressions against them.

Finally, in "Voluspá" we learn that, at Ragnarok, a ship made of fin-gernails leaves Muspelheim, filled with fire giants "en Loki stýrirm,"[4] literally meaning "with Loki steering." Loki has at this point abandoned the gods altogether and joined the ranks of their enemies. The argument from Loki supporters is that this is only natural, after the way the gods treated him throughout their relationships with him and, as we've seen, at the end of Lokasenna. This could perhaps be seen as valid, if not for Loki's continual misbehavior in nearly every myth in which he appears. It seems more reasonable to look at the range of Loki's behavior prior to his final breaking of frith by murdering a servant and taunting Skadhi. Yes, he gives gifts to the gods, and they bind him anyway. However, his gifts come with ever-escalating prices, as he struggles to make reparations for the harm he causes in the first place. He is the one who breaks the community frith and then is punished. He is the one who murders and, most importantly, refuses to pay weregild for it. Weregild was a means of giving recompense to the family of the slain, and, once it was paid, the murderer was generally forgiven. Loki knows this, and steers his course regardless. In the end, he declares himself an enemy of the gods. As we've seen in previous chapters, heathens tend to be very loyal to their gods, and this is a good part of why many heathens reject the worship of Loki altogether.

For those who accept Loki and give honor to him, he is a trickster figure in the Norse mythology. Some scholarship supports this theory. However, it is important to remember that trickster figures are more than simply laughing clowns and pranksters. True trickster figures can cause a great deal of chaos; they are often the impetus for major changes, and these changes can be disastrous for the people caught in the middle. Loki may, in fact, be the cause of much-needed change among the Aesir and Vanir. He certainly is ranked among them throughout much of the mythology. He travels with Thor, Tyr, and Odin. He might, or might not, be an apostasis of one of the original three creator gods. He brings, or helps to bring, many important gifts to the gods. While these always come at a price, it seems that Loki is willing to pay it. An interesting look at Loki from the point of view of a Lokean can be found at Ravencast, a heathen podcast. It is Episode 8, dated April 2007. It can be found here: http://ravencast.podbean.com/2007/04/.

Ultimately, it is up to the individual to decide how he or she feels about the "Loki issue." It is up to the individual to decide his or her devotion—or neutrality, or even enmity—to Loki. At the same time, it is important to know the complexities of the situation, and to be a good guest. A good guest will ask his or her host if Loki is allowed in their rituals or not, and behave accordingly. On the other side of this coin, a good host lets his or her guest know if Loki is welcome in advance of any rituals, so that the guest is well-informed. For some, this means staying away from certain houses where Loki is, or is not, welcome. This, too, is a matter of personal choice.

Notes on Appendix

1. Snorri Sturluson, The *Prose Edda* (London: Everyman, 1987), 35.

2. Snorri Sturluson, The *Prose Edda* (London: Everyman, 1987), 35–36.

3. Snorri Sturluson, The *Prose Edda* (London: Everyman, 1987), 59–60.

4. Ursula Dronke, trans., The *Poetic Edda, Volume II: Mythological Poems* (Oxford: Clarendon Press, 1997), 20.

Glossary

Aegir—an etin (jotun) who is best associated with the deep sea. He is a friend and ally to the Aesir and Vanir.

Aesir—plural form of "As," or god. The Aesir specifically are one of the two main groups of deities living in Asgard and is worshipped by ancient and modern heathens.

alf/alfar—singular and plural forms referring to the entities of the land, sea, and sky. These beings live primarily in Alfheim, but are also considered locational. Some may be considered similar to the male ancestral dead.

Alfheim—literally "alf-home," this is the land most of the alfar reside in.

Althing—a type of annual meeting similar to a Thing, where legal matters were decided. The Althing was held at Thingvellir from roughly 930-1798 CE.

Alvis—lit. "All-Wise," a dwarf who arrives in Asgard and plays a riddle-game with Thor. Thor delays Alvis until dawn comes, at which time Alvis turns to stone.

ancestor/ancestor worship—the practice of venerating, honoring, or otherwise making offerings to the respected dead.

Angrboda—a jotun and the mother of the wolf, Fenris, the Midgard Serpent, and Hella.

animism—the belief that there is a "spirit" or "life" to everything that exists.

Ásatrú—(plural Asatruar) also Asatru, from "As," meaning "god" and "tru," meaning true or loyal to. The name of the religion and cultural worldview of modern heathens.

Asgard—lit. "God-Yard," the home of the Aesir and selected Vanir.

Audhumla—the sacred cow which appears inside Ginunngagap. She licks the rime away and frees the first being, Ymir.

Austri—lit. "east," but also the name of the dwarf holding up the vault of the sky in that direction.

Axis Mundi—the singular "pole" or other high place used to indicate the center of all things. Yggdrasil represents the axis mundi in heathen belief systems.

Baldur—also Balder and Baldr, an As. Baldur dies as a result of a mistletoe dart and resides in Helheim until after the destructive Ragnarok.

Beowulf—the name of an early poem about the adventures of a hero named Beowulf.

Bestla—a giant and the mother of Odin, Vili, and Ve.

Bifrost—the name of the rainbow bridge connecting Asgard and Midgard.

Blót—also blot, one of two major heathen rituals. Blót involves sacrifice and the maintenance of a relationship with the deities, ancestors, and/or land spirits.

Bor—a giant and the father of Odin, Vili, and Ve.

Bragi—a member of the Aesir most closely associated with poetry and song.

Brisingamen—Freyja's necklace. Created by the four dwarves whose surname is "Brising."

Brokk—a dwarf and one of the sons of Ivaldi. Loki wagers Brokk that he cannot forge a certain number of gifts for the gods. Loki loses the wager and Brokk sews his lips together.

brownie—a type of helpful spirit.

Conversion Period—a period of time marked by the rise of Christianity and the decline of polytheism/paganism. In Europe this occurred approximately 300-1000 CE.

Dáinn—a dwarf whose name means "died."

dis/disir—one of the female ancestors who are known to follow a person throughout their lives, offering protection and support.

Disablót—A ritual honoring the disir held at the end of January or early February.

Draupnir—an item forged by Brokk and Eitri. It is a magical golden ring. Every nine nights it drops another golden ring.

dwarf/dwarves—also called a Svartalf/Svartalfar, a class of beings created from the maggots consuming the corpse of Ymir.

Einherjar—Odin's chosen army of warriors, who train every day and feast all night. Denizens of Valhalla, this army forms the defense of Asgard during the final battle, Ragnarok.

Eir—one of Frigga's handmaidens, most closely associated with healing and mercy on the battlefield.

Eitri—a dwarf. Brokk's brother and assistant at the forge.

Etin—another term for "giant." Etins is the plural form.

Ex nihilo—creation from nothing. Norse mythology runs in the opposite—something existed before creation. In this sense, Muspelheim, Niflheim, Ginnungagap, and the World Tree, Yggdrasil, all existed before creation began.

Fenris/Fenrir—the monstrous wolf sired by Loki. Fenris remains bound until Ragnarok, at which time he kills and consumes Odin.

Fire giant—a class of giants living in Muspelheim.

Folkvang—"people's plain" or sometimes "battle plain," this is the region of Asgard under Freyja's purview.

Forseti—the son of Baldur and Nanna, Forseti is most closely associated with justice in its many forms.

Freki—one of Odin's wolves.

Frey—one of the gods of the Vanir. Frey was brought to Asgard as part of the hostage exchange which ended the war between the Aesir and the Vanir.

Freyja—also Freya, one of the goddesses of the Vanir. No one knows quite how Freyja came to Asgard; she was not part of the hostage exchange. She is known as second in rank after Frigga.

Frigga—also Frig, the chief goddess of the Aesir, and wife to Odin. It is said she can see all of wyrd, but she remains silent about what she knows.

Frisia—an ancient country that once spanned from the coastlines of northwestern Netherlands into northwestern Germany and northward to the border of Denmark.

frith—a concept meaning an inviolable peace, particularly between members of an innangardh.

Fulla—one of Frigga's handmaidens, Fulla is a virgin who takes care of Frigga's shoes and her casket.

fulltrui—a term used to distinguish a sworn-oathed relationship to a particular deity.

futhark—the named used to refer to specific rune sets. Named for the first runes in the first aett (row): fehu, uruz, thurisaz, ansuz, raido, and kenaz.

galdr—a harsh, atonal chant or "singing" of the runes for magical effects.

Gefjon—one of Frigga's handmaidens. Gefjon used her sons, transformed into oxen, to carve out a land for herself. It is generally held that this is Sjaelland, originally part of Sweden but now a part of Denmark.

Gerdh—also Gerdhr, the etin-bride Frey marries.

Geri—one of Odin's wolves.

Germania—a book written by the Roman, Tacitus, describing his observations of the Germanic peoples.

Germanic Iron Age—a period of time marked by the rise and prominence of iron in forging, materials, and weaponry, approximately 600-800 CE.

Ginnungagap—the chasm or void lying between Muspelheim and Niflheim.

Gjallarhorn—Heimdal's horn, which he sounds at the beginning of Ragnarok, to alert the gods and goddesses that their enemies are approaching.

gnosis—a knowledge of spiritual/mystical information.

Gullinbursti—meaning "golden bristles," the name of the boar Frey rides.

Gullveig—"gold-greedy," the name of the witch whose arrival presaged the war between the Aesir and the Vanir.

hamingja—this refers to several things. In some cases it can refer to an individual's "spirit body," but it most often refers to the store of luck in an individual, often due to his or her family line's collective luck.

Hár—also Hárr. A byname for Odin, meaning the "High One." The *Poetic Edda's* "Hávamál" is also called "The Sayings of Hár."

heathen—an umbrella term used by Asatruar to refer to themselves and other groups that follow the Aesir, Vanir, and cultural worldviews of the Pre-Christian peoples.

Heid—also Heidh, the name of the Volva speaking to Odin in "Voluspa." She may also be Freyja.

Heimdal—one of the Aesir, Heimdal guards Bifrost, the rainbow bridge. His senses are acutely sharp, and his blowing of Gjallarhorn, his horn, presages Ragnarok.

Heimskringla—a book written by Snorri Sturluson. It covers the lives of the early Norwegian kings.

Hel—the half-living, half-dead child of Loki. She is set to govern Helheim and all of the dead that reside in it.

Helheim—literally, Hel's land. This is the place where most of the dead go when they die.

hight—"named" or "called." As an example, "a tree, Yggdrasil hight" would also mean "a tree named Yggdrasil" or "a tree, Yggdrasil it is called."

Hlidskjalf—the name of Odin's high seat, where he can sit and see everything in the nine worlds.

Hod—a blind god, son of Odin and brother to Baldur. He shoots the mistletoe dart that slays Baldur.

Hoenir—one of the three creator gods, his gift to humanity is óð, or inspiration.

Hof—a building or other sacred enclosure where heathens performed their worship.

Howe—another name for a place, in this case more often a mound, where heathens performed sacred rituals.

Hræsvelgr—"Corpse Eater," the name of the eagle who sits in the north. His wings cause the north winds to blow.

Hrym—a giant.

Huldfolk—also called the "hidden people," or "mound-folk."

Hugin—also Huginn, one of Odin's ravens. The word roughly translates to "thought."

husvaett—plural husvaettir. The "Vaettir," or spirits, living in and around a house.

Hvergelmir—the well located in Niflheim. All rivers flow from it.

ice giant—a class of giants living in Niflheim.

Idunna—one of the Aesir whose duty it is to care for the golden apples that the deities need to eat in order to stay young and vital.

Innangardh—literally "in-yard," used to denote those people whom you have chosen to make an "in-group" with.

Ivaldi—a dwarf, the father of Brokk and Eitri.

Jord—also Iord, the name of the earth, the personified goddess of the planet itself.

Jotun—one name for "giant." Jotnar is the plural form.

Jotunheim—"hall" or "land" of the jotnar. This is where the giants live.

Jormungandr—the Midgard Serpent, monstrous child of Loki. The serpent encircles all of Midgard. Jormungandr is Thor's mortal enemy and is slain by Thor at Ragnarok.

kenning—a kenning is a word or phrase used by poets to refer back to a specific item, concept, or being. A kenning for Freyja, for instance, would be "bright-gold weeper," for she is known to shed tears of gold when her husband, Ód, leaves her. Kennings allowed for creativity in poetry and song, and were also used to maintain proper poetic meter.

kindred—a chosen working group, typically structured under a "chosen family" model.

kobold—the German name for a house-spirit.

lá—one of the three gifts the creator gods gave to humans. It refers to "comely hue."

landvaettir—the spirits of a particular place of land, or of land in general.

ljosalf/ljosalfar—the word for the "light" elves, or alfar.

Ljosalfheim—the land of the light elves, or alfar.

Lofn—one of Frigga's handmaidens, she brings together marriages that would otherwise be forbidden.

Loki—one of the Aesir, who later betrays them and fights alongside the thursar at Ragnarok.

Mani—the god who guides the moon across the skies at night.

Midgard—literally "middle-yard," the center of the Norse cosmology, and the place where all humans live.

Migration Age—the period marked by the travels of the Germanic tribes from Northern Europe throughout the continent, roughly 300-600 CE.

Mjolnir—the name of Thor's mighty hammer.

mound—in this case, typically either a burial site or an entrance to the Otherworld.

mound-dweller(s)—see also huldfolk, the "invisible people," who in this case may be ancestors, who live under the earth.

Munin—one of Odin's ravens. The word translates roughly to "Memory."

Muspelheim—one of the nine worlds. Muspelheim is a land composed of fire. The thurs Surt lives there, as do the destructive fire giants.

Naglfari—the name of the boat, made of human fingernails and toenails, that the thursar ride into Ragnarok.

Nanna—one of the Aesir, Baldur's wife.

Nerthus—a goddess described by Tacitus in his work *Germania*. He refers to her as Mother Earth, and her time is known as one of peace and prosperity.

Niflheim—a realm of ice, cold, and frozen things. The ice giants live here.

nisse—(plural nissen), the Norwegian name for house-spirits and mound-dwellers.

Njord—one of the Vanir, Njord has to do with wealth and the boatyard.

Nordic Bronze Age—a period of time categorized by the use of bronze materials and weaponry, approximately 1700–500 BCE.

Nordri—literally north, but also the name of one of the dwarves holding up the vault of the sky.

oð—inspiration, one of the gifts the creator gods gave to humanity.

Odin—one of the chief gods, and an Aesir. Odin is known for having given up one eye and for his ravens Hugin and Munin.

offering(s)—items of food, clothing, drink, or other gifts given to the gods, ancestors, and/or wights in thanks for their many gifts.

omnibenevolent—being "all-good."

omnipresent—the ability to be in all places simultaneously.

omniscient—being "all-knowing."

önd—breath, one of the gifts the three creator gods gave to humanity.

örlög—literally translates as "ur-law," and refers to the beginning point of our lives by which our entire lives are bound.

Poetic Edda—also called the "Elder Edda," this is a compilation of poems, most with unknown authors. Some of the poems date to the Viking Age, while others are most likely early Medieval in origin.

polytheist—from "poly-," meaning "many," and "theist," or belief in one or many gods. A polytheist believes in the existence of many deities.

Prose Edda—also called the "Younger Edda," this is a work by the author Snorri Sturluson and was most likely written around 1222-1235 CE.

Proto-Indo-European—a reconstructed language considered to be the "root" of many modern European languages, including modern English, Icelandic, Norwegian, and German.

Ragnarok—often translated to "Twilight of the Gods," this is the final battle in the mythic cycle. The gods and goddesses of Asgard, the Einherjar, and all their allies battle against the thursar, the monsters, and the armies of the dead. Ultimately most of the gods are killed and the nine worlds are set on fire by the thurs Surt.

Ran—a goddess who lives under the sea. It is said that she gathers the souls of drowned sailors in her nets.

reconstruction (reconstructionist)—a term used when one is using extant source material (in this case, the myths, sagas, histories, and archeology) to re-create that which was lost. Usually used as a method to guide modern heathen practices.

rune—a word referring to a set of symbols used in writing, magic, and divination.

saga—a written record of events. The sagas may be historical or biographical, or may be what we would now call fiction.

Sága—one of Frigga's handmaidens. Frigga and Sága are remarkably similar, and Sága may or may not be a byname for Frigga.

scop—a name for a poet, singer, or other storyteller. Some scops were attached to particular lords, while others traveled.

seidh—also "seidhr." A trance-based magical practice that included prophesy, blessings, cursings, and so forth.

seidhjallr—the high seat a seidhworker sits in or ascends to in order to work seidh.

seidhkona—literally "seidh-woman," a female practitioner of seidh.

Sessrumnir—the name of Freyja's hall.

siðu—roughly meaning "tradition" or "common practice," this Old Norse word is applied to indicate the wide variations among Asatruar (heathens) both in the ancient and modern worlds.

Sif—one of the Aesir, Sif is Thor's wife. Her hair was stolen by Loki and replaced with strands of gold.

Sigyn—Loki's wife. It is said that she holds a bowl over Loki's face to catch the venom dripping down from a serpent's fangs.

Sjofn—one of Frigga's handmaidens, Sjofn turns people's hearts toward love.

skald—another word for a poet, singer, or storyteller. The individual may have traveled from place to place, or might have been attached or sworn to a particular leader or household.

Skidbladnir—the name of Frey's boat, one of the magical items forged by Brokk and Eitri.

Skadhi—an etin, the daughter of Thiazi, who marries Njord and later divorces him.

Skínfaxi—a horse that pulls the chariot of the sun across the daytime skies.

Skirnir—one of Frey's servants. It is Skirnir who woos Gerdh on Frey's behalf.

Skuld—one of the three Norns who feed Yggdrasil and care for the Well of Wyrd.

Sleipnir—the eight-legged horse sired by Loki. Odin rides Sleipnir, and Sleipnir can travel to all the worlds, including the realms of the dead.

Snotra—one of Frigga's handmaidens.

spá—also "spae." A branch of seidh which typically includes prophecy of some sort.

Sudri—literally "south," but also the name of one of the dwarves holding up the vault of the sky.

sumble—one of two main Asatru rituals. Sumble is a ritualized drinking ceremony which is meant to strengthen bonds within a community.

Sunna—the goddess who embodies the sun.

Surt—a destructive thurs who dwells in Muspelheim. He battles Frey during Ragnarok, defeats him, and then sets fire to all nine worlds.

svartalf/svartalfar—a word for the "dark" elves, or alfar. These are often dwarves.

Svartalfheim—the world where the svartalfar live.

Syn—one of Frigga's handmaidens; she is known to guard doorways and other gates.

Tacitus—a Roman historian who recorded his time spent with various Germanic-speaking tribes.

theod—the word literally translates as "tribe," and indicates a group formed by taking oaths along an "oath tree" which includes a sacral leader and his/her followers.

Theodism—a branch of heathenry all its own, Theodism is based around a hierarchical structure where there is one leader, often considered sacral, and his/her oath-sworn followers.

Thiazi—also "Thiassi." A giant. With Loki's assistance, Thiazi steals Idunna and her golden apples. He is killed by the gods when he flies over Asgard. Thiazi is the father of Skadhi.

Thing—Icelandic local assemblies where legal matters were decided. A Thing served as both a court of law and a form of legislation, as well as a gathering for religious purposes.

Thor—one of the chief gods of the Aesir. Thor is known as the friend of man and as a mighty warrior and giant-slayer.

Thrymheim—Thiazi's home.

thurs—(plural thursar), a class of giants that represent chaotic and destructive forces.

tomten—the Swedish word for house-spirits.

Trundholm Sun Chariot—an archeological artifact dating from the late Bronze Age.

tusse—(plural tussen), house-spirits and mound-dwellers as they are called in Denmark.

Tyr—one of the Aesir. He has only one hand, and is known to hold sway over legal matters and the Althing.

Ullr—a god known as a hunter and, possibly, one who witnessed oaths.

UPG (Unverified or Unsubstantiated Personal Gnosis)—the spiritual or mystical information one gleans from one's own information and subjective, personal experience.

Uppsala—a famous archeological site in Sweden, known for its extensive burial mounds. Records indicate that heathen worship thrived there.

Urdh—also "wyrd."

Utangardh—literally "out-yard," including anything not in one's innangardh. In other words, anyone or anything, including geography, that is unknown, neutral, or unwelcome among you and your in-group.

vaettir—the word for "spirits." These can be of the land, the house, the apartment, or any other indoor or outdoor location. The word itself is fairly generic and is most often used as a root for more specific terms—landvaettir, husvaettir (hus = house), and so on.

Vafthrúthnir—a giant known to be wise. He enters into a knowledge contest with Odin and loses the game, and his head.

Vafthrúthnismal—also "The Lay of Vafthrúthnir," found in the *Poetic Edda*. It is the story of the contest between Odin and Vafthruthnir.

Valkyrie—translated as "chooser of the slain," Valkyries were said to fly over battles and choose the most heroic and mighty warriors to die and become Einherjar, the warrior-dead living in Valhalla. The Valkyries were also known to serve Odin and the Einherjar.

Valhalla—translated as "slain-hall," this is the home of Odin and his Einherjar, where they feast all night before going out to battle every day.

Vali—one of Odin's sons, he avenges Baldur's death.

Vanaheim—literally, "van-home," where the Vanir live and Njord, Frey, and Freyja come from.

Vanir—the plural form of Van, one of the tribes of gods and goddesses that heathens worship.

Var—one of Frigga's handmaidens, she keeps contracts, particularly marriage contracts.

Vardhlokkur—"ward-songs," the songs used, presumably, to protect a seidhworker while seidh was being performed.

Verdandi—one of the three Norns who feed and care for Yggdrasil using waters from the Well of Wyrd.

Vestri—literally "West," but also the name of one of the dwarves holding up the vault of the sky.

Vor—one of Frigga's handmaidens, Vor is known as the careful and observant one.

weregild—the amount of money or other goods given as recompense for a murder or other killing. This payment was imposed by law and was a means by which blood feud could be avoided.

wight—a word referring to any living being, physical or spiritual in nature. Animals, plants, rocks, humans, and gods can all be called wights.

wyrd—(see also urdh) a concept reflecting one's path or pattern in life.

Ydalir—the home of Ullr.

Yggdrasil—the World Tree, on which Odin (one of his bynames is Ygg) "rides" when he sacrifices himself to himself in order to gain knowledge.

Ymir—the founder of the race of giants who is slain by Odin, Vili, and Ve. His body parts were used to create Midgard, the clouds, rocks, and other things.

Bibliography

Algeo, John, and Thomas Pyles. *The Origins and Development of the English Language*. Fifth ed. Boston: Thompson Wadsworth, 2005.

Archeology in Europe. http://www.archeurope.com/index.php?page=trundholm-sun-chariot. Accessed March 16, 2011.

Aristotle. *Nicomachean Ethics*. Translated by W. D. Ross. Great Books of the Western World. Edited by Robert Maynard Hutchins. Encyclopedia Brittanica, Inc. Chicago: William Benton, 1953.

Arnold, Martin. *The Vikings: Culture and Conquest*. London: Continuum Books, 2006.

Aswynn, Freya. *Leaves of Yggdrasil*. Saint Paul, MN: Llewellyn Publications, 1990.

Bauschatz, Paul C. *The Well and the Tree: World and Time in Early Germanic Culture*. Amherst: The University of Massachusetts Press, 1982.

Bede. *The Ecclesiastical History of the English People*. Leo
Sherley-Price, trans. London: Penguin Books, 1990.

Berman, Harold J. "The Background of the Western Legal
Tradition in the Folklaw of the Peoples of Europe." *The
University of Chicago Law Review* 45:3. p. 553–97. 1978.

Campbell, Dan and Anna Wiggins, translators. *Völuspá: A Dual-
Language Edition with Complete Glossary*. Hillsborough:
Iðavelli Hof, 2011.

Cleasby, Richard, and Gudbrand Vigfusson. *An Icelandic-English
Dictionary*. http://www.ling.upenn.edu/~kurisuto/germanic/
oi_cleasbyvigfusson_about.html. Accessed November 6, 2011.

Cook, Robert, trans. *Njal's Saga*. London: Penguin Books, 2001.

Davies, Owen. *Popular Magic: Cunning-Folk in English History*.
London: Hambledon Continuum, 2003.

Dronke, Ursula, trans. *The Poetic Edda, Volume II: Mythological
Poems*. Oxford: Clarendon Press, 1997.

DuBois, Thomas. *Nordic Religions in the Viking Age*. Philadelphia:
University of Pennsylvania Press, 1999.

Dumézil, Georges. *Gods of the Ancient Northmen*. Editor Einar
Haugen Berkeley: University of California Press, 1973.

Elliott, Ralph W. V. *Runes*. New York: Saint Martin's Press, 1959.

Ellis Davidson, H. R. *Myths and Symbols in Pagan Europe*.
Syracuse: Syracuse University Press, 1988.

———. *The Road to Hel*. New York: Greenwood Publishing
Group, 1968.

———. *Roles of the Northern Goddess*. New York: Routledge,
1998.

———. *Gods and Myths of the Viking Age.* New York: Barnes and Noble Books, 1996.

Fletcher, Judith. "Women and Oaths in Euripides." *Theatre Journal.* 55:1. 29–44, 2003.

Flowers, Stephen E. *The Galdrabók: An Icelandic Book of Magic.* 2nd edition. Smithville, TX: Runa-Raven Press, 2005.

———. *The Rune Poems, Volume One.* Smithville: Runa-Raven Press, 2002.

Flowers, Stephen E. and James A. Chisholm, trans. *A Source-Book of Seid.* Smithville, TX: Runa-Raven Press, 2002.

Gordon, E. V. *An Introduction to Old Norse.* 2nd ed. A. R. Taylor (revised). Oxford: Clarendon Press, 1992.

Grammaticus, Saxo. *The History of the Danes.* Books I-IX. Fisher, Peter, trans. Cambridge: D. S. Brewer, 1979.

Gundarsson, KveldulfR. *Elves, Wights, and Trolls.* New York: iUniverse, 2007.

———. *Teutonic Magic.* Saint Paul, MN: Llewellyn Publications, 1990.

Gundarsson, KveldulfR, et al. *Our Troth Volume One: History and Lore.* Second edition. North Charleston, SC: BookSurge, 2006.

Halsall, Maureen. *The Old English Rune Poem: a Critical Edition.* Toronto: University of Toronto Press, 1981.

Haywood, John. *The Penguin Historical Atlas of the Vikings.* London: Penguin Books, 1995.

Heaney, Seamus, trans. *Beowulf.* New York: W. W. Norton and Co., 2007.

Hollander, Lee M., trans. *The Poetic Edda.* 2nd edition. Austin, TX: University of Texas Press, 2004.

James, Edward. *The Franks*. Oxford: Basil Blackwell, 1998.

Jerome, C. A. *The Orðasafn of Gamlinginn*. Albuquerque, NM: Hrafnahús, 1991.

Kvideland, Reimund and Henning J. Sehmsdorf, eds. *Scandinavian Folk Belief and Legend*. Minneapolis, MN: University of Minnesota Press, 1998.

Larrington, Carolyne, trans. *The Poetic Edda*. Oxford: Oxford University Press, 1996.

Lafayllve, Patricia. *Freyja, Lady, Vanadis: An Introduction to the Goddess*. Denver: Outskirts Press, 2006.

Levinson, Sanford. "Constituting Communities Through Words That Bind: Reflections on Loyalty Oaths." *Michigan Law Review*. 84:7. 1440–70, 1986.

Lindow, John. *Norse Mythology: A Guide to the Gods, Heroes, Rituals, and Beliefs*. Oxford: Oxford University Press, 2001.

Magnusson, Magnus and Hermann Paulson, trans. *The Vinland Sagas: The Norse Discovery of America*. London: Penguin Books, 1965.

Mirhady, David Cyrus. "The Oath-Challenge in Athens." *The Classical Quarterly*. New Series. 41:1. 78–83, 1991.

Page, R. I. *Runes: Reading the Past*. Berkeley: University of California Press, 1987.

Paxson, Diana. *Essential Asatru: Walking the Path of Norse Paganism*. New York: Citadel Press, 2006.

———. *The Way of the Oracle: Recovering the Practices of the Past to Find Answers for Today*. San Francisco: Weiser Books, 2011.

Pollington, Stephen. *Leechcraft: Early English Charms, Plantlore, and Healing*. Norfolk: Anglo-Saxon Books, 2000.

Robert Cook, trans. *Njal's Saga*. London: Penguin, 2001.

Rosedahl, Else. *The Vikings*. Second edition. Susan A. Margeson and Kirsten Williams, trans. London: Penguin, 1998.

Russell, James C. *The Germanization of Early Medieval Christianity: A Sociohistorical Approach to Religious Transformation*. Oxford: Oxford University Press, 1994.

Sheffield, Ann Gróa. *Frey: God of the World*. 2nd edition. Lulu .com, 2007.

Simek, Rudolf. *Dictionary of Northern Mythology*. Angela Hall, trans. Cambridge: D. S. Brewer, 1996.

Stead, Lewis. *Ravenbok*. http://www.ravenkindred.com/Ravenbok .html. Accessed December 14, 2011.

Sturluson, Snorri. The *Prose Edda*. Anthony Faulkes, trans. London: Everyman, 1987.

———. The *Prose Edda*. Jesse Byock, trans. New York: Penguin Books, 2005.

———. The *Prose Edda*. Jean Young, trans. Berkeley: University of California Press, 1954.

———. *Heimskringla*. Lee M. Hollander, trans. Austin: University of Texas Press, 1964.

Tacitus. *The Agricola and the Germania*. Revised edition. H. Mattingly, trans. Revised translation by S. A. Handford. London: Penguin Books, 1970.

The Troth. http://www.thetroth.org. Accessed December 19, 2011.

Thorsson, Edred. *Futhark: A Handbook of Rune Magic*. York Beach, ME: Samuel Weiser, Inc., 1994.

Thorsson, Örnólfur, ed. *The Sagas of the Icelanders*. New York: Penguin Books, 2000.

Widson, John A. "The Oath in Ancient Egypt." *Journal of Western Studies.* 7:3. 129-36, 1948.

York, Michael. *Pagan Theology: Paganism as a World Religion.* New York: New York University Press, 2003.

Index

GET MORE AT LLEWELLYN.COM

Visit us online to browse hundreds of our books and decks, plus sign up to receive our e-newsletters and exclusive online offers.

- **• Free tarot readings • Spell-a-Day • Moon phases**
- **• Recipes, spells, and tips • Blogs • Encyclopedia**
- **• Author interviews, articles, and upcoming events**

GET SOCIAL WITH LLEWELLYN

Find us on   @LlewellynBooks

www.Facebook.com/LlewellynBooks

GET BOOKS AT LLEWELLYN

LLEWELLYN ORDERING INFORMATION

 Order online: Visit our website at www.llewellyn.com to select your books and place an order on our secure server.

 Order by phone:
- Call toll free within the US at 1-877-NEW-WRLD (1-877-639-9753)
- We accept VISA, MasterCard, American Express, and Discover.
- Canadian customers must use credit cards.

Order by mail:
Send the full price of your order (MN residents add 6.875% sales tax) in US funds plus postage and handling to: Llewellyn Worldwide, 2143 Wooddale Drive, Woodbury, MN 55125-2989

POSTAGE AND HANDLING

STANDARD (US):
(Please allow 12 business days)
$30.00 and under, add $6.00.
$30.01 and over, FREE SHIPPING.

INTERNATIONAL ORDERS,
INCLUDING CANADA:
$16.00 for one book, plus $3.00 for each additional book.

Visit us online for more shipping options. Prices subject to change.

FREE CATALOG!

To order, call
1-877-
NEW-WRLD
ext. 8236
or visit our
website